SPANDRELS OF TF

Among the various conceptions of truth is one according to which 'is true' is a transparent, entirely see-through device introduced for only practical (expressive) reasons. This device, when introduced into the language, brings about truth-theoretic paradoxes (particularly, the notorious Liar and Curry paradoxes). The options for dealing with the paradoxes while preserving the full transparency of 'true' are limited. In *Spandrels of Truth*, Beall concisely presents and defends a modest, so-called dialetheic theory of transparent truth.

Jc Beall is Professor of Philosophy at the University of Connecticut.

Spandrels of Truth

JC BEALL

CLARENDON PRESS • OXFORD

OXFORD
UNIVERSITY PRESS

Great Clarendon Street, Oxford OX2 6DP

Oxford University Press is a department of the University of Oxford.
It furthers the University's objective of excellence in research, scholarship,
and education by publishing worldwide in

Oxford New York

Auckland Cape Town Dar es Salaam Hong Kong Karachi
Kuala Lumpur Madrid Melbourne Mexico City Nairobi
New Delhi Shanghai Taipei Toronto

With offices in

Argentina Austria Brazil Chile Czech Republic France Greece
Guatemala Hungary Italy Japan Poland Portugal Singapore
South Korea Switzerland Thailand Turkey Ukraine Vietnam

Oxford is a registered trade mark of Oxford University Press
in the UK and in certain other countries

Published in the United States
by Oxford University Press Inc., New York

British Library Cataloguing in Publication Data
Data available

Library of Congress Cataloging in Publication Data
Data available

Printed in the United Kingdom by
Lightning Source UK Ltd., Milton Keynes

ISBN 978-0-19-926873-3 (Hbk)
ISBN 978-0-19-926874-0 (Pbk.)

For Graham, who saw falsity even through opaque truth

PREFACE

This book has a single aim: to concisely lay out and defend a simple, modest approach to *transparent truth* and its inevitable paradoxes, where transparent truth is entirely 'see-through' truth, a notion of truth such that x *is true* and x are intersubstitutable in all (non-opaque) contexts, for all (meaningful, declarative) sentences x of our language.

I present what is called a 'dialetheic' position on transparent truth and paradox, and so join Graham Priest (2006b) in the basic dialetheic claim: there are some true falsehoods. What I hope is clear, however, is that my position stems from a particular conception of truth, one not shared by Priest, and is very much a modest position on the whole. (Priest, in conversation, charges that the position is 'far too straight'. I take this as a compliment, reflecting the genuine modesty of my position. But the reader may judge.)

This book is decidedly a philosophy book, versus a logic treatise or the like. Given the topic, logic is important and plays a critical role; however, I have kept the mathematical details to a bare minimum, focusing instead on the basic, philosophical position. Indeed, logicians—at least those familiar with non-classical approaches to paradox—will find little new in this book. What I hope is of value is the overall philosophical position, modest as it may be. One virtue of the book, I hope, is that it lays out and defends a concrete, dialetheic theory of transparent truth.

Many of the basic ideas of this book have been published in earlier papers, papers that emerged from earlier drafts of this book. (In some sense, then, the papers borrowed from this book, even though the former saw the light of publication earlier than the latter did.) Philosophers familiar with Beall 2004, Beall 2005b, and also Beall and Armour-Garb 2003, have a flavor of some of the basic ideas; however, the position and overall theory is different in not insignificant details, including the logic.

In the remainder of this preface, let me briefly touch on the history, structure, and a few miscellaneous features of this book.

Structure of the book

I have tried to keep this book very short, and tried to streamline the discussion. As such, Chapters 1–3 simply lay out the basic position, pausing little (if at all) to take up objections. In particular,

» Chapter 1: marches through the basic idea of transparent truth qua constructed device (very much in the spirit, if not the letter, of deflationism about truth), and the basic 'merely semantic' view of resulting paradoxes.

» Chapter 2: takes up the issue of a 'suitable conditional' in our language; I endorse a very basic abnormal-worlds conditional, and briefly discuss its effect on the idea that validity is truth-preserving.

» Chapter 3: takes up an issue that, on the surface, seems to haunt dialetheists of any stripe, the topic of *just true*. I present my take on this issue, and, in addition to sketching other options for some such notion, briefly take up the topic of 'revenge' as related to the (alleged) problem of 'just true'.

As mentioned above, Chapters 1–3 pause little, if at all, for objections. Objections and replies are mostly left to the last chapter, namely Chapter 5.

Chapter 4, the longest chapter (because mostly expository), discusses what are probably the main alternative theories of *transparent truth* (see above). The chief alternative, which came about only recently, is the theory advanced by Hartry Field (2008). Were it not for Field's work, this book would have argued that, among the known approaches, there's exactly one rational option before us: namely, my modest dialetheic approach. Alas, thanks to Field's work, I do not argue as much. Indeed, as of now (the writing of this book), I do not know of any terribly strong arguments against Field's approach. My main reason for preferring my own account comes down, I'm afraid, to a fairly fuzzy sense that Field's approach not only misses an essential feature of negation, but might also be more complicated than we need. Regrettably, I do not know how to make the relevant sense of complexity (or, much to the same point, simplicity) precise enough to serve as an objection (it certainly isn't merely a matter of standard mathematical accounts of complexity); and I also do not know how to argue for the exhaustiveness of negation. Accordingly, Chapter 4, on the whole, leaves matters open. In the end, I hope that debate will carry forward, progressing to the point of showing which of the given approaches to transparent truth is ultimately best.

In addition to a few (somewhat technical) appendices to Chapters 1 and 2, there is also a final appendix to this book (viz., Appendix A), which provides a sketch of an alternative route to transparent truth and paradox, one not discussed in this book (except as sketched in the appendix). Though I've come to reject the given approach as not being as natural as my preferred account (presented throughout), I think that it is worth thinking about, and might well afford a sort of compromise between the main approaches to transparent truth and paradox— in effect, my own and those discussed in Chapter 4.

History of the book

This book was supposed to be longer—much longer—than it is. In fact, this book was to be but a blip (perhaps a chapter) in a much longer, fairly exhaustive discussion of truth theories in general—at least those theories that take a stand on paradox. For various reasons, this book—now intentionally very short—is on its own. I am still hoping to complete the longer book, which will aim to provide both the mathematical background involved in contemporary truth theories and a philosophical critique of such theories; however, that project is now separate (and currently joint work with Michael Glanzberg).

One principal reason for separating the projects is that this book, as above, is largely philosophical; it aims to present a modest, philosophical account of transparent truth and paradox. Another reason is that, as I quickly learned, the *projects* involved in current truth theories are wildly different, many stemming from 'intuitions' that have nothing to do with the core idea of transparent truth. [Indeed, Glanzberg's own theory (2001), like that of Simmons (1993) or McGee (1991) or Gupta and Belnap (1993) or Read (2008a, 2008b) or many others, including Priest's theory (2006b), stem from notions of truth that have nothing to do with simple transparency—notions that, I'm afraid, I still don't fully understand.] Since my position rests on a modest conception of *transparent* truth, it seemed that it would be overly distracting to tackle the other theories—and, in particular, their detailed mathematical features—here. Accordingly, if you are looking for a discussion of *revision theories*, or *contextualist theories*, or any theory that doesn't provide full transparency of truth, *this* book—the book you're reading—is *not* the place; the hope is that the book with Glanzberg, if it comes to fruition, will provide that. This book has the narrow focus of presenting a position on *transparent truth* and paradox—nothing more nor less.

It is perhaps also worth mentioning, qua 'history' of this book, that I nearly scrapped the project after I learned that Graham Priest and Hartry Field were both doing books on the topic of truth and paradox. While my position differs in significant respects from Priest's, we also have a lot in common, and certainly share the basic dialetheic insight, as mentioned above. As for Field (who thinks that transparent truth needs to be 'saved' from paradox!), we differ on dialetheism but—unlike Priest—agree on the essential transparency of truth, and 'methodological deflationism' in general. As such, it seemed to me that perhaps there was neither room nor need for my modest position being presented in book form. While I do as much in the Acknowledgments, I should pause here to thank Priest and Field for encouraging me to go ahead with this book. (Thanks.) There are others (e.g., Greg Restall) to whom I owe thanks for the same encouragement, but I leave that to the Acknowledgments.

Miscellany

In general, this is not a technical book, at least as far as truth-theoretic books go—at least those that, as they should, take paradox seriously. Indeed, for the most part, there's very little symbolism, except in the informally presented 'formal modeling' of things—wherein, again, there's little symbolism. For the most part, use–mention is left to context, although in some cases—where it matters—I use 'Quine quotes' as an appropriate naming device, and *not* as Quine quotes but rather as Gödel quotes (as it were). In effect, you can read $\ulcorner \alpha \urcorner$ as an appropriate name of α (e.g., in English, a quotation name or something similar), and that will be sufficient.

Along the same lines, I should note, in advance, that some notions are set out as explicit definitions, set off as if to be used in a proof. While the notions *are* used in various background proofs (almost all suppressed), the definitions, at least in the body of the text, are given simply to facilitate concise exposition— nothing more. (Even in several appendices, wherein the definitions have a slightly more proof-driven role, proofs are left to cited works. The appendices attempt to give just enough for the interested reader to fill in details, but they are kept at a minimum for the sake of concise discussion.)

I refer to whole chapters using 'Chapter n', where n is the given chapter number. I refer to proper parts of chapters (viz., sections or subsections) using '§$m.n$', which may be read 'section n of Chapter m'.

For convenience, I sometimes use 'iff' or 'just if' for *if and only if*. Additionally, for readability, I sometimes drop parentheses in 'symbolic sentences' like $\alpha \wedge \beta \to \beta$, which is short for $(\alpha \wedge \beta) \to \beta$. The guiding principle is that $\wedge$ and $\vee$ bind more tightly than any 'arrow' that appears in the book. Context will clarify.

« *Parenthetical remark.* I should note one other bit of style. Keeping the text relatively informal and short, as is my aim, sometimes requires footnotes or otherwise parenthetical notes. To avoid too many footnotes, I sometimes follow the practice pursued in Beall and Restall 2005, which employs 'parenthetical remarks' that are set off from the main text in the way that this paragraph is set off from the text. (There are quite a few of them. They can all be skipped without serious loss, though none of them are there without reason.) *End parenthetical.* »

Finally, Appendix B, at the back of the book, lists commonly used abbreviations; this is aimed to help when abbreviations like 'TP', 'PMP', 'LEM' and others fly around (as they in some places do).

ACKNOWLEDGEMENTS

This philosophical work rests on the logical labors of the Australasian Association for Logic (AAL) and the Logicians' Liberation League (LLL). Many AAL/LLL members are cited throughout, but a few should be mentioned at the outset: the Maximum Leader (to whom I'm also grateful for LLL archives), the Boss of Bloomington, the late Lady Plumwood, the late Peer of Plumwood, the Prince of Paradox, the One True Believer, the Prince of Darkness, the Protector of Oz, the Dominator of Something Vague, the Identity of Relevance, and Saint Alasdair. I am grateful for the work of all of these people, and hope that they see some value in the philosophical account herein. Thank you all.

Other acknowledgements. There are a great many people with whom I've enjoyed philosophical-cum-logical discussion on topics related to this book. Some of those people are as follows (I would say 'all' were it not for the near certainty of inadvertently omitting some): Brad Armour-Garb, Ross Brady, Phillip Bricker, Otávio Bueno, Colin Caret, Colin Cheye, Mark Colyvan, Aaron Cotnoir, Hartry Field, Jay Garfield, Michael Glanzberg, Patrick Greenough, Patrick Grim, Anil Gupta, Gary Hardegree, Dominic Hyde, Carrie Jenkins, Fred Kroon, the late David Lewis, Bill Lycan, Michael Lynch, Ed Mares, Vann McGee, Bob Meyer, Chris Mortensen, Daniel Nolan, Doug Owings, Graham Priest, Augustín Rayo, Stephen Read, Greg Restall, David Ripley, Marcus Rossberg, Gill Russell, Josh Schechter, Jerry Seligman, Lionel Shapiro, Stewart Shapiro, Reed Solomon, Koji Tanaka, Alasdair Urquhart, Bas van Fraassen, Achillé Varzi, Sam Wheeler, Robbie Williams, Tim Williamson, Crispin Wright, and Steve Yablo. In addition, I also thank all of those at *Arché* (St Andrews), particularly those involved in the logic- and maths-related projects, as well as the UConn Logic Group, the Melbourne Logic Group, and the University of Connecticut Philosophy Department.

I would also like to thank Peter Momtchiloff of Oxford University Press; he has been patient, encouraging, and nearly always witty. Thanks, Peter. I am also grateful to Tessa Eaton for steering the book through its final stages.

Thanks also to Tim Elder (Head of Department) and Ross McKinnon (former CLAS Dean) at the University of Connecticut; both have been very supportive of my work.

I am very, very grateful to various people who gave helpful comments on earlier drafts: Mark Colyvan, Aaron Cotnoir, Hartry Field, Ed Mares, Vann McGee, Graham Priest, Greg Restall, Dave Ripley, Josh Schechter, Lionel Shapiro, Reed Solomon, and Robbie Williams. For a variety of reasons (many schedule-related), some rather good suggestions from these readers have been left out. I hope, nevertheless, that the book remains useful and interesting.

I want to acknowledge a few people for a great deal of encouragement and useful discussion throughout. All of them are mentioned above, but deserve special mention again. Reed Solomon (of the UConn Logic Group) provided useful discussions of logical options at various points. Three people, who've been very helpful sounding boards over the last few years and particularly encouraging with respect to this book, are Hartry Field, Graham Priest, and Greg Restall. Thank you.

Finally, even though she never liked the ideas in this book, and came to rather strongly dislike my writing of the book (my writing it *three times over!*), Katrina Higgins remained supportive throughout—to say the least. I would dedicate this book to her if I thought that she'd ever keep a copy of it. Instead, let me simply say *thank you, Katrina.*

Jc Beall
Storrs, 2008

CONTENTS

1 The Basic Picture   1
  1.1 Ttruth qua constructed device   1
  1.2 Exhaustive negation   3
  1.3 Spandrels of ttruth   5
  1.4 A formal picture   6
  1.5 Basic picture: merely 'semantic' gluts   14
  Appendix: LPTT non-triviality   18

2 Suitable Conditional   25
  2.1 Capture and Release   25
  2.2 Curry and a suitable conditional   26
  2.3 Curry and Liars   33
  2.4 Truth preservation and validity   34
  2.5 Validity?   37
  Appendix: BXTT non-triviality   42

3 Just True   48
  3.1 Incoherent operators   48
  3.2 What *just true* is not   49
  3.3 What *just true* is: just *ttruth*   51
  3.4 Remarks on revenge   52
  3.5 Limited notions of 'just true'   57
  Appendix: a note on 'just true' in BX   63

4 A Look at the Field   65
  4.1 Broad background projects   65
  4.2 Kripke: basic paracomplete   67
  4.3 Field: advanced paracomplete   79
  4.4 Choosing among rivals?   94
  4.5 Summary and closing remarks   97

5 Objections and Replies   98
  5.1 Dialetheism, in general   98
  5.2 Negation, gaps, and unsettledness   101
  5.3 Truth, mathematics, and metaphysics   110
  5.4 Base-language gluts?   126
  5.5 Orthodoxy: Priestly dialetheism   130

A Overlap without Inconsistency?   134
  A.1 Philosophical picture: paranormal   134
  A.2 An alternative picture: merely instrumental gluts   137

B   List of Common Abbreviations   142

References   143

Index   151

1

THE BASIC PICTURE

Are some truths also false? Yes, but only in a fairly mundane, 'deflated' sense. The dialetheic position that I endorse stems from a particular conception of truth, combined with features of our base language (the fragment free of 'true' and related notions). The principal aim of this chapter is to sketch the basic philosophical position, leaving further issues and defense to subsequent chapters.

The chapter is structured as follows. §1.1 sketches the target conception of truth. §1.2 discusses relevant features of our base language, particularly negation. After briefly mentioning the target phenomenon (paradox) in §1.3, I sketch the basic logical framework in §1.4. Drawing on the canvassed ideas in preceding sections, the aim of §1.5 is to present the overall basic position.

1.1   Ttruth qua constructed device

God could use only the T-free fragment of English to uniquely specify our world. We are unlike God in that respect; we need a device that enables us to overcome finite constraints in our effort to describe the world. That device is 'true' or, for clarity, 'ttrue' (for 'transparent truth'), a device introduced via rules of intersubstitution: that $Tr(\ulcorner\alpha\urcorner)$ and α are intersubstitutable in all (non-opaque) contexts.[1] The sole role of *ttruth*—the reason behind its introduction into the language—is to enable generalizations that, given our finite constraints, we couldn't otherwise express.

According to the running metaphor, we once spoke only the 'ttrue'-free fragment of our language. For the most part, the given fragment served our purposes well. We could say that Max is a cat, that Gödel and Tarski were independently ingenious, that there will be cloned animals, and so on. Daily discourse, so long as it didn't generalize too much, worked well. But generalization is inevitable among beings with our desires. Even in daily discourse, let alone theoretical pursuits, we want to say (what, using *ttruth*, we say when we say) that all of So-and-so's assertions are ttrue, or that some claim in Theory X is tfalse (that is, that the negation of something in X is ttrue). As above, were we God, or even just beings with infinite time or capacities, we wouldn't need to use 'ttrue' in such generalizing contexts; we could simply assert each of So-and-so's assertions (or the negations thereof). But we're not, and so we introduced 'ttrue' to achieve

---

[1] Throughout, I use '$Tr(x)$' to represent our expressive device—*is ttrue*—and, as per the Preface, the corner quotes as some sort of appropriate naming device. (For the most part, I let context settle use–mention.)

the given sorts of expression. And *that*, and only that, is the job of 'ttrue' in our language.

The same end, as in Beall 2004, could have been achieved via the story of Aiehtela and Aiehtelanu (pronounced 'eye-ah-tell-ah' and 'eye-ah-tell-ah-noo', respectively), where 'Aiehtela accepts *x*' is intersubstitutable with *x*, and 'Aiehtelanu accepts *x*' is equivalent to the negation of *x*. For purposes of expressing what, using our device 'ttrue', we express via 'Whatever Max says is ttrue', we could have said that Aiehtela accepts whatever Max says. Similarly, for purposes of expressing what, using our device 'tfalse' (ttruth of negation), we express via 'Whatever Agnes says is tfalse', we could have said that Aiehtelanu accepts whatever Agnes says. So long as the logic of the story and respective acceptance behaviors of the key characters are laid out, the story of Aiehtela and Aiehtelanu would have done all that we in fact do with 'ttrue' (and, derivatively, 'tfalse')—yield generalizations that, for practical reasons, we cannot otherwise achieve.

Of course, if, when learning our language, we had been taught the story of Aiehtela and Aiehtelanu, we would have naturally reified the two characters. We would have asked after the 'nature' of Aiehtela and so on. Different theories of Aiehtela might have emerged, some suggesting that Aiehtela's acceptance behavior ultimately rests on a criterion of 'coherence', some suggesting something else. Such theories, while interesting, would ultimately miss the mark, at least if 'Aiehtela accepts' (derivatively, 'Aiehtelanu accepts') had in fact been introduced only as expressive devices—tools for reaching resources of our language that, for practical reasons, we couldn't otherwise reach.

In fact, we use 'true' instead of 'Aiehtela accepts', and similarly (and derivatively) 'false' instead of 'Aiehtelanu accepts'. Still, so long as the device is entirely see-through, with the aim of yielding generalizations that (for practical reasons) we couldn't otherwise achieve, it matters not at all what we use. The device tags no substantive 'nature', and wasn't intended to do so. As so-called disquotationalists have long said, 'true', at least its transparent usage (viz., 'ttrue'), is unlike ordinary predicates, which are introduced to 'name' some feature of the world. Our device 'true' (or 'ttrue', as I'm writing it) was not introduced to name any feature of the world; it is simply a tool constructed to facilitate the use of our ordinary predicates and language, generally.

The foregoing metaphors are in keeping, where not exactly in letter, with 'deflationism' or, more accurately, disquotationalism about truth (and related notions). For my purposes, the device *ttruth*—or the purely transparent notion of *truth*—is fundamental. With Hartry Field (1994) I embrace disquotationalism as a methodological stance. The basic argument for methodological disquotationalism invokes Ockham: if, as it (so far) appears, our relevant truth-talk can be explained (or, in some cases, explained away) in terms of *ttruth*, then we ought to recognize only *ttruth* and its derivatives; positing more than *ttruth* would be postulation without profit. Moreover, it is a sound methodological strategy, as Field notes, to pursue disquotationalism as far and earnestly as we can; for in so doing—and, plausibly, only in so doing—we will either see where it breaks down (where, e.g., more than mere *ttruth* is required) or we will see its vindication. Either way, we will learn the ttruth about truth.

Henceforth, methodological disquotationalism is assumed, where truth—or *ttruth*—is understood as above: a constructed, see-through, fully transparent device, one introduced for familiar expressive reasons. While various issues confront methodological disquotationalism (e.g., meaning, translation, and more), I leave those issues for another occasion. (I should also note that I'm in large agreement with Field 2001 on many of these issues, and so shall not take up space rehearsing that territory.) This discussion is aimed only at the issue of ttruth-theoretic paradox and what to make of it given the above conception of transparent truth. Part of the answer turns on our 'base language', the 'ttrue'-free language into which our device 'ttrue' was introduced, and in particular the behavior of negation.

« *Parenthetical remark.* Let me note, on a slightly technical issue, that I do not see the fundamental role of *ttruth* to be that of *mathematical* discovery along the lines sometimes suggested by Vann McGee (2005). On this matter, as well as related issues raised by Stewart Shapiro (2005), I entirely agree with Hartry Field's position (2005*b*). While *ttruth* may aid in mathematical discovery, it does so by doing its fundamental, generalization job over our whole language. I raise this issue for clarification, but henceforth set it aside. *End parenthetical.* »

1.2 Exhaustive negation

The principles of Excluded Middle (LEM) and Bivalence (BIV) may be understood as follows, where $\vdash$ records validity and $Tr(x)$ is our see-through device.

» LEM: $\vdash \alpha \vee \neg\alpha$
» BIV: $\vdash Tr(\ulcorner\alpha\urcorner) \vee Tr(\ulcorner\neg\alpha\urcorner)$

A background assumption, which I shall make throughout (and is certainly standard), is that *falsity* is truth of negation (i.e., *tfalsity* is *ttruth* of negation): α is false just if its negation $\neg\alpha$ is true. This is why BIV is put as it is, instead of explicitly in terms of the (derived) 'falsity' predicate.

With some (many?) philosophers, I accept both of these principles. Indeed, given *ttruth*, the principles are equivalent. By transparency, $Tr(\ulcorner\alpha\urcorner)$ and α are intersubstitutable in all (non-opaque) contexts, for all α. Hence, assuming that neither negation nor disjunction engenders opacity,[2] $\alpha \vee \neg\alpha$ implies $Tr(\alpha) \vee \neg Tr(\ulcorner\alpha\urcorner)$, and $\neg Tr(\alpha)$ implies $Tr(\neg\alpha)$, and so $\alpha \vee \neg\alpha$ implies $Tr(\ulcorner\alpha\urcorner) \vee Tr(\ulcorner\neg\alpha\urcorner)$. This is just the *transparency* of $Tr(x)$ doing its job; and the transparency sends the implications backwards too. Hence, at least as far as what is expressed *in* our language, the validity of LEM is equivalent to BIV—at least given our see-through notion of truth (viz., *ttruth*).

---

[2]This is an assumption I embrace throughout—despite, as in §1.4, negation enjoying an 'intensional semantics' in the formal picture.

To accept LEM is to accept that negation is *exhaustive*. I accept as much. Indeed, I accept that an essential role of negation is to be exhaustive, to exhaustively 'carve up' our claims (or sentences) into the true and false—equivalently (given *ttruth*), the ttrue and not ttrue. This is not to say that there's no sense in which negation fails its exhaustive job. As will be evident, at least in the formal picture (see §1.4), there may be 'points' or 'worlds' at which negation fails to be exhaustive. But—as will also be evident—such 'points' are abnormal, both in a technical sense (to be given in §1.4) and an ordinary sense. For now, it is safe to assume, at least with respect to my account, that negation is 'essentially exhaustive' (in some sense of 'essentially', though I use this word only suggestively).

Perhaps the most serious worry for any exhaustive account of negation is 'vagueness'. How does one accommodate vagueness—and the appearance of 'unsettledness', generally—in the language if negation is exhaustive? This is an important issue, but it's one that, except for some brief discussion in Chapter 5, I leave aside in this work. What I should emphasize is that, unlike some other philosophers (Colyvan, 2009; Hyde, 1997; Priest, 2008; Routley, 1992), I reject that vagueness involves gluts. Indeed, for present purposes, one may assume that some classical approach to vagueness is part of the overall account, although I leave *which* classical account open (except for some brief remarks in Chapter 5, where a classical but non-epistemic approach is briefly sketched).

Similar issues arise with other (non-paradoxical) fragments of the language—for example, ethical discourse—that, like vagueness, are sometimes classified as 'factually defective' (Field, 2001). I set this aside too, not because the issues are unimportant but because, as with vagueness, they are likely to overly distract from the main topic of ttruth and paradox. Again, for present purposes, one may simply assume that my account involves a *classical* approach to such issues. Indeed, in the case of ethical discourse (or similar non-vagueness-related phenomena), I think it entirely natural to say that ethical claims (or the like) are one and all either true or false—provided, of course, that truth and falsity are ttruth and tfalsity, as we are assuming. But, as said, I do not go into these issues further in this work (except in Chapter 5, where related issues are briefly discussed).

Transparent truth theorists who reject LEM are generally led to recognize (or posit) some stronger notion of truth than ttruth, say, 'determinate truth' or the like. (See Chapter 4 for some discussion of this.) This is unnecessary in the present context. Given LEM, all sentences—including the 'factually defective' ones (whatever, if anything, they may be)—are ttrue or tfalse. Whether such an account leaves out—or, perhaps, blocks out—important features of our language is for debate to tell. For present purposes, I raise the issues of vagueness and other 'factually defective' phenomena to set them aside.

1.3 Spandrels of ttruth

Spandrels of x are inevitable, and frequently unintended, by-products of introducing x into some environment. Originally, the term applied chiefly to architectural spandrels, those inevitable V-shaped areas that are by-products of arches. If you want arches in your design, you're going to have spandrels. Spandrels, however, are not peculiar to architecture. Evolutionary spandrels (Gould and Lewontin, 1978), for example, include the male nipple, which was not itself selected by Mother Nature for a particular role but, rather, is the inevitable by-product of other selected items (viz., female nipples). If you introduce something to play a particular role in some environment, you also—perhaps inadvertently—introduce whatever spandrels thereby result.

Once spandrels enter the picture, one must decide what to do with them. One might ignore the spandrels; one might decorate the spandrels; one might try to hide the spandrels; one might do something else. Whatever one does, one cannot take them away, at least not without taking away the intended feature (e.g., arches) that brought them about.

Language has its own spandrels. This is particularly the case when a given bit of the language is introduced for a particular role, much like *ttruth*. The guiding metaphor, as above, has us introducing 'ttrue' not to name some property in the world but, rather, to enable generalizations about the world and its features. The simplest way to achieve such a device is as above: that, for any (declarative) sentence α, $Tr(\ulcorner\alpha\urcorner)$ and α are intersubstitutable in all (non-opaque) contexts. But 'ttrue' is a predicate, and introducing it into the grammatical environment of English yields spandrels, unintended by-products of the device.

The first displayed sentence in §1.3 is not ttrue.

As always with spandrels, one needs to decide what to do with them. In our case, the task is to figure out what such (paradoxical) spandrels teach us about our language.

The short answer, on my account, is dialetheic: there are 'gluts', sentences that are ttrue and tfalse.[3] Assuming, as I do, that α implies α for all α, the transparency—that is, intersubstitutability—of $Tr(x)$ gives us familiar 'Release and Capture' rules.

RR. $Tr(\ulcorner\alpha\urcorner) \vdash \alpha$

RC. $\alpha \vdash Tr(\ulcorner\alpha\urcorner)$

Given these rules, plus the exhaustive nature of negation, the first displayed sentence in §1.3 is ttrue and not.[4] This is a sentence such that both it *and* its

---

[3]The terminology of 'glut' is from Kit Fine (1975) and the term 'dialetheism' from Priest and Routley (1989, p. xx).

[4]Also required is so-called *Reasoning by Cases* or '∨-Elim' in the following form.

If $\alpha \vdash \gamma$ and $\beta \vdash \gamma$ then $\alpha \vee \beta \vdash \gamma$.

While some philosophers have rejected this principle (or rule), I shall assume it—as do the main alternatives discussed in Ch. 4.

negation are ttrue, which is what is meant by a *glut*. Given such gluts, the broad logic of our language is 'paraconsistent', that is, a language for which arbitrary β does not follow from arbitrary α and $\neg\alpha$.

While the position is dialetheic, the dialetheism is fairly mundane—deflated dialetheism, as it were. In particular, the gluts—the ttrue tfalsehoods—are essentially tied to our given see-through device *ttruth* (or related notions). There's no suggestion that the gluts arise in our base language. In short, the gluts are 'merely semantic', where 'semantic', on my usage (throughout), simply picks out terms that are traditionally classified as semantic (e.g., 'ttrue of', 'satisfies', 'denotes', 'exemplifies', etc.).[5]

Before expanding on this, it will be useful to have a formal sketch of the basic logical framework (sans 'suitable conditional', which is taken up in Chapter 2). After giving the basic framework, I return, in §1.5, to the overall philosophical picture—the matter of spandrels, gluts, and the 'merely semantic' aspect of the account.

1.4 A formal picture

For ease of terminology, let us call conjunction, disjunction, and negation our 'Boolean' connectives. This is not non-standard terminology, though it is potentially misleading. To call the given connectives *Boolean* may mislead one to think that we're treating such connectives along *classical*, Boolean lines. We are not doing that! (If we did, then we couldn't have transparent truth in our language.) This isn't to say that the connectives exhibit no classical behavior at all; they do, as we will see. The point is that 'Boolean connectives' is herein just a term to name the familiar trio: conjunction, disjunction, and negation.

One might suggest another familiar term for the given trio, namely, 'extensional connectives'. As it turns out, this will not do. Following the Routleys (1972) and, in effect, Urquhart (1972), I give a *non-extensional* treatment of negation, in particular, a non-extensional 'worlds' treatment. As such, I use the term 'Boolean connectives' for the given trio, trusting that, given the foregoing caveat, no confusion will arise.

The plan, then, is to first give the semantics for the Boolean connectives, and then indicate how this is generalized to quantifiers and, in turn, the basic ttruth theory (sans conditional, which is taken up in Chapter 2). The result is a known ttruth theory, notably, the dual of Kripke's familiar Strong Kleene truth theory,[6] but a truth theory that, as far as I know, has been insufficiently appreciated, let alone endorsed.

---

[5] As far as I know, Mares 2004*b* is the first use of the term 'semantic dialetheism' in print. The truth theory that I advocate in this book certainly counts as a version of 'semantic dialetheism' in Mares' sense; however, Mares himself does not advocate a particular truth theory in the given work, and indeed may well advocate a less than transparent truth theory. See too Kroon 2004.

[6] In particular: the Kripke least fixed point, empty-ground-model construction using the Strong Kleene scheme—on the *non-classical reading* of the construction (versus KF or the like). (See Ch. 4 for some discussion of this construction.)

« *Parenthetical remark.* Dowden (1984) may have endorsed the theory, but it is not clear. Similarly, Woodruff (1984) discussed the theory, as did Visser (1984), but neither seemed to endorse it. While I endorse the theory, it is not the full theory that I endorse, as it lacks a suitable conditional—a topic on which the given works by Dowden, Woodruff, and Visser are silent. As will be evident in Chapter 2, the conditional is a very serious issue, but one that I leave for Chapter 2. *End parenthetical.* »

1.4.1 The Boolean picture

As above, I follow the Routleys (1972) and Urquhart (1972) in giving a 'worlds' or 'points' semantics for the target logic. I first present the familiar *classical* picture in the given framework, and then present the fuller, non-classical picture.

On an historical note, the given 'star' approach to negation, at least from a purely algebraic point of view, is set forth in Białynicki-Birula and Rasiowa 1957. Alasdair Urquhart (1972, §5), concerned with various 'relevance' or 'relevant' logics, independently discovered the idea, but did not make much of its philosophical value. The Routleys (1972), after whom the approach is usually named (viz., *Routley star*, short for *Routley & Routley star*), independently presented the approach in a familiar 'worlds' setting and emphasized the approach as a philosophically interesting framework for 'relevant logic'. (I should emphasize that, as may be clear in Chapter 2, my own interest is *not* 'relevant logic' per se, but only a viable framework for a simple ttruth theory.)

1.4.1.1 Boolean connectives: the classical picture.

Classical 'world' or 'point' semantics is familiar to all contemporary analytic philosophers. On the classical 'worlds' picture, our Boolean connectives are entirely extensional: for any purely Boolean sentence α, the value of α at point w is determined entirely by what's happening at w; the value of α doesn't turn on what's happening at other points.

For present purposes, it is worthwhile seeing that the basic classical picture, with respect to Boolean connectives, is a special case of a more general picture. As will be clear, if our language were classical, then the 'worlds' picture, described below, would be superfluous (at best)—except, perhaps, for standard aletheic modalities ('necessarily', etc.), none of which are at issue here. Given that we enjoy *ttruth* in our language, our language is not classical, and so the broader framework proves to be useful.

The framework is as follows. Interpretations—or models, as I will sometimes say—are structures $\langle \mathcal{W}, \mathcal{N}, @, \star, \models \rangle$. One may think of these as typical 'universal access' structures with a few slight twists. In particular, in addition to the familiar non-empty set $\mathcal{W}$ of 'worlds' or points and 'actual world' or 'base world' $@$, we also have $\mathcal{N}$, our so-called 'normal worlds', which is a non-empty subset of $\mathcal{W}$ such that $@ \in \mathcal{N}$.[7] In turn, we call $\mathcal{W} - \mathcal{N}$ the set of *abnormal* points, which may

---

[7]For purposes of giving the *logic*, which, though not belabored here, is of chief concern (at least as concerns our ttruth theory), having $@$ in the picture is inessential; however, it is useful in various ways.

or may not be empty. Another twist is $\star$, which is an operator on $\mathcal{W}$ such that $w^{\star\star} = w$. (The constraint that $w = w^{\star\star}$ ensures double-negation equivalence via clause S2 below. Remarks on 'star worlds' are given below in §1.4.1.2 under 'gluts and abnormal gaps', and also in Chapter 5.) Finally, $\models$ is a relation from worlds to sentences; intuitively, $\models$ is the *true at a point* (in a model) relation, and so '$w \models \alpha$' may be read as α *is true at* w and '$w \not\models \alpha$' as α *is not true at* w.

We say that a *classical model* is any such structure such that the following conditions are met. Unless otherwise specified, w is any $w \in \mathcal{W}$, and α, β any *sentences* (closed wff).

S0. $w = w^\star$. (This is the *Classical Constraint.*)

S1. $w \models \alpha$ or $w^\star \not\models \alpha$ for all $w \in \mathcal{N}$. (This is *Normal Exhaustion.*)

S2. $w \models \neg\alpha$ iff $w^\star \not\models \alpha$.

S3. $w \models \alpha \vee \beta$ iff $w \models \alpha$ or $w \models \beta$ (or both).

S4. $w \models \alpha \wedge \beta$ iff $w \models \alpha$ and $w \models \beta$.

Note that $\star$ shows up in 'truth conditions' only in S2, which reflects the apparent 'non-extensional nature' of negation. But the appearance, given S0, is mere appearance in the classical framework. I return to this below.

Towards defining validity (among other things), let us say that α is *verified in a model* just if, in the model, $@ \models \alpha$. *Validity*, then, is defined only over base (or 'actual') worlds:[8] any model that verifies the premises verifies the conclusion. In other words, where $\vdash_c$ is our (classical) consequence relation, and $w \models \Sigma$ iff $w \models \beta$ for all $\beta \in \Sigma$,

Definition $CPL^\star$ validity. *Let Σ be a set of sentences and α any sentence. Then $\Sigma \vdash_c \alpha$ iff $@ \models \alpha$ if $@ \models \Sigma$ for all classical models.*

Comments. There are, undoubtedly, philosophical questions that arise with the given framework. What, for example, is the 'nature' of such 'star worlds'? What of 'abnormal' worlds? And there are other questions that may arise. Though some of them may be addressed along the way, such questions are largely left to Chapter 5; this chapter (and the next) aim only to concisely present the basic proposal—leaving defense for Chapter 5. For now, a few comments about the resulting logic will be useful.

Classical Boolean logic. Clauses S3 and S4 are simply the classical clauses for conjunction and disjunction, merely relativized to points or 'worlds' (as in familiar modal logic). Moreover, given S0, S1, and the fact that *validity* is restricted to 'actual' points, S2 is simply the classical clause for negation. From S0, we have the equivalence of S2 and the familiar classical clause for negation, namely,

$$w \models \neg\alpha \text{ iff } w \not\models \alpha$$

---

[8]Note that, with respect to the logic, one may equivalently define validity over all *normal points* of all given models.

From S1, we have 'exhaustion' (or 'bivalence') over all *normal* points. But, now, given that validity is defined only over base points, negation—like the other Boolean connectives—winds up being perfectly classical. Indeed, for reasons just given, negation is perfectly *extensional*; the value of $\neg\alpha$ at a point turns only on the value α at that point.

Accordingly, despite the extra baggage involved in our models—notably, the possibly *abnormal* points and the star—Boolean connectives, on the classical picture, behave exactly as per classical (Boolean) logic. The classical constraint (viz., S0) undoes the idea that negation is non-extensional; it results in the usual extensional account of negation.

While the classical framework is part of the picture, it is only a proper part. Given transparent truth, the fuller picture is one in which the classical constraint (viz., S0) breaks down.

1.4.1.2 *Boolean connectives: a better picture.*

We say that w and $w^\star$ are *star mates*, for any $w \in \mathcal{W}$. The classical constraint S0 demands that all star mates collapse—that 'they' be the same point. This reduces negation to classical (and merely extensional) negation, which conflicts with having transparent truth, at least given other assumptions about other connectives in the language (e.g., disjunction, 'reasoning by cases', and so on).

What the spandrels of *ttruth* teach us is that, sometimes, our star mates come apart. If, as I've suggested, the spandrels of ttruth are both ttrue and tfalse, then we have some α such that both α and $\neg\alpha$ are ttrue. This can't happen at *any* world with the classical constraint, a fortiori not at @. Consider the formal picture above. Suppose that α is glutty at w, that is, that $w \models \alpha$ and $w \models \neg\alpha$. By S2, $w \models \neg\alpha$ just if $w^\star \not\models \alpha$, and so we have $w \models \alpha$ and $w^\star \not\models \alpha$. But by S0, the classical constraint, $w = w^\star$, in which case we have $w \models \alpha$ and $w \not\models \alpha$, which is impossible.

What the spandrels of ttruth teach us, then, is that S0 needs to be rejected, at least as a general constraint. And this is precisely the recipe we want. In particular, we keep everything as above except for S0, which is now dropped as a requirement on models. We define an $LP^\star$ model to be any of the former structures $\langle \mathcal{W}, \mathcal{N}, @, \star, \models \rangle$ that satisfy S1–S4.

Definition $LP^\star$ model. *Let $\mathcal{W}$ be a non-empty set of 'worlds' or 'points', with $\mathcal{N} \subseteq \mathcal{W}$ and $@ \in \mathcal{N}$. Let $\star$ be an operator on $\mathcal{W}$ such that $w = w^{\star\star}$ for all $w \in \mathcal{W}$. Let $\models$ be a relation from worlds to sentences. Then $\langle \mathcal{W}, \mathcal{N}, @, \star, \models \rangle$ is an $LP^\star$ model iff the following four constraints hold for all sentences α and β.*

S1. $w \models \alpha$ or $w^\star \not\models \alpha$ for all $w \in \mathcal{N}$. (Normal Exhaustion)

S2. $w \models \neg\alpha$ iff $w^\star \not\models \alpha$.

S3. $w \models \alpha \vee \beta$ iff $w \models \alpha$ or $w \models \beta$ (or both).

S4. $w \models \alpha \wedge \beta$ iff $w \models \alpha$ and $w \models \beta$.

In turn, *validity* remains as before, defined over all base (or 'actual') worlds of all LP^* models: any LP^* model that verifies the premises verifies the conclusion. Where $\vdash$ is our consequence relation, and $w \models \Sigma$ iff $w \models \beta$ for all $\beta \in \Sigma$,

Definition LP^* validity. *Let Σ be a set of sentences and α any sentence. Then $\Sigma \vdash \alpha$ iff, for all LP^* models, $@ \models \alpha$ if $@ \models \Sigma$.*

Gluts and abnormal 'gaps'. Notice that, as required by the spandrels of *ttruth*, gluts now find a place in the picture. Let $w \in \mathcal{N}$ and suppose that $w \models \alpha$ and $w \models \neg\alpha$. This, as we saw, is impossible given the classical constraint S0; but that constraint is no longer in force, at least in general. So long as $w \neq w^*$, we can have our given glut at w. How? A look at S2 provides the answer: namely, that $w^* \not\models \alpha$ and $w^* \not\models \neg\alpha$. In other words, w's star mate, namely w^*, is a world—or point—at which α is 'gappy' in the sense that neither α nor $\neg\alpha$ is true at w^*. Since the job of negation is to be exhaustive, w^* is a point at which *negation is on holiday*. Of course, given Normal Exhaustion (constraint S1), all such 'gappy points' are *abnormal*; they're points w^* at which negation is forced on holiday due to overactivity (viz., glutty behavior) at w^{**}, that is, at w. (That the given w^* is abnormal follows from S1. Suppose that our given w^* is normal. By S1, either $w^* \models \alpha$ or $w^* \not\models \alpha$. The former does not hold, and the latter, given that $w = w^{**}$, also fails to hold.)

The spandrels of ttruth require negation to work overtime (gluts); and negation stays healthy by relaxing (gaps) elsewhere. Metaphor aside, it is clear that the LP^* framework affords gluts, and that it does so by affording 'abnormal gaps', abnormal points at which neither α nor $\neg\alpha$ is true for some α.

The resulting logic. The resulting logic is a familiar logic, namely, what Priest (1979) has called LP, which is the 'gap'-free fragment of the more general FDE (Anderson and Belnap, 1975; Anderson, Belnap and Dunn, 1992; Dunn, 1969). A few notable features of the logic are as follows, where, by definition, $\alpha \supset \beta$ is equivalent to $\neg\alpha \vee \beta$.

> » LEM: $\vdash \alpha \vee \neg\alpha$
> » Explosion (EFQ) *fails*: $\alpha, \neg\alpha \nvdash \beta$
> » *Material* Modus Ponens (MMP) *fails*: $\alpha, \alpha \supset \beta \nvdash \beta$
> » Disjunctive Syllogism (DS) *fails*: $\alpha \vee \beta, \neg\alpha \nvdash \beta$

That we have LEM follows from S1, S2, and the restriction of $\vdash$ to normal points. That we do *not* have the validity of EFQ, MMP, or DS follows from a single counterexample. In particular, consider a model in which β is not true but α is a glut, that is, a model such that $@ \not\models \beta$ but $@ \models \alpha$ and $@ \models \neg\alpha$. In each of the given rules, the model verifies the premises but not the conclusion. (More fully, let $@^* \in \mathcal{W} - \mathcal{N}$. Let $@ \models \alpha$ and $@ \models \neg\alpha$, in which case, S3 delivers both that $@ \models \alpha \supset \beta$ and $@ \models \alpha \vee \beta$. Now let $@ \not\models \beta$.)

There are many objections that one might raise at this stage, particularly concerning the 'loss' of rules such as EFQ, MMP, and DS. I address such objections in Chapter 5, and offer a few relevant comments in §1.5. For now, the aim is simply to lay out the basic picture. Before turning to a fuller picture, one more comment concerning classical logic is in order.

Classical logic. Classical Boolean logic remains a so-called (proper) extension of our Boolean logic *LP*. Where $\vdash_c$ is classical consequence and $\vdash$ our broader, *LP* consequence relation, we have that

$$\text{if } \Sigma \vdash \alpha \text{ then } \Sigma \vdash_c \alpha$$

Whatever is valid in our 'real' Boolean logic (viz., *LP*) is classically valid. That this is so follows from the fact that any classical model is an *LP** model, since any classical model, by definition, is a relevant structure that satisfies S0–S4, and hence satisfies S1–S4. Moreover, though slightly more involved to establish, we have it that every classically valid sentence (versus 'rule') is valid in *LP* and vice versa. (I do not prove this here, as the result is available in many places, e.g. Priest 1979; Priest 2006*b*. The proof turns on the fact that our Boolean clauses subsume the classical clauses, and that validity is defined only over normal worlds or, more specifically, base points.)

That classical logic is an extension of our 'real' logic carries some important philosophical consequences, to which I return in §1.5 and, particularly, Chapters 3 and 5. For now, I briefly sketch the fuller picture, moving beyond the Boolean fragment (but short of a 'suitable conditional', which is taken up in Chapter 2).

1.4.2 *A fuller picture: predicates, quantifiers, and ttruth*

The spandrels (and, hence, paradoxes) of *ttruth* arise at the predicate level. While much of the logical action in the going non-classical approach is evident at the Boolean level (in particular, negation), it is important to have a slightly fuller story, in particular, how predicates and quantifiers are treated. Fortunately, much of this is familiar, and I simply sketch the basic idea. (Again, the topic of a conditional is set aside for Chapter 2.)

We expand our models by adding a domain $\mathcal{D}$, and a function I that assigns a denotation $I(t) \in \mathcal{D}$ to each name t at each world—the *same* denotation throughout, and so the subscript in '$I_w(t)$' is dropped—and assigns an extension to predicates at each world, in particular, $I_w(\varphi(x_1, \ldots, x_n)) \subseteq \mathcal{D}^n$.

« *Parenthetical remark.* In the standard many-valued semantics, one gives the usual extension and *anti-extension*. Since we are avoiding a many-valued semantics, we can get away with only an extension. (Towards sketching a non-triviality proof for the conditional-free truth theory, the standard many-valued framework is briefly sketched in the appendix to this chapter.) *End parenthetical.* »

With models in hand, an atomic sentence $\varphi(t_1, \ldots, t_n)$ is evaluated as *true at w (in a given model)* just if the relevant n-tuple is in the extension of predicate $\varphi(x_1, \ldots, x_n)$ at w. In other words, for any given model,

$$w \models \varphi(t_1, \ldots, t_n) \text{ iff } \langle I(t_1), \ldots, I(t_n) \rangle \in I_w(\varphi(x_1, \ldots, x_n))$$

Clauses for our Boolean connectives, which determine the values of non-quantified molecular sentences (at worlds in models), remain as in $LP^\star$.

For the quantifiers, we assume, for convenience, that every object $o \in \mathcal{D}$ serves as a name of itself, and let $\varphi(t/x)$ be the result of replacing all free occurrences of x in φ with term t (with clashes removed). The quantifiers, then, have the following familiar clauses.

Q1. $w \models \forall x\, \varphi$ iff $w \models \varphi(o/x)$ for all $o \in \mathcal{D}$.

Q2. $w \models \exists x\, \varphi$ iff $w \models \varphi(o/x)$ for some $o \in \mathcal{D}$.

Validity remains exactly as per the propositional $LP^\star$ case, defined only over 'actual worlds' of all models: any model that verifies the premises verifies the conclusion.

As in the Boolean case, classical semantics may be 'regained' by imposing appropriate constraints on the foregoing semantics, and in particular on what counts as an admissible interpretation or model. Specifically, one reinstates the classical clause S0 on our 'stars', which forces negation to be classical, having the effect that $I(\varphi) \cap I(\neg\varphi) = \emptyset$ for all I and predicates φ, where $\neg\varphi$ is the 'negation compound' of φ.

Ttruth device. We model our *ttruth* predicate by adding a distinguished (logical) predicate $Tr(x)$. This predicate is supposed to be entirely 'see-through' in the sense of being intersubstitutable with x in all (non-opaque) contexts, for all sentences x. With respect to the formal picture, such 'see-through-ness' may be understood via the following *transparency principle* TP (where relativity to worlds is left implicit).

TP. Let β be any sentence in which sentence α occurs. Then the result of substituting $Tr(\ulcorner\alpha\urcorner)$ for any occurrence of α in β has the same semantic value or same semantic status as β.

In the present context, TP is equivalent to the following constraint, which might be called *weak transparency* (though the term is not important).

WT. $w \models Tr(\ulcorner\alpha\urcorner)$ iff $w \models \alpha$ for all α and $w \in \mathcal{W}$.[9]

For present purposes, I shall use WT as a constraint on what counts as a *model*, or as what counts as an 'admissible interpretation' of our extended language with $Tr(x)$. In other words, we now say that an $LP^\star$ model is any of the above models that satisfy WT.

One can prove that, for the current language (sans conditional), every model satisfies TP, since every model, by definition, satisfies WT, and WT, *in the current context*, implies TP.

---

[9] If we were setting things up using functions ν from worlds and sentences into a set of semantic values, WT would take the form $\nu_w(Tr(\ulcorner\alpha\urcorner)) = \nu_w(\alpha)$ for all α and $w \in \mathcal{W}$. (And if, as in the appendix to this chapter, we avoid 'worlds' altogether, then WT takes the given equation form but drops the subscript to worlds.)

« *Parenthetical remark.* The implication from WT to TP fails when our language is extended with a 'suitable conditional', but I leave this for Chapter 2. That the implication from WT to TP holds over the given language falls out of a 'translation' between our current 'worlds' semantics and standard, many-valued semantics for LP on which the result is clear. (The 'translation' scheme and the standard many-valued semantics are sketched in the appendix to this chapter.) The one issue, in the current context, concerns negation contexts. In particular, with respect to TP and the case where β is $\neg\alpha$, the worry is whether, given the 'intensionality' of negation, negation and $Tr(x)$ commute, that is, whether

$$w \models Tr(\ulcorner \neg\alpha \urcorner) \ \text{ iff } \ w \models \neg Tr(\ulcorner \alpha \urcorner)$$

for all $w \in \mathcal{W}$ and all models. But we do have this. Suppose, for example, that β is $\neg\alpha$, and that $w \models \neg\alpha$, in which case $w^\star \not\models \alpha$. By WT, $w^\star \not\models Tr(\ulcorner \alpha \urcorner)$, and hence $w \models \neg Tr(\ulcorner \alpha \urcorner)$. The case in which $w \not\models \neg\alpha$ is similar. *End parenthetical.* »

LPTT: *the conditional-free theory.*   For convenience (but mostly for appendices and some issues in Chapter 5), I shall sometimes use 'LPTT' for the 'conditional-free' theory that I advocate. By 'conditional-free' I simply mean the theory so far advanced, where the language has only the logical resources so far discussed—in effect, standard first-order resources. (The next chapter expands the language— and, in turn, the ttruth theory—by adding a so-called suitable conditional.) LPTT, in short, contains all ttruths and is closed under the logic LP and the transparency principle TP. (To say that the theory is closed under LP is to say that if α is in the theory, then so too are all LP consequences of α. Likewise for being closed under TP.)

The question, of course, is whether there are any models of the theory, in particular, *non-trivial* models—models in which not every sentence is verified. Indeed, a stronger question, at least philosophically, is equally pressing. Are there 'natural' models, models in which, for example, the base language—or even simply arithmetic—is classical? Indeed, as discussed below, I advance LPTT as a ttruth theory that is entirely classical in its base language—the gluts in the theory arise only in (weird parts of the) semantic fragment. The question at hand about non-trivial, natural models is whether there are models of LPTT so understood.

That there are non-trivial, indeed 'natural', models may be seen from a Kripke-like construction sketched in the appendix to this chapter. The construction in question, for simplicity, is given in a familiar, many-valued, non-worlds semantics; however, it may be recast via 'translation'. (See the appendix to this chapter for the construction, and Definition 1.7 in the appendix for the 'translation' scheme.) In the end, there are models in which our base language (i.e., *ttruth*-free etc. fragment) is entirely classical; it's just the spandrels, which fail to 'ground out' classically, that wind up being gluts.

It is worth noting that, since $\alpha \vdash \alpha$ and $\vdash \alpha \supset \alpha$ hold in LP (the logic resulting from above), the transparency principle TP yields 'Release' and 'Capture' in both Rule and 'Conditional' forms.[10]

RR. $Tr(\ulcorner \alpha \urcorner) \vdash \alpha$
RC. $\alpha \vdash Tr(\ulcorner \alpha \urcorner)$
CR. $\vdash Tr(\ulcorner \alpha \urcorner) \supset \alpha$
CC. $\vdash \alpha \supset Tr(\ulcorner \alpha \urcorner)$

Of course, these last two are not terribly interesting given that, as mentioned above, MMP is invalid. This is why, in the next chapter, we expand the theory with a 'suitable conditional', more on which in the next chapter.

For now, it is important to return to the overall, basic philosophical picture, which is the chief concern.

1.5 Basic picture: merely 'semantic' gluts

With the foregoing ideas in hand, the basic philosophical position, which I take to be a modest one, comes together. Let me rehearse the basic background picture, expand from §1.3 on the treatment of spandrels, and then briefly discuss the 'merely semantic' and 'deflated' features of the position.

1.5.1 *Background picture: ttruth qua constructed device*

For purposes of describing the world, our given base language is in principle sufficient. Indeed, the trouble is not so much with the language as it is with us. Given our finitude, we cannot use the full reaches of our base language; there are various, familiar generalizations that, due to our finitude, we cannot express. The fix is a constructed see-through device, namely, *ttruth* (though, in English, spelled 'truth'). The device is not introduced to name some important property or, in general, to generate 'new claims' about the world; it is introduced to be *transparent*, to 'reveal' claims that—given our finite situation—we couldn't otherwise express.

1.5.2 *Spandrels and (a-)symmetry*

Despite the best intentions, 'new claims' nonetheless arise. As in §1.3, introducing our transparent device into the grammatical environment of English (or similar languages) yields spandrels of the device, in particular, *ttruth-ineliminable* sentences—sentences from which 'ttrue' cannot be eliminated via the governing intersubstitutability rules. An example is the first displayed sentence in §1.3, but there are many others, for example, typical truth-tellers like

$\sqrt{}$ The ticked sentence in §1.5.2 is ttrue.

Like Liars, this is a *ttruth*-ineliminable sentence, a sentence such that 'ttrue' cannot be eliminated via the governing intersubstitutability rules. Unlike typical

---

[10]For more on this terminology, see Ch. 2.

Liars, the ticked sentence in §1.5.2 may be 'classically treated', not *forced* to be a glut.

For present purposes, I shall follow the simplest approach: I treat all such sentences as *gluts*. But this is ultimately defeasible; I am fully open to an *asymmetry* among the target sentences. In the end, various theoretical or practical pressures may push for an asymmetric treatment. For example, it may be that, as with typical truth-tellers, when a glut isn't *forced*, some of the given sentences are best treated along classical lines. I do not see that a lot hangs on this.

Priest (2006*b*) has argued that 'uniformity' or 'symmetry' plays a big role here, urging that all such target sentences be uniformly treated as gluts. (Matters are more complicated with a 'suitable conditional', which is discussed in Chapter 2.) My reply is that the symmetry constraint is not clearly well-motivated in the current context. On some conceptions of truth, it might make sense to think that the 'nature' of truth is partial to symmetry, that symmetry is tied up with the given 'nature' (whatever it might be). Yet, on the going transparent conception, wherein truth is merely a constructed see-through device and devoid of any 'nature', such considerations seem to me to be misplaced—or, at least, not obviously relevant. If, as I'm assuming, truth is just ttruth, then it seems that there's no demand from symmetry unless it's required by the job—the given transparency role—of ttruth. At least on the surface, the given job appears not to require as much.

While open to an 'asymmetric' treatment, I shall, as above, follow a simple, uniform approach: gluts across the board for the target ineliminable-ttruth sentences.

1.5.3 *Supervenience*

According to the driving picture, *ttruth* is a constructed see-through device, one brought in to overcome practical difficulties that we otherwise confront with our (otherwise quite sufficient) base language. Given that the device is constructed to be entirely transparent, one expects a sort of supervenience to hold. In particular, one expects ttruth to supervene on the base-language facts—the base-language ttruths.

The expectation of such supervenience, I think, is natural. If one were to insist on such supervenience across the board, then one would need to reject that some of the given spandrels are gluts, since such sentences are ttrue without their ttruth 'depending' on base-language ttruths. But I see no reason to so insist. As with the symmetry constraint, insistence seems to me to be misplaced, at least given the going conception of truth. Why insist as much when the constructed device might yield spandrels that buck supervenience? That the base language serves as a subvenient base for ttruth makes sense, I admit, for those sentences in which 'ttrue' is eliminable via the fundamental intersubstitutability rules—for the 'normal' sentences. What, though, of the inevitable spandrels? Why think that the ttruth of the first displayed sentence in §1.3 (or etc.) depends on the ttruth (or tfalsity) of base-language sentences? As far as I can see, there is no reason to think as much. If anything is to determine the ttruth or tfalsity of such sentences, it's at most the overall logic (or rules) of the language. Extending the otherwise sensible supervenience constraint to such sentences seems, as I said, to be simply misplaced.

1.5.4 *Merely semantic gluts*

One more element of the picture, alluded to throughout, needs to be discussed: that the gluts in our language are entirely 'semantic', involving no base-language predicates. Our base language is entirely *classical*. When we bring in our constructed see-through device *ttruth*, we overcome practical, expressive limitations that we faced with respect to our base language. The spandrels of *ttruth* bring gluts into our language, but they do not 'spill' gluts back into our otherwise classical base language. In this way, the resulting dialetheism is very limited.

Let $\mathcal{L}$ be our base language, that is, the language 'prior' to *ttruth* (and other 'semantic' notions). One simple way of modeling the 'merely semantic' idea is to restrict our class of LP* models: take only those such that @ $\models \alpha$ just if @* $\models \alpha$, for any $\alpha \in \mathcal{L}$. In other words, take only those LP* models in which @ $\not\models \alpha \wedge \neg\alpha$ for any base-language α. The effect is that there is no model in which our base-language sentences are gluts. This reflects the going idea that, as above, what drives the inconsistency is *ttruth* playing with itself, as opposed to acting properly on (what Kripke would call) 'grounded' sentences.

« *Parenthetical remark.* In the standard many-valued semantics (see appendix to this chapter), the restriction takes models to be those such that $\nu(\alpha) \neq \frac{1}{2}$ for any α in the base language. *End parenthetical.* »

One notable virtue of the proposed, restricted account concerns negation.[11] Some philosophers think it to be 'conceptually true' that, for example, DS is valid, and perhaps similarly EFQ, where these are understood in rule form.

» DS: $\neg\alpha, \alpha \vee \beta \vdash \beta$

» EFQ: $\alpha, \neg\alpha \vdash \beta$

I do not want to put much weight on the 'conceptually true' claim, as I do not know quite what to make of the idea of conceptual truth, especially, perhaps, concerning valid rules. Nonetheless, conceptual truth or not, the idea that such rules are (in some sense) 'essential' to negation is respected on the current proposal, at least in a restricted sense. Of course, as in §1.4.1.2, neither rule is valid simpliciter. Still, on the proposed account, the given rules are 'valid' in a significant but restricted sense: namely, when α is a base-langage sentence. On the proposed restriction, there's no model in which α is a glut, for any α in the base language. As such, DS and EFQ are without counterexample when restricted to the relevant fragment. In a sense, then, provided that one remains in the right

---

[11]I'm grateful to various philosophers for emphasizing this apparent virtue, particularly Carrie Jenkins and Ed Mares, but also Daniel Nolan and Michael Glanzberg.

fragment, typical rules such as DS and EFQ are without counterexample; the validity relation, when restricted to the given fragment, contains DS and EFQ.

Deflated dialetheism

In this chapter I've laid out the basic position. The position is dialetheic, but only in a modest, 'deflated' way; the 'true falsehoods' are merely transparently true and transparently false; they are ttrue sentences whose negations are also ttrue.

My account agrees with the common (though not universal) thought that negation is essentially exhaustive—that its job is to cut an exhaustive line between the ttrue and tfalse. Sometimes, due to spandrels of *ttruth*, negation's exhaustive behavior results in *overactivity*; negation, in concert with *ttruth*, yields gluts—sentences α such that α and $\neg\alpha$, and $\neg\neg\alpha$, and $\neg\neg\neg\alpha$, and so on are one and all ttrue.

While the gluts are oddities—and, as mentioned, generally unintended—our overall language, according to my (modest) account, is otherwise entirely standard. Our base language is entirely classical.

There seems to me to be nothing terribly radical in the proposed position, let alone anything absurd. Perhaps, if truth were more than ttruth—more than a mere constructed see-through device—then 'true falsehoods' might be alarming (if not absurd, depending on the account of truth). Perhaps. But on the transparent conception, such true falsehoods are not only rather mundane; they are not surprising, given the see-through device that we enjoy and its inevitable spandrels.

CHAPTER ONE APPENDIX: NON-TRIVIALITY

In this appendix, I briefly sketch the standard many-valued semantics for (quantified) LP, which, in turn, may be used to give a Kripke-like construction that establishes the non-triviality of the given *transparent* truth theory, namely, LPTT. Another advantage of the many-valued semantics for LP is that it may be easier to get a feel for the basic 'Boolean' or, more generally, conditional-free logic and the resulting truth theory of the given (conditional-free) fragment.

This appendix is mainly for those who want a sense of how the non-triviality Kripke construction goes in this context. Details are left to cited work, and much is presupposed. I swiftly sketch the many-valued semantics, and then sketch the Kripke construction that serves as a non-triviality proof for the target (though only conditional-free) ttruth theory.

Many-valued LP semantics

The many-valued semantics for LP is the result of designating the middle value in the Strong Kleene semantics (see Chapter 4), where the middle value is now thought of as representing 'gluts'. This idea goes back to Asenjo (1966), but is best known from Priest's work (1979, 2006b) from which the name 'LP' derives.[12]

In short, we let $\mathcal{V} = \{1, \frac{1}{2}, 0\}$ be the set of semantic values, with $\{1, \frac{1}{2}\}$ the set of *designated* values, where the designated values are the ones in terms of which the consequence relation is defined.

With respect to the Boolean framework, we let interpretations be functions from our sentences into $\mathcal{V}$, in particular all of those functions ν that satisfy the following conditions.

1. Negation: $\nu(\neg\alpha) = 1 - \nu(\alpha)$.
2. Conjunction: $\nu(\alpha \wedge \beta) = \min\{\nu(\alpha), \nu(\beta)\}$.
3. Disjunction: $\nu(\alpha \vee \beta) = \max\{\nu(\alpha), \nu(\beta)\}$.

With respect to the broader, quantificational language, we follow a standard approach in many-valued semantics. In particular, our interpretations (or models) are structures $\langle \mathcal{D}, I \rangle$, where $\mathcal{D} \neq \emptyset$ (our domain), and, in addition to assigning denotations to all names, I also assigns a pair of sets $\langle \varphi^+, \varphi^- \rangle$ to each n-ary predicate φ. Here, φ^+ is the extension of φ (under I), and φ^- the anti-extension (under I). The key stipulation, to ensure the essential 'exhaustiveness' of negation, is that $\varphi^+ \cup \varphi^- = \mathcal{D}$ for all predicates φ. The corresponding 'exclusion' constraint, according to which $\varphi^+ \cap \varphi^- = \emptyset$ for all φ, is (of course) dropped, since some sentences may be gluts. (This is just the 'opposite' or, technically, the

---

[12] Along these lines, Halldén (1949) espoused the 'weak' version of LP, which designates the middle value but uses Weak Kleene operators rather than the Strong ones at play in LP (and Strong Kleene, for which see Ch. 4).

'dual' of the setup in Strong Kleene.) The semantic values of *atomic* sentences, in turn, are defined in a natural fashion.

» $\nu(\varphi(t_1,\ldots,t_n)) = 1$ iff $\langle I(t_1),\ldots,I(t_n)\rangle \in \varphi^+$ and $\langle I(t_1),\ldots,I(t_n)\rangle \notin \varphi^-$.
» $\nu(\varphi(t_1,\ldots,t_n)) = \frac{1}{2}$ iff $\langle I(t_1),\ldots,I(t_n)\rangle \in \varphi^+ \cap \varphi^-$.
» $\nu(\varphi(t_1,\ldots,t_n)) = 0$ iff $\langle I(t_1),\ldots,I(t_n)\rangle \in \varphi^-$ and $\langle I(t_1),\ldots,I(t_n)\rangle \notin \varphi^+$.

The Boolean compounds are given as above (see clauses for Conjunction, etc. above). Quantifiers may be treated as generalized conjunctions and disjunctions, with the simplifying assumption that every $o \in \mathcal{D}$ serves as a name of itself.

» $\nu(\forall x\,\varphi) = \min\{\nu(\alpha(o/x)) :$ for all $o \in \mathcal{D}\}$
» $\nu(\exists x\,\varphi) = \max\{\nu(\alpha(o/x)) :$ for all $o \in \mathcal{D}\}$

Validity, finally, is defined via the designated values 1 and $\frac{1}{2}$. For convenience, let us say that a model *verifies* a sentence α just if $\nu(\alpha) \in \{1,\frac{1}{2}\}$, and that a model verifies a set Σ of sentences just if it verifies all sentences in Σ. Then $\Sigma \vDash \alpha$ just if every model that verifies Σ verifies α.

Monotonicity.   One feature of the given semantics, which is critical for the non-triviality construction, is called *monotonicity*. The basic idea may be put as follows.

Let us say that ν is *classical* with respect to α just if $\nu(\alpha) \in \{1,0\}$. (So, ν is not classical with respect to α iff $\nu(\alpha) = \frac{1}{2}$.) Let us also say that ν and ν' *agree with respect to* α just if $\nu(\alpha) = \nu'(\alpha)$. Now, define $\preceq$ to be the relation that holds between LP valuations just if ν and ν' agree with respect to any α with respect to which ν is classical.

Definition $\nu \preceq \nu'$ *iff there's no* α *such that* $\nu(\alpha) \in \{1,0\}$ *but* $\nu'(\alpha) \neq \nu(\alpha)$.

Finally, let $\preceq^A$ be $\preceq$ *restricted to all atomic sentences*.

Definition $\nu \preceq^A \nu'$ *iff there's no* atomic p *such that* $\nu(p) \in \{1,0\}$ *but* $\nu'(p) \neq \nu(p)$.

Then the crucial 'monotonicity' property of the given semantics may be put as follows.

Proposition (M_{LP}) *If* $\nu \preceq^A \nu'$ *then* $\nu \preceq \nu'$ *for all* ν *and* ν'.

I herein omit the proof (which is achieved via induction). M_{LP}, combined with some set-theoretic facts, yields the target non-triviality construction, to which I now briefly turn.

« *Parenthetical remark.* It may be easier—and, for the construction, somewhat illuminating—to put the monotonicity slightly differently, directly in terms of the (many-valued) LP operators. Here, in this parenthetical remark, we let $\preceq$ be an arbitrary partial ordering, not our defined one above. Let $\langle \mathcal{V}, \preceq \rangle$ be a partial order (so that $\preceq$ is now an ordering of $\mathcal{V}$ that is reflexive, anti-symmetric, and transitive). Let g be any n-ary operator on $\mathcal{V}$, and let $v_i, v_i' \in \mathcal{V}$ for $1 \leq i \leq n$. Then g is *monotonic* with respect to $\preceq$ iff for any v_i and v_i',

$$\text{if } v_1 \preceq v_1' \text{ and } \ldots \text{ and } v_n \preceq v_n' \text{ then } g(v_1,\ldots,v_n) \preceq g(v_1',\ldots,v_n')$$

Then the (many-valued) *LP* operators are monotonic on the following partial ordering of $\mathcal{V} = \{1, \frac{1}{2}, 0\}$. (The name 'A3' is from Gupta and Belnap 1993.)

FIG. 1.1. A3

Visser (1984) proves a general result that, when combined with the above monotonicity of *LP* (many-valued) operators, provides an algebraic proof of 'fixed point interpretations' for our *LP* transparent truth theory LPTT. (Visser proves his results for other, more general schemes, but they apply in the *LP* case. Fitting (1986), Woodruff (1984), and—in a very user-friendly fashion—Gupta and Belnap (1993) give related results.) For our purposes, the given structure may serve as a picture of one part of the overall construction. *End parenthetical.* »

Stars and many values: translation

Before turning to the non-triviality (Kripke) construction for the proposed truth theory LPTT, which construction is done via the many-valued semantics (versus star semantics) for *LP*, the relation between the star-based and many-valued-based semantics should be noted. As mentioned in Chapter 1, the equivalence of our 'official' star-based semantics and the foregoing many-valued semantics may be established via translation. The translation is as follows.

Definition *(Translation: star and many-valued LP) Let $\nu(\alpha)$ be the semantic value of α on LP model ν. Then the two-way 'translation scheme' runs thus.*

» $@ \models \alpha$ *and* $@^\star \models \alpha$ *iff* $\nu(\alpha) = 1$
» $@ \models \alpha$ *and* $@^\star \not\models \alpha$ *iff* $\nu(\alpha) = \frac{1}{2}$
» $@ \not\models \alpha$ *iff* $\nu(\alpha) = 0$

A warning is in order: while—given the above translation—the official, star-based semantics is equivalent to the many-valued one *for the conditional-free language* so far discussed (in Chapter 1), the equivalence breaks down once we add a suitable conditional (see Chapter 2). One may still safely think in many-valued terms for the conditional-free fragment, but this is the case *only* for the given fragment.

Kripke construction

The target 'Kripke' construction comes from various philosophers, including Dowden (1984), Woodruff (1984), Brady (1989) and Priest (1991). For present purposes, I simply sketch the construction; details are available in the cited works. The main reason for sketching the construction is not that it is in doubt (see cited works), but rather because it plays a role in the less familiar Brady–Priest construction for our target (conditional-*ful*) language. (See Chapter 2.)

What we're doing. What we want to show is that our *LP*-based transparent truth theory LPTT is non-trivial in the target, 'natural' way, a theory enjoying a classical base language, extended with $Tr(x)$, and closed under *LP* and TP. We do this by constructing a model in which $Tr(x)$ is entirely transparent, in the sense of satisfying TP, but not all sentences are true (in the model)—in fact, that the base language is entirely classical. In the end, non-triviality results from the fact that the model is entirely standard with respect to arithmetic, which will serve as our base language.

« *Parenthetical remark.* As mentioned in a parenthetical remark above, there is a slightly simpler, algebraic proof of non-triviality due to Visser. Since I rely on Brady's construction for the more general non-triviality result (see appendix to Chapter 2), and Brady's construction follows the more familiar Kripke 'inductive' construction, I leave the algebraic proof aside. *End parenthetical.* »

What we want. Let $\mathcal{L}$ be the language of arithmetic, and $\mathcal{L}^+$ be $\mathcal{L}$ augmented with the predicate $Tr(x)$.[13] The aim is to construct a model that has the following features.

D1. Arithmetic is standard (i.e., standard model for arithmetic fragment).

D2. $Tr(x)$ is entirely transparent, in the sense that TP holds.

Because our current language is entirely extensional, D2 is achieved if (and only if) our model is a 'Kripke fixed point' model. (Matters change when we introduce a 'suitable conditional' in Chapter 2.)

How we do it. The strategy, following Kripke (1975), is to construct a transfinite sequence of interpretations that 'end' with the right sort of model. More clearly, let a *standard interpretation* of $\mathcal{L}^+$ be one for which $\mathcal{L}$ has the standard interpretation. Let an interpretation be *transparent* just if TP holds for the interpretation. The strategy, then, is to construct a (transfinite) sequence of standard interpretations such that, at some stage in the sequence, we achieve a transparent interpretation.

What is important is that our sequence satisfies 'monotonicity'. What we want (and need) is that if stage i is less than (or equal to) stage k, then $\nu_i \preceq \nu_k$, where ν_i and ν_k are the given valuations at the given stages.[14] As above, we want (and need) more than this: we want that the sequence is not only monotonic

---

[13] For simplicity, we also assume that $\mathcal{L}$ contains function symbols for each primitive recursive function, and no other function symbols. I should note that, while using the language arithmetic simplifies the construction, the construction goes through for the language of set theory.

[14] Actually, the more general construction requires that if $0 < i < k$, then $\nu_i \preceq \nu_k$. I do not present the construction in its properly general form, but rather only sketch the idea behind the construction. (I return to this qualification below.)

(in the given sense), but that it results in better and better interpretations—eventually, reaching an entirely transparent one. Provided we have the requisite monotonicity, various background set-theoretic facts ensure that we reach our requisite transparent, standard model.

The basic idea. Since $\mathcal{L}$ is to remain standard, the main task is to specify the interpretation(s) of our predicate $Tr(x)$. If we start with a less than transparent interpretation, we need to 'reset' the interpretation of $Tr(x)$ in some systematic way. Kripke's 'reset' approach does the trick: set $Tr(\ulcorner\alpha\urcorner)$ to 1 if there's a prior stage at which α is 1, and to 0 if a prior stage at which α is 0, and otherwise leave $Tr(\ulcorner\alpha\urcorner)$ at $\frac{1}{2}$. This is the basic 'reset' rule, which takes us from a given interpretation of $Tr(x)$ to a better one, at least given an appropriate starting interpretation. (The 'reset rule', so given, requires an appropriate starting model. To prove the required monotonicity, the rule needs to be slightly more complicated. I return to this below.)

The question is: how shall $Tr(x)$ be *initially* set? There are various options but I shall follow the simplest.[15] In particular, we 'overstuff' our base interpretation of $Tr(x)$: all sentences of the form $Tr(\ulcorner\alpha\urcorner)$ are assigned $\frac{1}{2}$. The idea, then, is that we initially set $Tr(x)$ at the bottom point of A3 (see fig 1.1), and we let our 'reset rule' resolve $Tr(x)$ to better and better interpretations. In particular, if α starts at a classical value, then our reset rule takes $Tr(\ulcorner\alpha\urcorner)$ up A3 to the given classical value. If α never gets to a classical value (i.e., stays at the bottom of A3), then $Tr(\ulcorner\alpha\urcorner)$ will itself remain at the bottom of A3, and α and $Tr(\ulcorner\alpha\urcorner)$ will have the same value.

« *Parenthetical remark.* For simplicity, I also assume that sentences of the form $Tr(t)$, where t does not 'denote' a *sentence* (i.e., does not resolve to the code of a sentence), shall be assigned 0. This is not strictly necessary, but it is convenient. This stipulation is omittted from the following discussion, but should be taken as implicit. *End parenthetical.* »

In slightly more detail, the construction goes as follows. Our initial, base interpretation (with valuation ν_0) is such that, where $|\alpha|^{\mathbb{N}}$ is the standard interpretation of α,

» $\nu_0(\alpha) = |\alpha|^{\mathbb{N}}$ if α is in $\mathcal{L}$.
» $\nu_0(Tr(\ulcorner\alpha\urcorner)) = \frac{1}{2}$.
» Compounds: these are determined—at *every* stage—by LP operators.

Given M_{LP}, our base ν_0 is a standard interpretation but a *non-transparent* one.[16] After all, $\nu_0(1 = 0) = 0$ but $\nu_0(Tr(\ulcorner 1 = 0\urcorner)) = \frac{1}{2}$, and so we do not have WT even for all atomic α. (Indeed, ν_0 fails to satisfy the rule 'Release', since $Tr(\ulcorner 1 = 0\urcorner)$ is designated but $1 = 0$ is not.)

---

[15]The approach in question is the exact dual of Kripke's empty-ground-model construction for Strong Kleene. See Ch. 4.

[16]For convenience, I sometimes call ν_i an interpretation, even though, strictly speaking, this is the given valuation function of the given interpretation.

What we want, as above, is to move from ν_0 to better and better—more and more transparent—interpretations. Following the Kripke 'reset' rule, we are able to do so. In particular, for $k \neq 0$ (successor or limit), we reset $Tr(\ulcorner \alpha \urcorner)$ to a classical value if α is classical 'below', and otherwise leave $Tr(\ulcorner \alpha \urcorner)$ at $\frac{1}{2}$. Specifically, the reset rule—given our base ν_0 above—is the following.

$$\nu_k(Tr(\ulcorner \alpha \urcorner)) = \begin{cases} 1 \text{ if } \nu_i(\alpha) = 1 \text{ for some } i < k \\ 0 \text{ if } \nu_i(\alpha) = 0 \text{ for some } i < k \\ \frac{1}{2} \text{ otherwise.} \end{cases}$$

So, for example, even though $\nu_0(1 = 0) = 0$ but $\nu_0(Tr(\ulcorner 1 = 0 \urcorner)) = \frac{1}{2}$, the reset rule adjusts the latter at stage one: $\nu_1(Tr(\ulcorner 1 = 0 \urcorner)) = 0$ since, as above, $1 = 0$ has value 0 at the base stage (viz., zero). Of course, ν_1 is still far from transparent, since, for example, $\nu_1(Tr(\ulcorner 1 = 0 \urcorner)) = 0$ but $\nu_1(Tr(\ulcorner Tr(\ulcorner 1 = 0 \urcorner) \urcorner)) = \frac{1}{2}$. But, again, the reset rule rectifies this at stage two: $\nu_2(Tr(\ulcorner Tr(\ulcorner 1 = 0 \urcorner) \urcorner)) = 0$ since, as above, $Tr(\ulcorner 1 = 0 \urcorner)$ is 0 at stage one. And so on.

What is important is that, given our starting model, this reset rule yields the required monotonicity for the sequence of interpretations, namely,

Proposition *(KLP) For any stages i, k and corresponding interpretations ν_i and ν_k, if $i \leq k$ then $\nu_i \preceq \nu_k$.*

In other words, if ν_i is classical with respect to α, then ν_i and ν_k agree with respect to α, for any $k \geq i$. The proof, which I skip here, is via induction, and invokes the basic monotonicity M_{LP} of the LP semantics (and the definition of interpretations of $Tr(x)$ at various stages).

« Parenthetical remark. Stricktly speaking, the given 'reset rule', as noted above, actually presupposes the relevant monotonicity. To establish the given monotonicity, the following, more general rule, which deals with so-called limit stages, is employed.

$$\nu_k(Tr(\ulcorner \alpha \urcorner)) = \begin{cases} 1 \text{ if } \exists i \neq 0 \, \forall j (\text{if } i \leq j < k \text{ then } \nu_j(\alpha) = 1) \\ 0 \text{ if } \exists i \neq 0 \, \forall j (\text{if } i \leq j < k \text{ then } \nu_j(\alpha) = 0) \\ \frac{1}{2} \text{ otherwise.} \end{cases}$$

Since the aim, in this appendix, is only to give a feel for the target construction and (non-triviality) model, I have used the simpler 'reset' rule. See cited works for general definitions and proofs. *End parenthetical. »*

What we get. As Kripke (1975) and others[17] have shown, various basic set-theoretic facts ensure that, eventually, we reach a 'fixed point' stage k such that $\nu_k = \nu_{k+1}$. Given Proposition KLP, such a stage provides our desired *transparent* and *standard* model. Let me briefly say something about each of these features.

---

[17]Dowden 1984; Visser 1984; Woodruff 1984; Priest 1991; Brady 1989; Gupta and Belnap 1993.

Fixed point. Why do we reach a 'fixed point'? I skip the set theory here (see any of the cited references), but the basic idea is as follows. Our language is countable, and so we can list our sentences $\alpha_1, \alpha_2, \ldots$ What Proposition KLP gives us is that there are two key possibilities for any α_n, namely, that it never gets a classical value at any stage, or it gets a classical value and keeps it 'forever'. Now, suppose that, as you go up each stage i in the construction, you cross off any α_n that gets a classical value. At stage 0 (the base stage), you cross off all α in $\mathcal{L}$ (i.e., the arithmetic sentences), although none of the sentences of the form $Tr(\ulcorner \alpha \urcorner)$ are crossed off (at stage zero). At stage 1, we cross off $Tr(\ulcorner \alpha \urcorner)$ for all α that were crossed off at the prior stage, and also cross off any compounds that are classical at this stage. And so on. What's important to notice is that you must cross off something at each stage; otherwise, you're at a (fixed) point k such that $\nu_k = \nu_{k+1}$, a stage at which any 'potential cross-offs' have already occurred. Since, as above, our given language is countable, your crossing-off activity can only go on countably many steps, and so you'll *have* to reach such a fixed point. That's the basic idea.

« *Parenthetical remark.* Actually, I should note that, with respect to the 'real' proof of such fixed points, it is important that we accept classical set theory, which I do accept. This is not to say that a paraconsistent set theory couldn't provide the required 'fixed point' result; however, as far as I can see, it might not. In any event, I accept classical set theory, e.g. ZFC, which is assumed in our formal modeling. (See Chapter 5 for further discussion concerning the lesson(s) of Russell's paradox.) *End parenthetical.* »

Standard interpretation. What the fixed point gives us is our desired *transparent* model. That the model is also *standard* is clear. (The proof, again, is via induction, but I just point to the basic idea here.) As above, our base interpretation ν_0 itself is standard; the fragment $\mathcal{L}$ is interpreted via the standard model. But, now, given the relevant monotonicity (viz., Proposition KLP), $\mathcal{L}$ remains standard throughout.

The upshot: LPTT is non-trivial in a 'natural' way

What we have, then, is a proof that our ttruth theory (over, e.g., arithmetic plus 'ttruth') is non-trivial, and non-trivial in the requisite way: namely, that the base language is entirely classical; it's just the *ttruth*-ineliminable spandrels that wind up glutty.

2

SUITABLE CONDITIONAL

Chapter 1 presented the basic transparent truth theory that I advocate. This chapter extends the account by addressing the pressing issue of a 'suitable conditional'. My main aim, as in Chapter 1, is simply to present the target account, leaving defense largely to Chapter 5; however, the related issue of validity and 'truth preservation' is addressed in the last two sections.

2.1 Capture and Release

On many conceptions, truth is thought to play Capture and Release: $Tr(x)$ fully captures the information in x, and similarly releases x. In familiar guise:

Capture. $\alpha \Rightarrow Tr(\ulcorner \alpha \urcorner)$

Release. $Tr(\ulcorner \alpha \urcorner) \Rightarrow \alpha$

Here, $\Rightarrow$ may be either a turnstile (representing valid argument or rule) or a conditional (giving rise, when conjoined, to the familiar T-biconditionals). The terms 'Capture' and 'Release' are used not to proliferate terminology, but rather to further emphasize that, at least in the case of *ttruth*, the whole role of the device is to 'capture' and 'release' information. (Another reason for the generic terminology is that it nicely unifies common features of many operators, e.g., common Release features of 'it is known', 'it is necessary that', etc.) As in Chapter 1, I sometimes use 'cc' and 'cr' to abbreviate *conditional Capture* and *conditional Release* (i.e., the conditional reading of $\Rightarrow$), and use 'rc' and 'rr' for the *rule forms* (i.e., the turnstile reading).

Regardless of other conceptions of truth, the question is whether Capture and Release hold for *transparent truth*, our see-through device *ttruth*. Since, on the going account, *ttruth* is introduced via rules of intersubstitutability (see Chapter 1), the rule form of Capture and Release will hold provided that α is a consequence of itself, for all α in the language. As in Chapter 1 (see §1.4), we do have $\alpha \vdash \alpha$, and so, via transparency (intersubstitutability rule), we have both rc and rr, namely,

Rule Capture. $\alpha \vdash Tr(\ulcorner \alpha \urcorner)$

Rule Release. $Tr(\ulcorner \alpha \urcorner) \vdash \alpha$

So, we have rc and rr. What about cc and cr? The only connectives so far discussed, beyond the quantifiers, have been the 'Boolean' ones: disjunction, conjunction, and negation. Our only 'conditional', then, is the 'material conditional', the so-called *hook*, which is defined via negation and disjunction.

The hook. $\alpha \supset \beta$, by definition, is $\neg \alpha \vee \beta$.

Do we have CC or CR for our hook? Yes. Given the transparency of our $Tr(x)$, what is necessary and sufficient for CC or CR for the hook is the validity of $\alpha \supset \alpha$. That we have $\vdash \alpha \supset \alpha$ is clear. The exhaustive 'nature' of our negation gives us LEM, namely, $\vdash \alpha \vee \neg\alpha$. By definition of the hook, $\alpha \supset \alpha$ just is $\neg\alpha \vee \alpha$, and so we have the validity of $\alpha \supset \alpha$. From the transparency of $Tr(x)$, we get both *Hook Capture* and *Hook Release*.

> *Hook Capture.* $\vdash \alpha \supset Tr(\ulcorner\alpha\urcorner)$
>
> *Hook Release.* $\vdash Tr(\ulcorner\alpha\urcorner) \supset \alpha$

As a result, we have the validity of all *hook Tr-biconditionals*, namely,

$$Tr(\ulcorner\alpha\urcorner) \equiv \alpha$$

Here, $\alpha \equiv \beta$ abbreviates $(\alpha \supset \beta) \wedge (\beta \supset \alpha)$, and $\alpha \supset \beta$ abbreviates $\neg\alpha \vee \beta$. Accordingly, our *hook Tr-biconditionals*, unpacked via the definition of the hook, have the following disjunctive form.

$$(\neg Tr(\ulcorner\alpha\urcorner) \vee \alpha) \wedge (\neg\alpha \vee Tr(\ulcorner\alpha\urcorner))$$

The bare disjunctive form of our hook Tr-biconditionals raises an issue. As mentioned in Chapter 1, our hook does not detach; it does not satisfy MPP (rule Modus Ponens):

> » MPP. $\alpha, \alpha \Rightarrow \beta \vdash \beta$

When $\Rightarrow$ is the hook, we have 'material modus ponens' MMP, which is not valid. In the formal account, a countermodel, as in Chapter 1, is a model that verifies α and $\neg\alpha$, and hence also verifies $\neg\alpha \vee \beta$, but fails to verify β. Hence, our hook Tr-biconditionals fail to detach.

The question is whether we have *detachable* Tr-biconditionals (i.e., *ttruth*-biconditionals). If we do, then such biconditionals are not our usual 'material biconditionals', as noted above. I think that we do enjoy detachable Tr-biconditionals, and the next two sections briefly address this topic.

2.2 Curry and a suitable conditional

Most truth theorists emphasize the importance of the T-biconditionals or, generally, the T-schema.[1] I also take the T-biconditionals seriously, but, as above, its status is derivative when the relevant T is our see-through $Tr(x)$: if we have a conditional $\Rightarrow$ that satisfies Identity (i.e., $\vdash \alpha \Rightarrow \alpha$), then the Tr-biconditionals fall out of the fundamental intersubstitutability of $Tr(\ulcorner\alpha\urcorner)$ and α. One desideratum, then, is that our conditional satisfy Identity. As above, our hook satisfies this desideratum, but it fails to satisfy another desideratum, namely, MPP.

Beyond such basic desiderata (e.g., Identity, MPP), there is an obvious other desideratum: non-triviality! If, as I propose, we simply accept that our transparent device is inconsistent—that there are 'ttrue'-ful gluts—we need to rethink so-called contraction principles.

---

[1] Parts of this chapter are from Beall 2005*b*, though the account herein is different.

Contraction and Curry. Consider common versions of contraction, where, for now, $\Rightarrow$ is some detachable conditional, that is, $\Rightarrow$ satisfies MPP.

» $(\alpha \wedge (\alpha \Rightarrow \beta)) \Rightarrow \beta$
» $(\alpha \Rightarrow (\alpha \Rightarrow \beta)) \Rightarrow (\alpha \Rightarrow \beta)$
» $\alpha \Rightarrow (\alpha \Rightarrow \beta) \vdash \alpha \Rightarrow \beta$

Such principles give rise to triviality (everything being ttrue) in virtue of Curry's paradox (Beall, 2008; Curry, 1942; Meyer *et al.*, 1979; Priest, 1987). Spandrels such as 'If this sentence is ttrue, then every sentence is ttrue' pose a problem if the given conditional detaches, satisfies Identity (yielding the Tr-biconditionals), and also contracts. To see this, consider a typical Curry sentence γ of the form $Tr(\ulcorner\gamma\urcorner) \Rightarrow \bot$, where $\bot$ is an explosive sentence—implies everything—and $\Rightarrow$ satisfies both Identity and MPP. (γ, e.g., might be the sentence 'If this very conditional is ttrue, then everything is ttrue'.) An explosive Curry is cooked as follows.

$$\frac{Tr(\ulcorner\gamma\urcorner) \Rightarrow (Tr(\ulcorner\gamma\urcorner) \Rightarrow \bot)}{Tr(\ulcorner\gamma\urcorner) \Rightarrow \bot} \qquad \cdot \text{ T-schema (Simplification)}$$
$$\cdot \text{ Contraction for } \Rightarrow$$
$$\frac{(Tr(\ulcorner\gamma\urcorner) \Rightarrow \bot) \Rightarrow Tr(\ulcorner\gamma\urcorner)}{Tr(\ulcorner\gamma\urcorner)} \qquad \cdot \text{ T-schema (Simplification)}$$
$$\cdot \text{ Modus Ponens for } \Rightarrow$$
$$\frac{}{\bot} \qquad \cdot \text{ Modus Ponens for } \Rightarrow$$

The other contraction-principles similarly yield triviality. As a result, if the detachable conditional employed in our Tr-biconditionals avoids Curry-generated triviality, then it doesn't contract in the given ways.

Let us say that a conditional is *suitable* if it satisfies MPP, Identity, and avoids Curry-generating contraction. What we want, then, is a suitable conditional for our ttruth theory. And, of course, we also want safety from Curry in general, not just for a single suitable conditional. If there are other conditionals in the language (as there may well be), the language must be 'robustly contraction-free', to use Restall's terminology (1993a). In effect, this means that the language is free from *definable* conditionals that contract in the relevant ways. (For extensive discussion of contraction in paraconsistent settings, see Restall 1994; Restall 2000.) That the following proposal is indeed safe (i.e., the proposed theory robustly contraction-free) is ensured by the non-triviality proof in the appendix to this chapter.

« *Parenthetical note.* Those familiar with Łukasiewicz's conditionals might suggest the ∞-valued conditional as a suitable one. This meets the minimal desiderata but it generates ω-inconsistency (Restall, 1992; Hájek *et al.*, 2000) . I briefly return to this in Chapter 4 in discussion of Kripke's account. *End parenthetical.* »

2.2.1 *Towards a suitable conditional*

We already have worlds or points (see Chapter 1), and a natural thought is to use them. In particular, just as negation enjoys a 'modal' treatment, so too with our target conditional. The natural thought is the familiar one, namely,

$$w \models \alpha \rightarrow \beta \quad \text{iff} \quad \text{for all } w' \in \mathcal{W}, \text{ if } w' \models \alpha \text{ then } w' \models \beta$$

Call this the *normal* condition. According to the normal condition, our target conditional is true at a point just if the consequent is true at any point at which the antecedent is true.

While the normal-condition approach is both natural and familiar, it does not yield a suitable conditional, at least as it stands. In particular, notice that various contraction principles are validated, where validity, as in Chapter 1, is defined only over normal or 'base' worlds. Consider *pseudo modus ponens*,[2] namely,

» PMP. $\alpha \wedge (\alpha \rightarrow \beta) \rightarrow \beta$

Given the going account, this is false at a point (normal or otherwise) just if there's some point at which both α and $\alpha \rightarrow \beta$ are true but at which β is not true. But this is ruled out by the normal condition in its current form. Let w be a point at which the antecedent of PMP is true, that is, $w \models \alpha$ and $w \models \alpha \rightarrow \beta$. Since $w \models \alpha \rightarrow \beta$, the normal condition requires that there be no point at which α is true and β not, and so $w \models \beta$. Hence, any point—a fortiori, any normal or base point—at which PMP's antecedent is true is a point at which its consequent is true. Hence, PMP is validated if the normal condition (as given) is imposed. So, the current approach, as given, fails to yield a suitable conditional.

For contraction to fail, we need points at which both α and $\alpha \rightarrow \beta$ are true but β not. But for $\rightarrow$ to satisfy MPP ('real Modus Ponens', as it were), no *normal* world can be like that. This suggests that contraction is avoided, but MPP retained, in virtue of our conditional behaving differently—abnormally, as it were—at *abnormal* worlds, that is, at worlds or points in $\mathcal{W} - \mathcal{N}$. In particular, *we let the normal condition govern (the valuation or semantic status of) conditionals at normal worlds* (i.e., points in $\mathcal{N}$), but we let conditionals behave differently at abnormal worlds.

How shall conditionals be evaluated at abnormal worlds? One approach, due to Routley and Loparić (1978), is to simply let $\alpha \rightarrow \beta$ be *arbitrarily* evaluated at abnormal worlds. In this case, we can have $w \models \alpha$ and $w \models \alpha \rightarrow \beta$ but $w \not\models \beta$, for some (abnormal) world $w \in \mathcal{W} - \mathcal{N}$. Moreover, provided that validity is defined only over normal (or base) worlds, we still enjoy MPP. In other words, even though, towards avoiding PMP (and other contraction principles), we have points at which $\alpha \wedge (\alpha \rightarrow \beta)$ is true but β not true, there are no *normal* points like that, and so no counterexample to MPP.

This approach is both simple and, I think, natural in various ways, and it yields a 'suitable conditional' in our running sense (i.e., Identity, MPP, and avoids Curry-related contraction). On the other hand, without further constraints, the conditional fails to satisfy *equivalents replacement* or *substitutivity of equivalents*, as $\alpha \leftrightarrow \beta$ does not imply $(\gamma \rightarrow \alpha) \leftrightarrow (\gamma \rightarrow \beta)$. For purposes of a *ttruth* theory—wherein *ttruth* is supposed to be fully see-through (i.e., fully intersubstitutable)—it is important to have a conditional that satisfies substitutivity of equivalents.

---

[2]The term is from Priest 1980; Restall 1994.

There are various ways to tweak the given account that provide the given *equivalents replacement* rule, but I shall follow a different—though related—approach from the simple, 'arbitrary evaluator' one.

« *Parenthetical remark.* See Beall 2005*b* for one way of (perhaps ultimately ad hocly) tweaking the above approach to get substitutivity, and Priest 1992 for another approach. The latter approach is done in terms of 'propositions', and the given substitutivity falls out of the framework without requiring ad hoc constraints. It is worth noting that the failure of 'equivalents replacement' is a consequence of a more general weakness of the above approach. In particular, virtually all rules involving embedded conditionals are lost. Perhaps this has its virtues, but, as above, I shall pursue a different path. *End parenthetical.* »

2.2.2 *The proposal*

Let us assume that the normal condition, as in §2.2.1, is right for *normal* worlds, though not for *all* worlds—specifically, not for abnormal ones. The issue at hand concerns abnormal worlds, in particular, the behavior of our target conditional at such worlds. The proposal I shall follow is ultimately due to Routley and Meyer (1973) and Priest and Sylvan (1992).

The proposal invokes a familiar thought: we acknowledge a relation on worlds. In standard modal semantics, our *unary* connective(s)—for example, 'necessarily' or the like—are treated via a *binary* relation on worlds. For example, where $\Box$ is our unary modal operator, we invoke a binary 'accessibility' relation R along the following lines, where Rww' holds just if w enjoys 'access' to w'.

» $w \models \Box\alpha$ if and only if $w' \models \alpha$, for all w' such that Rww'.

This approach has been useful for cashing out the logic of such (unary) connectives.

Along the same lines, we shall invoke a *ternary* relation for purposes of treating our *binary* conditional—at least for abnormal worlds, which is the current issue. One may, for present purposes, think of the ternary relation along familiar 'accessibility' lines: $Rww'w''$ holds just if the *pair* $\langle w', w'' \rangle$ is 'accessible' from world w. When $w' = w''$, this might just be the familiar 'access' involved in standard 'worlds semantics' (assuming $\langle x \rangle = x$), but I do not want to put too much weight on the philosophical import of the given relation. (I return to the issue of philosophical import in Chapter 5.) For convenience, let us say that $\langle w', w'' \rangle$ is a *w-accessible pair* just if $Rww'w''$.

The idea, then, is that the normal condition, as above (see page 28), governs our conditional at all normal (or base) points: $\alpha \to \beta$ is true at a *normal* world iff there's *no* world (normal or not) at which α is true but β not. At *abnormal* points, the conditional is constrained by the given ternary relation: $\alpha \to \beta$ is true at an abnormal point w iff there's no w-accessible pair $\langle w', w'' \rangle$ such that α is true at w' and β not true at w''. Whereas the normal condition (now restricted to normal worlds) involves looking only at (all) points taken by themselves (and checking whether the consequent is true at the point if antecedent is true), the abnormal condition involves looking at *pairs* $\langle y, z \rangle$ of points—and checking whether the consequent is true at z if antecedent is true at y. Of course, sometimes, $y = z$, in which case one is back to checking a point 'by itself', but sometimes $y \neq z$.

A formal picture. It will be useful to have a slightly clearer formal picture in hand. We expand our previous structures (see Chapter 1) by adding a ternary relation R on $\mathcal{W}$, so that our structures are now $\langle \mathcal{W}, \mathcal{N}, \mathcal{D}, @, R, \star, I, \models \rangle$. Quantifiers and Boolean connectives remain as in Chapter 1.

Our target conditional, which, unlike the hook, is a primitive connective in the syntax, has clauses for each 'type' of world—normal and abnormal. In particular, one clause specifies the behavior of our target conditional at normal worlds, and another clause specifies the conditional's behavior at abnormal worlds.

The clause for normal worlds—the clause governing the behavior of our conditional at normal worlds—is the 'normal condition' from above.

» *Normal.* Where $w \in \mathcal{N}$ and $w' \in \mathcal{W}$,
$$w \models \alpha \to \beta \quad \text{iff} \quad w' \models \beta \text{ if } w' \models \alpha, \text{ for } any \ w' \in \mathcal{W}$$

The 'abnormal condition', in turn, governs our conditional at abnormal points.

» *Abnormal.* Where $w \in \mathcal{W} - \mathcal{N}$ and $w', w'' \in \mathcal{W}$,
$$w \models \alpha \to \beta \quad \text{iff} \quad w'' \models \beta \text{ if } w' \models \alpha, \text{ for all } w\text{-accessible } \langle w', w'' \rangle$$

Recall the terminology from Chapter 1, according to which α is verified in a model just if $@ \models \alpha$. Since $@ \in \mathcal{N}$, we have it from the normal condition that $\alpha \to \beta$ is verified in a model just if there's *no* world (normal or abnormal) at which α is true and β not. This preserves the familiar force of the original 'normal condition', despite the restriction to normal points (i.e., the restriction that the normal condition governs the conditional only at normal points).

Finally, *consequence* is now defined as in Chapter 1: any such model that verifies Σ verifies α. Let me briefly turn to some virtues of the conditional.

« *Parenthetical remark.* An historical note: so-called non-normal points—what I'm calling *abnormal* points—were first invoked by Kripke (1965) to model weak Lewis systems (viz., systems in which Necessitation fails). Routley and Meyer (1973) and Routley and Loparić (1978) invoked such points for purposes closer to the current project, as have Priest (1992) and Mares (2004a). As above, I return to the philosophical import, if any, in Chapter 5. *End parenthetical.* »

2.2.3 *Virtues of the conditional*

The chief virtue of the conditional is that the target desiderata are achieved, as follows. Other virtues (and alleged 'defects') are taken up in Chapter 5.

Detachment. While we don't have *all-points detachment* (i.e., 'truth preservation' over all points), we do have it at all *base-points* (at $@$ for any given interpretation). To get a counterexample to MPP we would need $@ \models \alpha$ and $@ \models \alpha \to \beta$ but $@ \not\models \beta$. But this is impossible, since $@$ is normal (in all models); the normal condition has it that $\alpha \to \beta$ is true at $@$ iff β is true at every point at which α is true. So, MPP holds.

Identity. We have the validity of $\alpha \to \alpha$, and hence the Tr-biconditionals, given the fundamental intersubstitutability rules governing *ttruth*.[3]

Of course, so far, the MPP and Identity desiderata require no more than standard 'world' semantics. (Indeed, such desiderata are achieved with standard, *extensional* conditionals—e.g., RM_3 or Łukasiewicz's n-valued conditionals.) The role of our *abnormal* worlds emerges with the other desideratum regarding Curry.

Contraction. Counterexamples to the given contraction principles emerge in virtue of abnormal worlds. Consider an example, namely, PMP. Perhaps the simplest sort of countermodel to PMP is one in which w is abnormal, $w \models \alpha$ and $w \not\models \beta$, and there's no w-accessible pair $\langle w', w'' \rangle$ for any worlds w and w'. In this case, since there's no 'accessibility' for w, there's no $\langle w', w'' \rangle$ such that $w' \models \alpha$ but $w'' \not\models \beta$, and hence $w \models \alpha \to \beta$ by the abnormality condition. So, $w \models \alpha \wedge (\alpha \to \beta)$. But, then, there's a point (viz., abnormal w) at which α and $\alpha \to \beta$ are true but β not. Hence, as @ is normal, @ $\not\models \alpha \wedge (\alpha \to \beta) \to \beta$ regardless of the status of α or β at @. Similar models serve to invalidate the other contraction principles.

Substitutivity of Equivalents. We have that $\alpha \leftrightarrow \beta \vdash C(\alpha) \leftrightarrow C(\beta)$, for any context C. (I omit the proof, but see Priest and Sylvan 1992.)

2.2.4 *The logic BX and broader ttruth theory*

It is important, at least for the proposed ttruth theory, to say something about the resulting logic. The following axiom system is (strongly) complete with respect to the given 'formal picture' (i.e., formal semantics). See Routley 1980; Priest and Sylvan 1992 for proofs.

For present purposes, I simply lay out the system, which serves as the logic of my proposed *ttruth* theory. For further discussion (and completeness proof), see Priest and Sylvan 1992, wherein related systems are also discussed.[4]

In what follows, An is an axiom, and Rn a rule. Strong completeness requires so-called 'disjunctive' versions of various rules, which I do not herein give but nonetheless indicate with an asterisk.[5] Note that I assume appropriate adjustments for 'freedom and bondage' (e.g., *x not free in α in A12 or A15, and likewise for β in A13 and A14*). Finally, $\alpha(t/x)$, as in Chapter 1, is the result of replacing all free occurrences of variable x in α with (closed) term t.

A0. $\vdash \alpha \vee \neg\alpha$

A1. $\vdash \alpha \to \alpha$

---

[3] See the appendix to this chapter for a proof (sketch) that we continue to enjoy *ttruth* over our extended, conditional-ful language.

[4] For stronger—though, for my *ttruth*-related purposes, too strong—systems and corresponding ternary semantics, see Restall 1993*b*. (See also Fine 1974 for early work on related logics.)

[5] See Priest and Sylvan 1992 for details, but an example suffices for the idea: in addition to R2, we also have R2D (for Disjunctive): if $\vdash \alpha \vee \gamma$ and $\vdash \beta \vee \gamma$ then $\vdash (\alpha \wedge \beta) \vee \gamma$. The other Disjunctive versions are similar.

A2. $\vdash \alpha \wedge \beta \to \alpha$ and $\alpha \wedge \beta \to \beta$

A3. $\vdash \alpha \to \alpha \vee \beta$ and $\vdash \beta \to \alpha \vee \beta$

A4. $\vdash \alpha \leftrightarrow \neg\neg\alpha$

A5. $\vdash (\neg\alpha \vee \neg\beta) \leftrightarrow \neg(\alpha \wedge \beta)$

A6. $\vdash (\neg\alpha \wedge \neg\beta) \leftrightarrow \neg(\alpha \vee \beta)$

A7. $\vdash \alpha \wedge (\beta \vee \gamma) \to (\alpha \wedge \beta) \vee (\alpha \wedge \gamma)$

A8. $\vdash (\alpha \to \beta) \wedge (\alpha \to \gamma) \to (\alpha \to \beta \wedge \gamma)$

A9. $\vdash (\alpha \to \gamma) \wedge (\beta \to \gamma) \to (\alpha \vee \beta \to \gamma)$

A10. $\vdash \forall x\alpha \to \alpha(t/x)$

A11. $\vdash \alpha(t/x) \to \exists x\alpha$

A12. $\vdash \alpha \wedge \exists x\beta \to \exists x(\alpha \wedge \beta)$

A13. $\vdash \forall x(\alpha \vee \beta) \to (\alpha \vee \forall x\beta)$

A14. $\vdash \forall x(\alpha \to \beta) \to (\exists x\alpha \to \beta)$

A15. $\vdash \forall x(\alpha \to \beta) \to (\alpha \to \forall x\beta)$

R1*. If $\vdash \alpha$ and $\vdash \alpha \to \beta$ then $\vdash \beta$.

R2*. If $\vdash \alpha$ and $\vdash \beta$ then $\vdash \alpha \wedge \beta$.

R3*. If $\vdash \alpha \to \beta$ then $\vdash \neg\beta \to \neg\alpha$.

R4*. If $\vdash \alpha \to \beta$ and $\vdash \gamma \to \delta$ then $\vdash (\beta \to \gamma) \to (\alpha \to \delta)$.

The logic so axiomatized is called BX, which is a slightly stronger logic than the so-called *basic* (affixing) logic B, stronger in the sense of adding LEM.[6] Discussion of the logic, and its place in a family of paraconsistent logics, may be found in Dunn and Restall 2002, and also in works cited above.

BXTT*: the broader ttruth theory.* The official *ttruth* theory, then, is what, following usage in Chapter 1 with 'LPTT', we may call 'BXTT', which contains all ttruths and is closed under BX and TP, our transparency principle for *ttruth*. (See Chapter 1.) That, despite the additional conditional, we enjoy not only a non-trivial theory, but a 'natural', classical-base-language theory (in the sense discussed in Chapter 1) follows from a result ultimately due to Ross Brady. Since our non-triviality result for the LP^* theory LPTT, sketched in the appendix to Chapter 1, requires monotonicity of all connectives, the given construction does *not* establish non-triviality for our broader, conditional-ful theory BXTT. The reason is that our conditional is not monotonic in the requisite sense. Still, the basic

---

[6]It is worth noting that, given A0 and R1*, features such as transitivity, 'prefixing', and 'suffixing' are cases of R4*, where these, respectively, are

» If $\vdash \alpha \to \beta$ and $\vdash \beta \to \gamma$ then $\vdash \alpha \to \gamma$.

» If $\vdash \gamma \to \delta$ then $\vdash (\alpha \to \gamma) \to (\alpha \to \delta)$.

» If $\vdash \alpha \to \beta$ then $\vdash (\beta \to \gamma) \to (\alpha \to \gamma)$.

non-triviality construction is similar to the 'Kripke' construction for the LP^* theory; it employs an ingenious idea, due to Brady, for handling our non-monotonic conditional. The non-triviality construction is sketched in the appendix to this chapter.

2.3 Curry and Liars

In this section, I pause briefly to clarify the difference between—and the different treatment of—Curry sentences (at least 'real' ones) and Liars. I also briefly return to the issue noted in Chapter 1, namely, 'symmetry' considerations with respect to *ttruth*-ineliminable sentences.

2.3.1 *Liars and Curry*

Some philosophers might think that Curry paradoxes are just more Liars—the same phenomenon. Some Curry sentences arguably are just more Liars. In particular, if we restrict ourselves to the →-free fragment, so that our only 'conditional' is the hook, then Curry sentences are simply disjunctive Liars. Where 'If' is just the hook, a spandrel such as

√ If the ticked sentence in §2.3.1 is ttrue, then everything is ttrue.

is equivalent to

The ticked sentence in §2.3.1 is not ttrue or everything is ttrue.

In this case, we have a sentence λ equivalent to $\neg Tr(\ulcorner \lambda \urcorner) \vee \bot$. The result, by familiar reasoning (available in BX), is that the ticked sentence is simply a glut.

Whether such disjunctive sentences are called *Curry* sentences or Liars (or both) is unimportant, but it is useful to set terminology. Let a Curry sentence be a sentence that says of itself only that *if* it is ttrue, then $\bot$ is ttrue, where $\bot$ is an explosive sentence (e.g., 'everything is ttrue') and the given 'if' is our suitable conditional—not the hook. On this way of talking, the ticked sentence in §2.3.1 is not a Curry sentence (given the intended hook reading).

With terminology set, it does appear that Curry sentences are more of the same Liar-like phenomenon. The only real difference is that no Curry sentence is glutty while Liars are glutty. Given a detachable conditional, it is not rational to accept that such Curry sentences are *gluts*, since such sentences imply triviality.[7] On my account, Curry sentences are false; I reject that they're ttrue.

If we want, as we do, to reject that Curry sentences are ttrue, accept that they're tfalse, we need our conditional to allow for cases in which antecedent, consequent, and the conditional itself are all tfalse. This is what our conditional

---

[7] A so-called *trivialist*, who accepts that everything is ttrue (and, hence, tfalse), would accept as much. With Priest (2006a), I reject that trivialists are rational—at least if *ttruth* is the relevant truth predicate. One could, of course, reject RR and CR for 'true', and thereby accept that everything is 'true' (in some sense) without the consequence that everything is true, but I focus only on *ttruth* in this discussion (and assume RR and CR throughout).

allows. In the formal picture, Curry sentences wind up false in virtue of being true at abnormal worlds. Consider, again, the simple countermodel to PMP discussed in §2.2.3, wherein $\alpha \to \beta$ is false at @ even though α and β are false at @. All that's required is a point at which α is true and β false; and this is what an abnormal world provides in the case of Curry-like sentences.

One might think that Curry sentences require the existence of a *trivial world*, a world—or, more neutrally, point—at which *all* sentences are true. After all, in order for $\gamma \to \bot$ to be false, where γ is a Curry sentence equivalent to $\gamma \to \bot$, we need a point w at which γ is true. But, then, since γ is equivalent to $\gamma \to \bot$, and since our conditional $\to$ detaches (i.e., satisfies MPP), $\bot$ must be true at w too, and so everything is true at w, since $\bot$ implies everything.

This is a natural thought, but it reflects a misunderstanding. Curry sentences do not force the existence of a trivial world. While we do have the validity of MPP, validity is defined only over normal (or 'base') worlds. In other words, our conditional detaches at all normal (hence, 'actual') worlds, but it needn't—and, as the given example indicates, doesn't—detach at *all* worlds. Abnormal worlds live up to their name: our conditional doesn't always detach at such worlds; it behaves 'abnormally' at such worlds.

2.3.2 *Symmetry again*

Inasmuch as Curry sentences, like Liars, are *ttruth*-ineliminable sentences (i.e., as in Chapter 1, sentences from which 'ttrue' cannot be removed via the fundamental intersubstitutability rules), there is a straightforward sense in which 'symmetry' approaches to such sentences must be rejected—at least on my approach. In Chapter 1, I noted my openness to an asymmetric treatment of such sentences (e.g., treating some *ttruth*-ineliminable sentences as gluts, some classically), but officially embraced the simple approach according to which all such sentences are gluts—transparently true with transparently true negations. This position remains, but only for the conditional-free fragment.

There are a variety of objections and issues that arise with the proposed (fairly weak) conditional, but I leave many of those to Chapter 5. For the remainder of this chapter, I briefly discuss only one of the given issues, namely, validity and 'truth preservation'.

2.4 Truth preservation and validity

The notion of validity is often cashed out, at least intuitively, as 'necessary truth preservation'. At the very least, 'truth preservation' is commonly thought to be a necessary condition of validity, where 'truth preservation' is a conditional claim with a conditional as consequent, namely, VTP (for 'validity truth preservation').

> » VTP. If an argument is valid, then if its premises are (all) true, its conclusion is true.

Where $\Rightarrow$ is some conditional in the language, and $Val(x, y)$ the validity predicate (in and for the given language), VTP has the following form, where, for simplicity, I concentrate on single-premise arguments.

$$Val(\ulcorner\alpha\urcorner,\ulcorner\beta\urcorner) \Rightarrow (Tr(\ulcorner\alpha\urcorner) \Rightarrow Tr(\ulcorner\beta\urcorner))$$

As it turns out, such a claim—namely, that validity is (unrestrictedly) ttruth-preserving—needs to be rejected, and I reject it. In a fully classical setting (in which our logic is fully classical), we can retain the familiar (alleged) connection between validity and 'necessary truth preservation' by giving up a ttruth predicate (for the language) in which to express (in the language) such a connection. (One must resort to a 'richer metalanguage' and, hence, use something other than *ttruth*, or give up some of the Capture and Release behavior—and, hence, again give up *ttruth*.) By contrast, as Chapter 1 indicated, my approach gives us a ttruth predicate in and for the language; however, the familiar (alleged) connection between validity and ttruth preservation is lost or, at least, strained.

To see the problem, concentrate on the VTP principle, where $\Rightarrow$ is any suitable conditional in the language, for example, our suitable conditional $\rightarrow$ given above. Given the transparency of $Tr(x)$, we can think of VTP as V1, namely,

V1. $Val(\ulcorner\alpha\urcorner,\ulcorner\beta\urcorner) \Rightarrow (\alpha \Rightarrow \beta)$

Given that $\Rightarrow$ detaches (i.e., MPP is valid), plus plausible assumptions about conjunction (all of which hold in the proposed logic BX), we have

$$Val(\ulcorner\alpha \wedge (\alpha \Rightarrow \beta)\urcorner,\ulcorner\beta\urcorner) \tag{2.1}$$

But, then, by V1, (2.1) and MPP we immediately get PMP, namely,

$$\alpha \wedge (\alpha \Rightarrow \beta) \Rightarrow \beta \tag{2.2}$$

The trouble, as in §2.2, is that (2.2) is a notoriously easy recipe for Curry paradox, which results in triviality. If all claims of the form (2.2) are ttrue, then a fortiori every Curry instance is ttrue. For example, where γ is a Curry sentence equivalent to $\gamma \Rightarrow \perp$, and $\perp$ some triviality-yielding sentence, (2.2) implies triviality as follows.

$\gamma \wedge (\gamma \Rightarrow \perp) \Rightarrow \perp$	· Curry instance of (2.2), i.e. of PMP
$\gamma \wedge \gamma \Rightarrow \perp$	· Equivalents Subsitution: γ for $\gamma \Rightarrow \perp$
$\gamma \Rightarrow \perp$	· Equivalents Subsitution: γ for $\gamma \wedge \gamma$
γ	· Equivalency of γ and $\gamma \Rightarrow \perp$
$\perp$	· MPP for $\Rightarrow$

The upshot is that, 'intuitively right' as it appears, V1 and, hence, VTP must go.

One might suggest employing a 'mixed strategy' involving our hook and our suitable conditional. We can have, for example,

V2. $Val(\ulcorner\alpha\urcorner,\ulcorner\beta\urcorner) \rightarrow (\alpha \supset \beta)$

As such, we can ttruly say that valid arguments are ttruth-preserving where the given 'truth preservation' is expressed via the material 'conditional'. Moreover, while this implies a PMP lookalike, namely,

$$\alpha \wedge (\alpha \rightarrow \beta) \supset \beta \tag{2.3}$$

(2.3) is harmless for Curry-instances; the hook, as noted, fails to detach.

One might think that a salient cost of retaining ttruth preservation via V2 concerns the familiar relation between inference (or, indeed, deductions) and validity. The utility of (knowing that you have) a valid argument is often supposed to be that it is ttruth-preserving. The utility of such ttruth preservation, in turn, is often supposed to be that our inferences, if ttruth-preserving, 'won't go wrong'. The worry is that while V2 ensures that valid arguments are ttruth-preserving the utility of such ttruth preservation is now dubious: one can know that an argument is valid and know that its premises are all ttrue, but nonetheless remain without a valid argument that takes one from such information and the V2-ttruth-preservation of the argument to the given conclusion.

I agree that one doesn't have a valid argument from all instances of V2's consequent $\alpha \supset \beta$ and α to β, but I think that this does not undermine the familiar pragmatic utility of valid arguments. The worry about 'utility' is about what we do with valid arguments, and in particular about their role in regimenting (perhaps ideal) 'proper' or 'legitimate' reasoning. While I do not have a worked out theory of 'legitimate' or 'proper' reasoning, I assume that, for present purposes, the relevant feature of such reasoning is that its 'steps' go from ttruth to ttruth, unttruth (i.e., tfalsity) to ttruth, or unttruth to unttruth. For convenience, let a *proper step* be one that goes from ttruth to ttruth, unttruth to ttruth, or from unttruth to unttruth. Then what the running worry wants is an assurance that, where 'always' is (here) a logically necessary connection, one always makes proper steps via valid arguments. But *this* feature of valid arguments, properly understood, is intact. In particular, if one construes the 'steps' along 'rule' (e.g., turnstile) lines, one's valid steps are exactly as wanted: proper, and logically necessarily so. Formulating such properness in conditional form is what V2 affords: always and everywhere—logically necessarily—valid arguments 'step' from ttruth to ttruth, unttruth to ttruth, or unttruth to unttruth. The fact that one cannot, in turn, make a valid step from all instances of V2's consequent $\alpha \supset \beta$ and α to β may initially be surprising; however, it does not diminish the key fact that, in the case of valid arguments, one always steps properly. This, it seems to me, is sufficient 'utility' in valid arguments.

One might wonder whether, in addition to always yielding 'proper steps', valid arguments ever yield a step from ttruth to unttruth, where 'unttrue' is short for 'not ttrue' (i.e., tfalse). The answer is affirmative for predictable reasons. In particular, spandrels of *ttruth*, such as Liars, are not ttrue; however, we have valid arguments from ttrue premises to such spandrels' unttruth. So, some valid arguments go from ttruth to unttruth. The point is independent of the V2 approach to truth preservation: so long as we have valid arguments from ttrue premises to the ttruth of (say) Liars, we thereby have valid arguments from ttrue premises to unttrue conclusions. But none of this is problematic. Despite going from ttruth to unttruth, such valid steps—towards, for example, Liar gluts— remain perfectly proper; they go from ttruth to ttruth. Indeed, in stepping from the Liar to itself, one not only goes from ttruth to unttruth, but one also runs the gamut of 'proper' options—ttruth to ttruth, unttruth to ttruth, etc. In short,

Liars add a twist to validity: we can have sound arguments (i.e., valid with all ttrue premises) with unttrue conclusions (e.g., a Liar that is not ttrue). Still, for all the apparent oddity, our valid arguments always make proper 'steps'. And this is what is important or at least 'useful' about them.

One alternative to the V2 proposal should be mentioned, namely, rejecting the idea that we have a single *validity* relation defined over our entire language. This is the route proposed by John Myhill (1975, 1984). Details aside, the proposal is to trade in a single validity relation for a hierarchy of such relations, each relation defined over some proper fragment of the language. In turn, one introduces infinitely many corresponding conditionals, each 'indexed' (as it were) to a different validity relation. With these resources in hand, one can safely—that is, safely from Curry—ttruly assert that every (say) $valid_n$ argument is ttruth-preserving, where 'ttruth preservation' employs the corresponding conditional (say) $\Rightarrow_n$.

While I do not have any strong arguments against the Myhill approach— many conditionals, many validity relations—I do not endorse it. The proposal makes sense if there's some prior need to think that validity is ttruth-preserving. As far as I know, there is no such need. Indeed, it is not implausible to think that the alleged equation (perhaps ultimately a conflation) of validity and 'truth preservation' (of some necessary sort) arises from a Tarskian, 'hierarchical' account of truth. On such an account, one may easily *define* validity (for a given 'lower' language) in terms of truth-for-that-language. But even Tarski didn't think that such an account was an account of truth, let alone our device *ttruth*. Pending some need to think that validity is ttruth-preserving, I think that the Myhill approach is under-motivated.

« *Parenthetical remark*. On the surface, rejecting that validity is ttruth-preserving goes against the grain of 'logical pluralism' as given in Beall and Restall 2005, but I think that there may be a way of reconciling such rejection with the main thesis of that book. In short, one continues to take *validity* to be a notion defined via *truth in a case* conditions, and one is pluralist about such 'cases'. The difference is that one can no longer take validity to be *truth preserving*, only *truth in a case* preserving—rejecting that there's a case C such that α is true-in-C iff α is ttrue. Whether this successfully reconciles the logical pluralism of Beall and Restall 2005 is open. Given the limited aims of this book, I leave it as such. *End parenthetical.* »

2.5 Validity?

As above, I reject that valid arguments are ttruth-preserving in anything beyond the hook sense of V2. The salient question is what, in the end, *validity* is supposed to be if not 'essentially ttruth-preserving'. While I remain without a firm answer to this question, there are some options, all of which strike me as reasonable and, pending the discovery of problems, any of which I am happy to endorse. By way of closing this chapter, I briefly sketch three fairly natural options, though leave details wide open.

2.5.1 *No definition: primitive validity*

One option is that validity is simply a primitive relation, not definable in terms of ttruth or any derivative, stronger notion of truth. (See Chapter 4 for discussion of derivative, stronger notions of truth in prominent non-paraconsistent settings.) Though primitive, validity might enjoy many features that we often incorrectly take to be definitive of the relation. For example, validity might be ttruth-preserving over a large fragment of our language. We might have

$$Val(\ulcorner \alpha \urcorner, \ulcorner \beta \urcorner) \to (\alpha \to \beta)$$

for all α and β in such and so a fragment, though, as above, not for *all* α and β in the language. Indeed, such limited ttruth preservation holds in the $\to$-free fragment on my proposed account. Because the $\to$-free fragment may largely be the fragment on which 'intuitions' are built (although I am not prepared to put too much weight on that), we may have reasonably but nonetheless incorrectly conflated such limited ttruth preservation with a *definition* of validity. On the going account, however, there is no such definition, at least over the whole language.

Despite its primitive status, common thoughts about validity might still be retained in terms of *acceptance* and *rejection*, instead of ttruth. Example:

» One ought to reject the validity of a given argument if one accepts that it's possible for the given premises to be ttrue but conclusion tfalse.

Such a principle (or the like) is not to be seen as partially definitive of validity; it's not. Still, the primitive validity relation might well 'fit' with such a principle.

Further details aside, there are at least two issues that arise for the 'primitive' approach to validity. The first one is epistemological; the second concerns the role of model theory (or, more generally, formal semantics). Let me briefly address each issue.

The epistemological issue is straightforward. If validity is primitive, then how do we come to know what is valid? How do we come to know which, among the many relations over our language, is the validity relation? This is a serious and, I think, seriously hard issue. And I do not have an answer. What is clear is that the issue is not peculiar to the 'primitive' account. After all, even if, for some notion of truth or other, validity really were defined in terms of 'truth preservation' (of some necessary sort), standard epistemological questions of how we would know that *that* is a 'real counterexample' (or etc.) would arise. (Along these lines, note that, unless we're working with a hierarchy of validity relations, it is very difficult—even paradoxes aside—to see how one could *define*, in a non-circular fashion, the validity relation for one's own language.) This is not to say that the epistemological issue doesn't require an answer. It does. The point, again, is just that the issue is not peculiar to the 'primitive' approach.

The other question concerns the role of our model-theoretic account of consequence. More generally, if validity is primitive, what is the role of our formal semantics and, in particular, the formal account of validity in Chapter 1? The answer, given methodological disquotationalism and the driving conception of *ttruth*, is that the formal account is instrumental; it serves as a simple but almost entirely heuristic guide towards specifying what the validity relation amounts to. On the 'primitive' approach, validity is primitive; it is not defined via 'truth values' or 'semantic values' or in any other way. Still, we can construct useful model-theoretic accounts of various valid 'forms' in terms of such 'semantic values', and such is the chief service of formal semantics and a model-theoretic account of validity.

« *Parenthetical remark.* Model theory, of course, may also serve to give a consistency (or non-triviality) proof, as Dummett (1978) and Field (2008) have emphasized. Hartry Field, in works cited, has advocated this sort of 'merely heuristic' view of formal semantics, though he might reject some of my (brief) sketch. *End parenthetical.* »

The 'merely heuristic' account of model theory and, in general, of formal semantics is natural—perhaps inevitable—for transparent truth theorists (or, at least, methodological disquotationalists), especially on the conception advocated in this essay. I briefly return to this issue in Chapter 3. For now, I turn to another approach to validity that one might endorse in the current framework, one where our formal semantics plays more than a merely heuristic or instrumental role.

2.5.2 *Definition: two-step account*

Another approach to validity is very closely related to the 'primitive' account but, in contrast, advocates a definition of validity. The idea, on this approach, is to construct some formal language (with some class of models or interpretations) and use the account of validity *for that (artificial) language* to *define* validity in our language. In short, one follows two steps.

» *Step One:* one constructs some language $\mathcal{L}$ and defines what it is for $\mathcal{L}$-sentences to be *true-in-M*, for 'models' (or interpretations) M. In turn, one defines validity for $\mathcal{L}$ in terms of truth-in-M (over all given M). This is exactly what we did in Chapter 1, and is the standard approach in formal semantics (though terminology might vary). Let us call this $\mathcal{L}$-*validity* (just for a handy name).

» *Step Two:* one extracts the $\mathcal{L}$-valid 'forms' from Step One. In turn, where $\mathcal{F}$ comprises the extracted 'forms', one defines *validity*, for our 'real' language, relative to $\mathcal{F}$. In particular, an argument is valid just if its 'form' is in $\mathcal{F}$.

This two-step approach, like the 'primitive' approach, agrees that validity cannot be defined in terms of ttruth (or its derivatives). Unlike the 'primitive' account, the current approach takes one's formal account to be more than either heuristic or instrumental; it is now essentially used in defining 'real validity' (the validity relation over our language). In particular, the notion of truth-in-M, defined over one's formal language $\mathcal{L}$, is used to first define a notion of validity for some other (and entirely formal) language $\mathcal{L}$. This relation, over $\mathcal{L}$, yields 'valid forms' (however, ultimately, that is to be filled out). In turn, one uses the given class of 'forms' to *define* validity over one's language.

Notice that, on this approach, it is not surprising that some arguments (in our 'real' language) are not ttruth-preserving. What makes an argument valid on this approach is simply the 'form', where the relevant forms come from artificial, formal $\mathcal{L}$. Every $\mathcal{L}$-valid $\mathcal{L}$-argument is truth-in-M-preserving for all M (that's just what $\mathcal{L}$-validity is), but true-in-M is not *ttruth*.

As with the previous account, this 'two-step definition' approach faces epistemological issues. The epistemological questions, at bottom, are much the same (e.g., why *that* formal language versus *that* one), and such questions remain open.

Unlike the previous account, this approach requires a precise account of 'argument forms'. This is not an easy matter, and I leave the task undone—or, at least, to the work of others (e.g., Preyer and Peters 2002). For now, I turn to one more option, a sort of synthesis of the foregoing two.

2.5.3 *Partial definition: sufficient condition only*

The 'primitive' approach rejects that validity is to be defined. The 'two-step definition' approach advocates a definition, but one in terms of some artificial language whose connection to our 'real language' remains (at least for all I've said) unclear.

Another option is to take a middle ground: *validity* has at most a 'partial' definition. More accurately, *validity* enjoys only a *sufficient* condition, not a necessary and sufficient condition. (One could, of course, give multiple sufficient conditions, but I shall suggest just one.)

The lesson of Curry is that we must reject that valid arguments are (unrestrictedly) ttruth-preserving in anything more than the hook sense (viz., V2). In particular, as above, we cannot use our suitable conditional $\rightarrow$ and ttruly say that valid arguments are ttruth-preserving, that is, cannot ttruly assert

$$Val(\ulcorner\alpha\urcorner, \ulcorner\beta\urcorner) \rightarrow (\alpha \rightarrow \beta)$$

On the other hand, there is no trouble having the converse, namely

$$(\alpha \rightarrow \beta) \rightarrow Val(\ulcorner\alpha\urcorner, \ulcorner\beta\urcorner)$$

Indeed, given the account of our conditional in §2.2.1, this is what one should expect. After all, our conditional $\rightarrow$ covers *all* worlds (or points), normal (i.e., base) or abnormal, whereas validity (at least in the formal picture) is restricted only to normal (or base) worlds. More clearly, if you concentrate on a given model, the truth of $\alpha \rightarrow \beta$ in the model requires 'truth preservation' over all worlds of the model, be they normal or abnormal. On the other hand, only a *normal* (or, as it's set up, a *base*) world in the model serves as a 'counterexample' to a given argument form.

None of this is to suggest a conflation of the role of the turnstile (i.e., ⊢) in our formal picture and our 'real conditional' or 'real validity'. The former 'talks about' a class of models, whereas the latter—at least in our real language—talks about various worlds. The point, rather, is that our conditional may naturally serve as a sufficient condition for validity—our 'real' conditional and 'real' validity. This makes validity 'partially' defined, in some sense. As Curry teaches, we don't have a necessary and sufficient condition for validity, but we have a sufficient one, namely, the ttruth of our suitable conditional.

V3. $(\alpha \rightarrow \beta) \rightarrow Val(\ulcorner\alpha\urcorner, \ulcorner\beta\urcorner)$

This might not be everything that one would want from an account of validity, but it may be all that we need.

Summary

In this chapter, I have broadened the overall picture by adding a suitable conditional into the mix. Moreover, I have specified the logic of the proposed theory of ttruth, namely, BX and TP (giving the resulting theory BXTT). The overall theory, as discussed in Chapter 1, is intended to be a modest one: we have gluts, but they are 'merely semantic', arising only from our see-through device (or related 'semantic' notions); they do not arise at our otherwise classical base language.

While the conditional-free fragment enjoys a clear non-triviality proof (one in which, as desired, the base language is entirely classical), the addition of our suitable conditional changes matters. Fortunately, there is a non-triviality proof (one in which the base language, as desired, is entirely classical). This is sketched in the appendix to this chapter.

CHAPTER TWO APPENDIX: NON-TRIVIALITY

This appendix presupposes the Chapter 1 appendix. As with the Chapter 1 appendix, the main aim here is simply to sketch the target non-triviality construction, concentrating on a particular model instead of more general results. Proofs and full details are left to cited work. I first try to sketch the basic idea, and then simply specify the basic construction.

The basic idea

As in Chapter 1, we want a standard, transparent model of the—now conditional-ful—ttruth theory BXTT. Let $\mathcal{L}$ be the language of arithmetic and $\mathcal{L}^+$ be $\mathcal{L}$ extended with $Tr(x)$, and $\mathcal{L}_+^+$ be $\mathcal{L}^+$ extended with $\to$. A model is *standard* if $\mathcal{L}$ enjoys its standard interpretation (i.e., standard model), and *transparent* if TP holds over $\mathcal{L}_+^+$. (See Chapter 1 for TP and, relatedly, WT.) Let the target theory be in the language of $\mathcal{L}_+^+$ closed under TP and BX. What we want, then, is a standard, transparent interpretation of the theory.

The challenge. Recall that WT and TP are equivalent over $\mathcal{L}^+$. This is no longer the case in $\mathcal{L}_+^+$. Moreover, while the relevant 'monotonicity' features still hold over $\mathcal{L}^+$ (see Chapter 1 appendix), this is no longer the case for $\mathcal{L}_+^+$, as the conditional fails to be monotonic in the relevant sense. Accordingly, the 'Kripke' non-triviality construction for the $\mathcal{L}^+$-restricted theory does not carry over to $\mathcal{L}_+^+$ in a straightforward fashion. The challenge, then, is to figure out how to construct the requisite standard, transparent model of the given theory.

How we do it. The construction is ultimately due to Ross Brady (1989), although I will follow the notation of Priest (1991), who explicitly applied Brady's construction to truth theory. In effect, we follow a (repeated) two-step process. In the first step, we do what we did for the $\mathcal{L}^+$-restricted theory: we construct a 'Kripke' fixed point from a suitable ground interpretation of $Tr(x)$. The critical question is: in running the 'Kripke' procedure, how do we deal with claims of the form $\alpha \to \beta$, where $\to$ is supposed to be as per BX?

Brady's insight is to treat such claims as *atomic*, at least for purposes of generating the (Kripke fixed-point) interpretations of $Tr(x)$. In other words, the ground model—the base interpretation—simply assigns all claims of the form $\alpha \to \beta$ one of our LP values.[8] In turn, with such claims being treated as 'atomic', we simply run the Kripke construction as per Chapter 1, and get a transparent, standard model—assuming a suitable assignment of values in the ground model.

But how, then, does this approach provide a model of the BX theory? After all, if $\alpha \to \beta$ is treated as 'atomic' in the ground interpretation, we could have

---

[8]As in Ch. 1, we continue to use the many-valued LP semantics for our $\to$-free fragment.

an atomic α and 'atomic' $\alpha \to \beta$ both being designated but β not designated, in which case, such an interpretation will conflict with MPP, which is valid in BX.

This is correct. And this is why we have to run the process again (and again, and again, ...). Recall, from Chapter 1 (appendix), the situation with getting 'more and more transparent' interpretations of $Tr(x)$. We needed some 'reset rule' to adjust the subsequent interpretations of $Tr(x)$. The same is true with respect to our conditional. Not only do we need to 'reset' our interpretation of $Tr(x)$ at each stage, we also need to reset the interpretation of our 'atomic conditionals' at each new stage. And such 'resetting' is the second step of the construction. Before sketching the reset rule for the conditional, it might help to think of the situation as follows.

1. *Step one*: generate a Kripke fixed point for $Tr(x)$. As in Chapter 1 (appendix), we start with some suitable ground model ν_0. As above, we treat claims of the form $\alpha \to \beta$ as 'atomic'. In turn, we use the 'reset rule' for $Tr(x)$ to go through various stages $\nu_1, \nu_2, \ldots$ until we reach a Kripke fixed point at (some) stage κ. Let $\nu_0^* = \nu_\kappa$ be the (least such) fixed point of this process, starting with base ν_0. All of this, in effect, is just as in Chapter 1 (appendix), except that we now have claims of the form $\alpha \to \beta$ (which are treated as atomic).

2. *Step two*: reset all claims of the forms $\alpha \to \beta$ and $Tr(x)$, and repeat Step one. Specifically, use the values at 'previous' Kripke fixed points (i.e., previous points ν_i^*, where ν_i is a given ground model) to reset the values of $\alpha \to \beta$ for a *new* base model ν_j, and then run the Kripke construction for $Tr(x)$ to get $\nu_j^1, \nu_j^2, \ldots$ until you reach a fixed point ν_j^* for the given base model. Repeat this process, until you achieve a fully transparent (and standard) fixed point model.

Reset rule for the conditional

I give the basic construction below, but it is worth saying something about how the 'reset' rule for the *conditional* works. Brady's method, at least for our target theory, utilizes a particular (non-LP) operator on $\{1, \frac{1}{2}, 0\}$, an operator known as the RM_3 conditional (Dunn and Restall, 2002), which is defined as follows.[9] (Here, I use $\Rightarrow$ for the RM_3 conditional.)

$\Rightarrow$	1	$\frac{1}{2}$	0
1	1	0	0
$\frac{1}{2}$	1	$\frac{1}{2}$	0
0	1	1	1

With the RM_3 conditional in hand, the basic 'reset rule' for our 'atomic' sentences of the form $\alpha \to \beta$ is as follows.

---

[9] I should note that Brady's method can be employed for a variety of different logics. Indeed, Field's recent work (sketched in Ch. 4) employs Brady's approach for a novel (non-paraconsistent) logic.

> » Set $\alpha \to \beta$ to be 1 at stage k if the value of $\nu_i^*(\alpha) \Rightarrow \nu_i^*(\beta)$ is 1 for all stages $i < k$.
> » Set $\alpha \to \beta$ to be 0 at stage k if the value of $\nu_i^*(\alpha) \Rightarrow \nu_i^*(\beta)$ is 0 for all stages $i < k$.
> » Set $\alpha \to \beta$ to be $\frac{1}{2}$ at k otherwise.

Assuming an appropriate base model (see the next section), we keep 'resetting' our conditional by looking back at previous Kripke fixed-point models (for the truth predicate) and using the RM_3 operator, all the while treating sentences of the form $\alpha \to \beta$ as 'atomic'. In particular, one looks at the values of α and β at previous fixed-point models ν_i^*, and then evaluates the RM_3 conditional $\alpha \Rightarrow \beta$ at such fixed points. As above, we set $\alpha \to \beta$ to 1 at stage k just if $\nu_i^*(\alpha) \Rightarrow \nu_i^*(\beta)$ is 1 for all previous fixed points ν_i^*, and so on.

In effect, we're simply doing what we did in the appendix to Chapter 1, namely, constructing a Kripke fixed-point model for $Tr(x)$ from an appropriate base model ν_0. The difference is that, in addition to sentences of the form $Tr(\ulcorner \alpha \urcorner)$ and identities, we now have other sorts of 'atomics', namely, $\alpha \to \beta$. After we reach a fixed point ν_0^* for $Tr(x)$, we use that point to set a *new* base model ν_i, and run the Kripke construction for $Tr(x)$ again—and again, and so on until we finally reach a transparent and standard model. That's the idea. The next section briefly sketches the target construction (with target base model).

The basic construction

The target construction, following Chapter 1 (appendix), goes as follows. (Assumptions from Chapter 1 remain in place, e.g. that $\nu_i(Tr(t)) = 0$ if t does not 'denote' a sentence, and I continue to call ν_i an interpretation, even though it is the valuation function of our interpretations.)

Our initial, base interpretation (with valuation ν_0) is similar to that of Chapter 1 (appendix). Where $|\alpha|^{\mathbb{N}}$ is the standard interpretation of α, we set

> » $\nu_0(\alpha) = |\alpha|^{\mathbb{N}}$ if α is in $\mathcal{L}$.
> » $\nu_0(Tr(\ulcorner \alpha \urcorner)) = \frac{1}{2}$.
> » $\nu_0(\alpha \to \beta) = \frac{1}{2}$.
> » Compounds (except arrow) are determined at *every* stage by LP operators.

The relevant 'monotonicity', as per Chapter 1 (appendix), remains for a Kripke construction from this base model. (See cited work for proofs.) Let ν_0^* be the least fixed point for this base model ν_0. What we want is a standard, transparent model of BXTT, our given BX theory in $\mathcal{L}_+^+$. The current interpretation ν_0^* does not do the trick. (E.g., the monotonicity of the Kripke construction ensures that $\nu_0^*(\alpha \to \beta) = \frac{1}{2}$ for all α and β. Let α be $1 = 1$ and β be $1 = 0$, in which case $\alpha \to \beta$ and α are designated in ν_0^* but β not. Hence, ν_0^* doesn't even respect MPP, which holds in BX, and so fails to model the given theory.) This is where Brady's 'reset rule' for the conditional is essential.

What we want, as in Chapter 1 (appendix), is to move from ν_0^* to better and better interpretations—eventually, a standard, transparent one. Following the Brady 'reset' rule for the conditional, and the (in effect) Kripke reset rule for $Tr(x)$, we are able to do so. In particular, for $k \neq 0$ (successor or limit), we reset both sorts of atomic—namely, conditionals and 'truth ascriptions'—as follows.

$$\nu_k(\alpha \to \beta) = \begin{cases} 1 \text{ if } \forall j < k[\nu_j^*(\alpha) \Rightarrow \nu_j^*(\beta)] = 1 \\ 0 \text{ if } \exists j < k[\nu_j^*(\alpha) \Rightarrow \nu_j^*(\beta)] = 0 \\ \frac{1}{2} \text{ otherwise.} \end{cases}$$

In effect, then, we set our conditional to a classical value based on the value(s) of the corresponding RM_3 conditional at previous fixed points. If there's a previous fixed point at which the RM_3 value is 0, then our conditional gets set to 0 for the next base interpretation. If the RM_3 value is 1 at all previous fixed points, then our conditional is set to 1 for the next base interpretation. If neither of these conditions is met, then the conditional remains at $\frac{1}{2}$.

The Kripke 'reset rule' for $Tr(x)$ at stages $k > 0$ remains in effect. In particular, where ν_j^* is a Kripke fixed point for base ν_j, and so $\nu_j^*(\alpha) = \nu_j^*(Tr(\ulcorner \alpha \urcorner))$,

$$\nu_k(Tr(\ulcorner \alpha \urcorner)) = \begin{cases} 1 \text{ if } \nu_j^*(\alpha) = 1 \text{ for some } i \text{ and any } j \text{ such that } i \leq j < k \\ 0 \text{ if } \nu_j^*(\alpha) = 0 \text{ for some } i \text{ and any } j \text{ such that } i \leq j < k \\ \frac{1}{2} \text{ otherwise.} \end{cases}$$

With this reset rule, and the reset rule for the conditional, we simply go through our two-step process sketched above: start with our given ν_0, and do a Kripke construction to get a (Kripke) fixed point ν_0^*. In turn, use the 'input' from ν_0^* and the given reset rules to generate a new base model, and do the Kripke construction again—and repeat, and repeat, and so on.

Provided that we've got the right sort of base model (and we do), the target monotonicity holds: if $i \preceq j$ then $\nu_i^* \preceq \nu_j^*$. Accordingly, once our conditional reaches a classical value, it keeps it 'forever'. More generally, once any atomic (including our conditional) reaches a classical value, it keeps it. And this result, as in Chapter 1 (appendix), gives us what we want: a standard, transparent model of our given theory.

While proofs are left to cited works (Brady, 1989; Priest, 1991), let me briefly say something about each of the crucial features of the resulting model—namely, transparency, standard model, and our BX theory.

Transparent model. Let ν_κ be the least fixed point of the construction above; in other words, ν_κ is our given model. The question is whether ν_κ is transparent in the sense that TP holds.

Considerations from Chapter 1 (appendix) make it clear that WT holds in ν_κ. The trouble is that, as mentioned above, WT no longer implies TP. Fortunately, the given construction verifies TP. While neither Brady (1989) nor Priest (1991) explicitly establish this, the proof is fairly straightforward (and hereby omitted). Actually, there are various routes towards establishing TP in the given model. One route is via the Tr-schema and substitutivity of equivalents, both of which hold in the model. Another option is via something slightly stronger than TP, namely,

$$\nu_k^*(\beta) = \nu_k^*(\hat{\beta}) \text{ for all } k$$

where $\hat{\beta}$ is the result of substituting $Tr(\ulcorner \alpha \urcorner)$ for all occurrences of α in β. Here, $\hat{\beta}$ is defined inductively. For our atomics, we let $\hat{\beta} = \beta$ if α is not a subformula of β, and let $\hat{\beta}$ be $Tr(\ulcorner \alpha \urcorner)$ if β is α. The Boolean compounds and quantifiers are as expected, and the clause for our conditional is the following.

$$\text{If } \beta \text{ is } \gamma_0 \rightarrow \gamma_1 \text{ then } \hat{\beta} \text{ is } \hat{\gamma_0} \rightarrow \hat{\gamma_1}.$$

The proof, in turn, is via induction on β. For the induction case, we assume $\forall i < k \forall \beta (\nu_i^*(\beta) = \nu_i^*(\hat{\beta}))$ and aim to show $\nu_k^*(\beta) = \nu_k^*(\hat{\beta})$ for all β. The steps up to the conditional proceed as in the base case (which I've hereby skipped). For the conditional, we need $\nu_k^*(\gamma_0 \rightarrow \gamma_1) = \nu_k^*(\hat{\gamma_0} \rightarrow \hat{\gamma_1})$, which is established via the 'reset rule' for the conditional and the induction hypothesis (see above). I herein skip the proof. The important point is that ν_κ is a *transparent* model, in the sense that TP holds.

Standard model. We want not just a transparent model; we want a *standard* model, since we want a 'modest' position according to which our base language $\mathcal{L}$ is classical. In the current context, our base language is arithmetic. In Chapter 1 (appendix), we saw that $\mathcal{L}^+$ enjoys a standard model in the given Kripke construction (given our 'over-stuffed' base model). That the situation is the same for $\mathcal{L}_+^+$ and our given ν_κ should be plain—notwithstanding my omission of proofs. As in Chapter 1 (appendix), our base interpretation ν_0 itself is standard, and the fragment $\mathcal{L}$ is interpreted via the standard model. Given the relevant monotonicity (mentioned above), $\mathcal{L}$ remains standard throughout.

Model of our theory BXTT. So, the given model is both standard and transparent. The question, in turn, is whether it's a model of BX (and, hence, a model of our target ttruth theory BXTT underwritten by BX and TP). The answer, which is affirmative, is provided in detail by Ross Brady (1989), and discussed in Priest 1991; Priest 2002. Two key questions concern TP and the standard interpretation of $\mathcal{L}$. The final—and not non-tedious—step is to establish that, in our case, ν_κ verifies all BX axioms and supports (i.e., doesn't refute) the BX rules. That this is so is established by Brady (1989).

« *Parenthetical remark.* For those tempted to run through some of the axioms (or rules) of BX, it is important to recall that both 1 and $\frac{1}{2}$ are designated in this context. Some sentences—in effect, the $Tr(x)$-ineliminable (or, in Kripke's well-known terminology, 'ungrounded') sentences—will be such that $\alpha \rightarrow \alpha$ takes the value $\frac{1}{2}$ in ν_κ, but this is OK since, as above, $\frac{1}{2}$ is designated. *End parenthetical.* »

The upshot: BXTT is non-trivial in a 'natural' way

What we have, then, is a proof that our *conditional-ful* ttruth theory BXTT is non-trivial, and non-trivial in the requisite way: namely, that the base language is entirely classical; it's just the *ttruth*-ineliminable spandrels that wind up glutty.

3

JUST TRUE

Trivialism is the thesis that everything is ttrue. Trivialists are dialetheists, but trivialism—unlike dialetheism—is not a rational view. Rational dialetheists maintain that some (actually, many) ttruths are *just true*; they reject that all or even most claims are gluts. Indeed, on my account, it is only the spandrels of *ttruth* (or related notions) that are gluts; the rest are 'just true'.

« *Parenthetical remark.* The term 'trivialism', as far as I know, was coined by Priest (2000*a*, 2006*a*). It is important to note that I have used *ttruth* in characterizing trivialism. If we characterized trivialism using some other notion of truth that failed to satisfy Release—in either rule or conditional form—trivialism wouldn't be obviously irrational. One could accept that all sentences are true (in the given sense of 'true') without all sentences following therefrom. After all, if the relevant notion of truth (whatever it might be) fails to obey unrestricted Release, then one's theory could coherently contain $True(\ulcorner \bot \urcorner)$ without containing $\bot$. Our focus, though, is on *ttruth*, and so I shall pass over such options. *End parenthetical.* »

Truth, I maintain, is simply *ttruth*, a transparent device that behaves as per the theory advanced in Chapters 1 and 2. What does *just true* amount to?

This chapter discusses the question of *just true* and a few related issues. Some issues (e.g., acceptance and rejection, probability theory) are mentioned but taken up only in Chapter 5. After a brief discussion of incoherent operators, I set out what I take *just true* to be. In turn, I discuss a 'revenge'-related line of thinking that might lead some to think that there's more to *just true* than what I suggest. I close by discussing a few other ideas concerning 'just true'-like notions.

3.1 Incoherent operators

Before getting to 'just true', an important background issue needs to be covered. In particular, it is important to see that there are operators that cannot coherently exist if our language enjoys various features. Tarski's Theorem gives one concrete example of such a result, but another example might be useful.[1] Suppose, as is plausible, that, in addition to appropriate forms of self-reference, our language has the following features F1 and F2.

---

[1] Tarski's Theorem, in effect, is that (classical) arithmetical truth is not definable in (classical) arithmetic. For discussion of the theorem and its broader implications see Smullyan 1992. For a user-friendly discussion of what Tarski's Theorem does *not* teach us, see Yablo 2003, which is also a useful discussion of Field's account (which account is discussed in Ch. 4).

F1. There's a predicate $T(x)$, in and for the language, that 'obeys' (unrestricted) Release and Capture in at least Rule Form.

F2. Disjunction Principle [DP]: if α implies γ, and β implies γ, then $\alpha \vee \beta$ implies γ, for all α, β, γ.[2]

Any (expressively capable) language with features F1 and F2, on pain of triviality, has no operator Θ such that both E1 and E2 hold, where E1 is an *exhaustion* principle, E2 an *exclusion* or *explosion* principle, and $\perp$ is an explosive sentence (i.e., implies all sentences).

E1. $\vdash \alpha \vee \Theta\alpha$

E2. $\alpha, \Theta\alpha \vdash \perp$

Suppose that we do have such an operator. Given the predicate $T(x)$, we'll inevitably have spandrels involving the operator, for example, a sentence λ that 'says' $\Theta T(\ulcorner\lambda\urcorner)$. From E1, we have

$$T(\ulcorner\lambda\urcorner) \vee \Theta T(\ulcorner\lambda\urcorner)$$

which yields two cases.

1. Case one:
   - (a) $T(\ulcorner\lambda\urcorner)$
   - (b) Release yields:[3] $\Theta T(\ulcorner\lambda\urcorner)$
   - (c) E2 yields: $\perp$
2. Case two:
   - (a) $\Theta T(\ulcorner\lambda\urcorner)$
   - (b) Capture yields: $T(\ulcorner\lambda\urcorner)$
   - (c) E2 yields: $\perp$

The point, for present purposes, is modest but important: there are incoherent notions, notions that cannot coherently exist if our language enjoys various features. This bears on the question of 'just true'.

3.2 What *just true* is not

A principal question, at the heart of Liar studies, is this: what is our language like, given that it enjoys *such and so* features? More to the point: assuming that our language has a truth predicate that plays Capture and Release (in at least rule form), what are its other features? One might say that it fails to contain a fully exhaustive negation-like device (e.g., see Chapter 4), something that would yield E1 above. One might, instead, say that DP (see F2), at least in its given unrestricted form, fails for our language. As in Chapters 1 and 2, I say none of those things.

---

[2] Feature F2 is also sometimes called *Disjunction Elimination* or *Reasoning by Cases*. I simply call it 'DP' for Disjunction Principle.

[3] Intersubstitutability of Identicals is also involved here (and at the same place in Case two). This is usually assumed valid, but it, like so much in the area, has been challenged. See Skyrms 1970; Skyrms 1984.

On my theory, we enjoy a language with F2 and, in virtue of enjoying *ttruth*, F1. (In fact, we enjoy something much stronger, namely, full intersubstitutability, which is the see-through service of *ttruth*.) Moreover, we have an operator—namely, negation—which satisfies E1. What we don't have, according to the proposed theory, is an operator satisfying E2, at least unrestrictedly. (Given the 'classical base-language' restriction discussed in Chapters 1 and 2, there's a straightforward sense in which negation satisfies E2 *over the given fragment*, but it doesn't satisfy E2 without qualification.)

As noted above, such a language—enjoying *ttruth*, F1 and F2—cannot have an operator Θ that satisfies both E1 and E2. This means more than that there's no primitive operator that satisfies E1 and E2; it requires that there be *no* such operator. For example, one might think that there's an obvious way to model the notion of *just true*. In particular, we recognize, in addition to our other connectives, a connective $\mathbb{J}$ modeled as follows.

$$w \models \mathbb{J}\alpha \text{ iff } w \models \alpha \text{ and } w^* \models \alpha$$

This is a natural thought if the idea is to 'rule out gluts'. On this idea, $\mathbb{J}\alpha$ is never true (in a model) if α is a glut (in the model). Indeed, $\mathbb{J}\alpha$ is true (in a model) just when α is ... well, 'just true' (in a model). Moreover, the given connective, so interpreted, avoids the problem of satisfying both E1 and E2. In particular, E1 fails: if $@ \not\models \alpha$, then so too $@ \not\models \alpha \vee \mathbb{J}\alpha$.

The trouble, in the end, is that the idea crashes. Adding $\mathbb{J}$ to the formal picture would quickly trivialize the picture; it would produce incoherence. Put differently, and more to the point, $\mathbb{J}$ fails to model any coherent connective in our language. Consider, in particular, the compound operator (say, $\mathbb{F}$) that results from applying $\mathbb{J}$ to $\neg$ (so, $\mathbb{F}\alpha$ is just $\mathbb{J}\neg\alpha$), namely,

$$w \models \mathbb{F}\alpha \text{ iff } w \not\models \alpha \text{ and } w^* \not\models \alpha$$

This operator satisfies both Exhaustion and Exclusion (i.e., E1 and E2).

» E1. If $@ \models \alpha$ then $@ \models \alpha \vee \mathbb{F}\alpha$. If $@ \not\models \alpha$, then $@^* \not\models \alpha$, since $@ \in \mathcal{N}$ and $w \models \alpha$ or $w^* \not\models \alpha$ for all $w \in \mathcal{N}$. (See Chapter 1.) So, $@ \models \mathbb{F}\alpha$, and hence $@ \models \alpha \vee \mathbb{F}\alpha$. So, E1 holds for $\mathbb{F}$.

» E2. By definition, $@ \models \mathbb{F}\alpha$ only if $@ \not\models \alpha$. Hence, we can't have a model in which $@ \models \mathbb{F}\alpha$ and $@ \models \alpha$. So, E2 holds for $\mathbb{F}$.

Given the other features of our language—*ttruth* and DP—the argument from §3.1 applies, letting Θ be $\mathbb{F}$. (In this case, we have a Liar-like sentence involving $\mathbb{F}$, a sentence λ equivalent to $\mathbb{F}\lambda$ or, in primitive form, $\mathbb{J}\neg\lambda$. Given F1, F2, and, as above, E1 and E2 for $\mathbb{F}$, triviality ensues.) Accordingly, $\mathbb{J}$, so understood, does not model a coherent operator in our language.

The point is not just that $\mathbb{J}$, so understood, is problematic. The point is that, whatever else it may be, the notion of *just true* is not one that, in concert with other elements of the language, yields an exhaustive and exclusive operator in the sense of E1 and E2, at least unrestrictedly.

3.3   What *just true* is: just *ttruth*

Just true, whatever it may be, is not exhaustive and exclusive in the sense of
E1 and E2. What, then, does *just true* amount to? My answer, in short, is that
just true is just *ttruth*. On the surface, *just true* is a compound of 'true' and
'only' or 'just'. Since our truth predicate is transparent, 'true' in 'just true' is
our device *ttruth*. The surface import of 'just true', then, is either *ttrue and not
tfalse*, having the form

$$Tr(\ulcorner \alpha \urcorner) \wedge \neg Tr(\ulcorner \neg \alpha \urcorner)$$

or *ttrue and not both ttrue and tfalse*, having the form

$$Tr(\ulcorner \alpha \urcorner) \wedge \neg(Tr(\ulcorner \alpha \urcorner) \wedge Tr(\ulcorner \neg \alpha \urcorner))$$

Given the transparency of our ttruth predicate, these may be simplified, respectively, to

$$\alpha \wedge \neg\neg\alpha$$

and

$$\alpha \wedge \neg(\alpha \wedge \neg\alpha)$$

But these are equivalent, and indeed equivalent to α, and hence to $Tr(\ulcorner \alpha \urcorner)$, for
any α. And this, in short, is what I take *just true* to be: just *ttruth*.

It may be useful to reflect on the big picture. As in Chapter 1 (and throughout), truth is ttruth. We did not introduce the device so as to name some important property; we brought it in only for practical, expressive convenience. Before
recognizing gluts, we took it to be obvious that *ttrue* and *ttrue and not tfalse*
were equivalent. After recognizing gluts, the equivalence remains. Of course, if
one thought that truth itself were some 'weighty', more-than-transparent, more-
than-logical notion, then one might think that 'just true' is similar. One might,
along such lines, think that the job of 'just true' is to pick out (or express etc.)
some such 'weighty' or, at the very least, more-than-logical property. But I do
not think along such lines. As throughout, truth is ttruth, having nothing more
than a transparent, expressive role. When, in the face of various spandrels, we
recognize gluts, we are recognizing more ttruths; we are not suddenly bringing in
a predicate 'glut' to name an important, non-logical property. The 'category' of
gluts is itself derivatively expressive; it is shorthand for ttruths that have ttrue
negations. Why expect, then, that the notion of 'non-glut' or 'true only' (i.e.,
true non-glut) is any different? As above, I think that it's not different: *just true*
just is *ttruth*.

While I maintain, as above, that *just true* is just *ttruth*, we can, if need be,
appeal to a pragmatic difference. In the context of transparent truth theories,
rejection is not simply acceptance of negation. In dialetheic theories, one may
accept $\neg\alpha$ without rejecting α. (In non-dialetheic theories, such as Field's, one
may reject α without accepting $\neg\alpha$.) In this way, perhaps 'just true' carries
pragmatic implicatures not carried by (an utterance of) 'ttrue', something to
the effect that the speaker rejects the given negation. For example, if Max says

that α is *just true*, he says nothing more nor less than that α is ttrue; however, his assertion carries the implicature that Max rejects $\neg\alpha$. *Just true* and *ttrue*, on this account, remain equivalent; it's just that an utterance of the former carries 'autobiographical' implicatures that the latter doesn't.

« *Parenthetical remark.* I return to the issue of acceptance and rejection—and, relatedly, probability theory—in Chapter 5.

I should also note that if truth were less than transparent (something other than *ttruth*), other options would emerge. Graham Priest (2006*b*), for example, agrees that *just truth*, like truth itself, is inconsistent; however, he rejects that truth and 'just truth' are equivalent. Unlike me, Priest takes truth to be an important (semantic) property, rather than a merely logical (see-through) device, and the resulting theory is a non-transparent theory of truth. On Priest's (non-transparent) theory, 'just true' is defined as $T(\ulcorner\alpha\urcorner) \wedge \neg T(\ulcorner\neg\alpha\urcorner)$, where $T(x)$ is Priest's (non-transparent) truth predicate. Since, on Priest's approach, $T(\ulcorner\neg\alpha\urcorner)$ fails to imply $\neg T(\ulcorner\alpha\urcorner)$, the equivalence between $T(\ulcorner\alpha\urcorner)$ and $T(\ulcorner\alpha\urcorner)\wedge\neg T(\ulcorner\neg\alpha\urcorner)$ breaks down. My focus, as throughout, is on *transparent truth* and its paradoxes; however, in Chapter 5 I discuss some of Priest's well-known (dialetheic) views. *End parenthetical.* »

3.4   Remarks on revenge

Some might think that the foregoing discussion of 'just true' misses the real issue. The real issue, one might press, is that dialetheic positions face a typical 'revenge' problem involving *just true*. The thought is that there's clearly a notion of *just true* that is essentially used in constructing the formal account, but one that—on pain of triviality—cannot be expressed in the overall theory. The aim of this section is to briefly touch on this issue.[4]

In the following subsections, I first discuss a broad, background topic to set the stage. (See §3.4.1.) I then turn to the topic of 'revenge', in particular 'just true' qua revenge problem. (See §3.4.2.) Finally, in §3.4.3, I give my reply to the alleged problem.

3.4.1   *Models and reality*

Like much in philosophical logic, constructing a formal account of truth is 'model building' in the ordinary 'paradigm' sense of 'model'. The point of such a model is to indicate how 'real truth' in our 'real language' can have the target (logical) features we take it to have—Release and Capture features or, in our case, full intersubstitutability of $Tr(\ulcorner\alpha\urcorner)$ and α. In that respect, formal accounts of truth are idealized models to be evaluated by their adequacy with respect to the 'real phenomena' they purport to model.

Formal accounts (or theories) of truth aim only indirectly at being accounts of truth. What we're doing in giving such an account is twofold.

---

[4]The following subsections, in addition to parts of this chapter above, are from Beall 2007*a*, which is the introductory essay to Beall 2007*b*.

1. We construct an artificial *model language*—one that's intended to serve as a heuristic, albeit idealized, model of our own 'real' language—and, in turn, give an account of how 'true' behaves in that language by constructing a precise account of *truth-in-that-language*.

2. We then claim that the behavior of 'true' in our language, at least in relevant, target respects, is like the behavior of the truth predicate in our model language.

By far the most dominant approach towards the first task—viz., constructing a model language—employs a classical set theory. (This is certainly the approach employed in this book, though it has largely been a background assumption.) One reason for doing so is that classical set theory is familiar, well-understood, and generally taken to be consistent. A related reason is that, in using a classical set theory, one's formal account of truth may serve as more than merely a heuristic picture; it can also serve as a 'model' in the technical sense of *establishing non-triviality* or, in non-paraconsistent settings, *consistency*.

That a classical set theory is used in constructing our artificial language serves to emphasize the heuristic, idealized nature of the construction. We know that, due to paradoxical sentences, there's no truth predicate in (and for) our 'real language' if our real language is (fully) classical.

« *Parenthetical remark.* The same applies if the truth predicate has an extension: the extension isn't really a classical set. Every classical set S is such that $x \in S$ or $x \notin S$, which, given paradoxical sentences, results in inconsistency. (The point is independent of 'size' issues. Classical *proper classes* are likewise such that $x \in C$ or $x \notin C$.) If T is the extension of $Tr(x)$ and T is a set, a sentence λ that 'says' $\ulcorner \lambda \urcorner \notin T$ makes the point—assuming, as is plausible, suitable 'extension' versions of Capture and Release (e.g., $\alpha \Rightarrow \ulcorner \alpha \urcorner \in T$, etc.). *End parenthetical.* »

The project, as above, is to show how we can have a truth predicate in our 'real language', despite the various paradoxical spandrels that arise from introducing our truth predicate (our see-through device). And the project, as above, is usually—if not always—carried out in a classical set theory. Does this mean that the project, as typically carried out, is inexorably doomed? Not at all. Just as in physics, where idealization is highly illuminating despite its distance from the real mess, so too in philosophical logic: the classical construction is illuminating and useful, despite its notable idealization. But it is idealized, and, pending argument, on the surface only heuristic. That's the upshot of using classical set theory.

One might think it odd that we can enjoy classical set theory or classical logic, but it is not uncommon among theories of *ttruth*. So long as classical logic is an extension of our (weaker) logic, we can enjoy classical set theory (or the like). Since classical logic is an extension of LP, which is the logic of our conditional-free $\mathcal{L}^+$ (i.e., base language plus 'ttrue'), you can stand squarely in an appropriate fragment of $\mathcal{L}^+$ and enjoy a perfectly classical theory—like classical set theory.

In effect, this is the situation that we enjoy when we are utilizing a classical 'metalanguage' in constructing our formal 'model language'.

3.4.2 *'Just true' qua revenge problem*

As above, in giving a formal theory of truth, one does not directly give a theory of *truth*; rather, one gives a theory of $\mathcal{L}_m$-truth, an account, for some formal 'model language' $\mathcal{L}_m$, of how $\mathcal{L}_m$'s truth predicate behaves, in particular, its logical behavior. By endorsing a formal theory of truth, one is endorsing that one's own truth predicate is relevantly like *that*, like the truth predicate in $\mathcal{L}_m$, at least with respect to various phenomena in question (e.g., logical behavior).

In what follows, I use '$\mathcal{L}_m$-truth' to abbreviate *the (logical) behavior—e.g., the logic of—$\mathcal{L}_m$'s truth predicate* (i.e., the logic of $\mathcal{L}_m$ predicate set up to be the $\mathcal{L}_m$'s truth predicate). As discussed below, this is generally very different from the metatheoretic, model-dependent notion of *truth in $\mathcal{L}_m$*, which we normally use to specify $\mathcal{L}_m$-truth (i.e., specify the logic of $\mathcal{L}_m$'s given truth predicate).

Revenge qua objection—revenger's revenge—is an *adequacy objection*. Typically, the revenger charges that a given 'model language' is inadequate due to expressive limitation. Let L be our 'real language', English or some such natural language, and let $\mathcal{L}_m$ be our heuristic model language. (Recall that '$\mathcal{L}_m$-truth' abbreviates 'the behavior of $\mathcal{L}_m$'s truth predicate'.) In broadest terms, the situation is this: we want our (heuristic) $\mathcal{L}_m$, and in particular $\mathcal{L}_m$-truth, to illuminate relevant features of our own truth predicate, to explain how, despite paradoxical sentences, our truth predicate achieves the features we take it to have. Revenge purports to show that $\mathcal{L}_m$ achieves its target features in virtue of lacking expressive features that L itself (our real language) appears to enjoy. But if $\mathcal{L}_m$ enjoys the target features only in virtue of lacking relevant features that our real L enjoys, then $\mathcal{L}_m$ is an inadequate model: it fails to show how L itself achieves its target features (e.g., consistency). That, in a nutshell, is one common shape of revenge.

In our case, the objection might run as follows. Let $\mathcal{L}_m$ be our formal 'model language' (sketched in Chapters 1 and 2). In constructing $\mathcal{L}_m$, we use—in our metalanguage—classical set theory, and we define *truth-in-$\mathcal{L}_m$*, which, with other similar notions, is used to discuss $\mathcal{L}_m$-truth (the behavior of $\mathcal{L}_m$'s truth predicate). In particular, *truth-in-$\mathcal{L}_m$* is defined as *designated*, which, in our case, amounts to being true at @ in a given model (i.e., @ $\models \alpha$ iff α is designated in the given model). (In the standard many-valued approach, discussed in Chapter 1 appendix, designation amounts to being assigned something in $\{1, \frac{1}{2}\}$.) Moreover, we can prove—in our metalanguage—that, despite paradoxical sentences, a sentence $Tr(\ulcorner \alpha \urcorner)$ is true-in-$\mathcal{L}_m$ exactly if α is true-in-$\mathcal{L}_m$. (Indeed, we get WT and, more generally, TP, as discussed in Chapter 2.)

The familiar 'revenge' charge at issue is that $\mathcal{L}_m$, so understood, is not an adequate model of our real language; it fails to illuminate how our own ttruth predicate, despite paradoxical sentences, achieves non-triviality. In particular, the revenger's charge is that $\mathcal{L}_m$-truth achieves its non-triviality in virtue of $\mathcal{L}_m$'s expressive poverty: $\mathcal{L}_m$ cannot, on pain of triviality, express certain notions *that our real language can express.*

Example. First, notice that we have a notion of *just false in* $\mathcal{L}_m$, which, like the other notions used to discuss $\mathcal{L}_m$-truth, is defined via our semantic values; in particular, α is just-false-in-$\mathcal{L}_m$ iff α is not-true-at-@ (in a given model, i.e., @ $\not\models \alpha$). Suppose, now, that $\mathcal{L}_m$ contains a predicate $JF(x)$ that defines $\{\alpha : \alpha \text{ is just false in } \mathcal{L}_m\}$. Given the resources of $\mathcal{L}_m$, there will be a sentence λ that says $JF(\ulcorner\lambda\urcorner)$. But, then, we can immediately prove—in the metalanguage— that λ is true-in-$\mathcal{L}_m$ iff $JF(\ulcorner\lambda\urcorner)$ is true-in-$\mathcal{L}_m$ iff λ is just-false-in-$\mathcal{L}_m$ iff λ is not true-in-$\mathcal{L}_m$. But this is impossible, since—by construction—no sentence of $\mathcal{L}_m$ is both true-in-$\mathcal{L}_m$ and not true-in-$\mathcal{L}_m$. Hence, we conclude that $\mathcal{L}_m$ cannot express *just false in* $\mathcal{L}_m$.

The same objection can be put more generally (and more concisely) by skipping the 'just false' notion and simply using *not true in* $\mathcal{L}_m$. Just suppose that $\mathcal{L}_m$ contains a predicate $NT(x)$ that defines $\{\alpha : \alpha \text{ is not true-in-}\mathcal{L}_m\}$, and the reasoning is the same. In turn, one concludes that $\mathcal{L}_m$ cannot express *is not true-in-*$\mathcal{L}_m$.

The revenger's charge, then, amounts to this: that our model language fails to be enough like our real language to explain at least one of the target phenomena, namely, *ttruth's non-triviality.* Our metalanguage is part of our 'real language', and we can—because we do—define $\{\alpha : \alpha \text{ is not true-in-}\mathcal{L}_m\}$ in our metalanguage. Since, as above, the given model language cannot similarly define $\{\alpha : \alpha \text{ is not true-in-}\mathcal{L}_m\}$, the given model language is inadequate: it fails to illuminate the target features of *ttruth*, in particular, its non-triviality.

3.4.3 *Remarks on revenge*

The foregoing 'revenge' objection turns on the claim that *is not true in* $\mathcal{L}_m$ (or, more narrowly, *is just false in* $\mathcal{L}_m$) cannot be expressed in $\mathcal{L}_m$. The relevance of such a result, if it in fact goes through (a point to which I return below), is not obvious. After all, even if the notion is not expressible in the model language, the given notion is a *classically constructed* notion; it is a 'model-dependent' notion—a notion that makes no sense apart from the given (classically constructed) models—defined entirely in a classical metalanguage. As such, the given notion is not one of the target (say, model-independent, or 'absolute') notions in our real language L that $\mathcal{L}_m$ is supposed to model. The question is the relevance of the revenger's result, if the result goes through at all.

At this stage, a bit more detail on the 'model language', and in particular its resources, is in order. For present purposes, I mention only two situations: classical arithmetic and classical set theory. In the appendices of Chapters 1 and 2, the former was assumed for simplicity, but the latter is equally available.[5] What is important to note is that if (classical) set theory is used as one's base

---

[5] As mentioned in Ch. 1's appendix, the non-triviality results go through where set theory (versus arithmetic) is the base language, but it is in various ways simpler—and certainly more standard—to use classical arithmetic as the base language.

'model language', in addition to its serving as one's metalanguage (in which one proceeds, as discussed above, to define *true-in-*$\mathcal{L}_m$ etc.), then the revenger's argument towards the inexpressibility of *true-in-*$\mathcal{L}_m$ clearly fails. After all, $\mathcal{L}_m$ enjoys classical set theory as a part, and hence can express any classical set-theoretic notion—a fortiori, *true-in-*$\mathcal{L}_m$. So, quite plainly, the revenger's arguments do not establish that such set-theoretic notions are not expressible in set theory. Instead of establishing that notions like *true-in-*$\mathcal{L}_m$ are not expressible in $\mathcal{L}_m$, the revenger's argument at best establishes that such notions do not play the role in $\mathcal{L}_m$ that $\mathcal{L}_m$'s truth predicate plays—namely, being a (transparent) truth predicate in $\mathcal{L}_m$. The relevance of such a result is not clear.

In the case in which classical arithmetic is the base model language, which case I have been assuming here (because of its use in earlier Chapters), the same question of relevance arises but for a slightly different reason. In particular, it is clear that set theory is not expressible in arithmetic, and so the revenger's argument(s) needn't be given to establish as much. What the arguments do establish—or, if need be, can be tweaked to do—is again that such model-dependent, set-theoretic notions do not play the role in $\mathcal{L}_m$ that $\mathcal{L}_m$'s truth predicate plays. This is correct, but, again, the relevance of the result is unclear.

Now, one might think that, regardless of which sort of model language is in play (arithmetic or set theory), the relevance of the revenger's argument(s) is plain. One might, for example, think that the semantics for $\mathcal{L}_m$ is intended to reflect the semantics of L, our real language. Since the semantics of the former essentially involves, for example, *not true-in-*$\mathcal{L}_m$, the semantics of our real language must involve something similar—at least if $\mathcal{L}_m$ is an adequate model of our real language. But, now, if there's nothing in $\mathcal{L}_m$ that plays exactly the role—and enjoys exactly the same (logical) behavior—in $\mathcal{L}_m$ as *true-in-*$\mathcal{L}_m$ plays in the formal semantics, we should conclude that $\mathcal{L}_m$ is an inadequate model of our real language L since our real language clearly does enjoy such a notion (viz., *true-in-*$\mathcal{L}_m$ itself).

Such an argument might serve to turn the revenger's result into a plainly relevant and powerful objection; however, the argument itself relies on various assumptions that involve quite complex issues. One conspicuous assumption is that the 'semantics' of $\mathcal{L}_m$ is intended to reflect the semantics of our real language L. This needn't be the case. For example, suppose that, with 'deflationists', one rejects that semantics—the semantics of our real language—is a matter of giving 'truth conditions' or otherwise involves some explanatory notion of truth. In the face of Liars (or other paradoxes), one still faces questions about one's truth predicate, and in particular its logical behavior. By way of answering such questions, one might proceed as above: construct a model language that purports to illuminate how one's real truth predicate enjoys its relevant features (e.g., Capture and Release) without collapsing from paradox. In constructing and, in turn, describing one's 'model language', one might give truth-conditional-like semantics for the model language by giving truth-in-a-model conditions for the language. If so, it is plain that the 'semantics' of the model language are not intended to reflect the 'real semantics' of one's real language; they may, in the end, be only tools used for illuminating the logic of our real language, versus illuminating the 'real semantics' of our real language. Indeed, this is the perspective that I endorse, namely, that our formal tools are just that: tools. The formal account of *ttruth* is given to elucidate the logical behavior of *ttruth*; it isn't intended to reflect the 'real semantics' of our real language, whatever such 'real semantics' might come to. So, a critical assumption in the argument above—the argument towards the relevance of the given inexpressibility results— requires argument.[6] Of course, pending a full theory of meaning—something I am not prepared to give—such an 'instrumentalist' reply is at best promissory, but there are some promising 'use-theoretic' approaches to meaning that might finish the job (e.g., Field 2001).

Meaning aside, I should note that Ross Brady (1989), in a closely related context, gestures at the sort of response to 'just true' qua revenge problem that I've advocated here. I do not know—and, in fact, somewhat doubt—whether Brady intends the 'instrumentalist' reply above, but his diagnosis of conflating model-dependent versus absolute (what he calls 'ordinary') is in agreement with the way I look at the matter. Brady writes (and here I take some liberty in paraphrasing in brackets):

> It seems to me that ... the [relevant notion] used in generating the [alleged problem] involves reference to the details of the model [used in our 'formal account']. That is, '*p* takes the value **t**', or some equivalent, makes reference to the specific values of a model ... and thus goes beyond natural language expressions which just refer to truth and falsity. (Brady, 1989, p. 467)

The point, as I (perhaps idiosyncratically) read Brady, is along the lines that I've suggested. While we can—in our 'real', natural language—classically construct various notions such as 'just true in a model' or etc., we mustn't forget that these are classically constructed (i.e., bound by classical logic) and thereby not the non-model-dependent notions that we really care about. With respect to our formal, model-theoretic picture, we have our classically behaving 'just true' and so on; however, as Brady points out (and I endorse), this is all simply model-dependent. Our 'absolute' notion of *just true*, as I've said, is just *ttruth*.

3.5   Limited notions of 'just true'

I maintain, as above, that our notion of *just true* is just *ttruth*. The thought, perhaps based on taking the formal picture too seriously (see previous section),

---

[6]Hartry Field (2008), as I understand him, takes a very similar position. Indeed, though I've long endorsed such an 'instrumentalist' view of the formal account, I am indebted to Field's work for forcing me to be more forthright about the matter. Field's basic account of *ttruth* is sketched in the next chapter (although his position on similar revenge-like objections is left to his work). I should also emphasize that Field, unlike other (formal) truth theorists, is explicit in his use of set theory—versus arithmetic—as the base 'model' language. This affords responses to revenge-type arguments that I have not herein discussed, and for brevity leave to Field 2008.

that we need to recognize a notion of truth stronger than ttruth seems to me to be in need of argument. Still, what is worth noting is that there may be various notions of 'just true' available, should they be needed. In fact, there are clearly some such operators in the theory already advanced. By way of closing this chapter, I briefly discuss two natural options, one that's already available, one merely speculative.

To clarify the issue, suppose that we're after a notion of *just true* that is stronger than *ttruth*. In particular, far from having intersubstitutability (the chief see-through service of *ttruth*), the target 'just true' doesn't even satisfy Capture (either RC or CC). The thought is that while any α that is just true is ttrue, the converse, presumably, fails. The thought, more clearly, is that α may be ttrue without thereby being *just true*—on the target, stronger notion of 'just true'. At a minimum, then, our 'just true' operator $\mathbb{J}$, whatever it may be, satisfies Release (at least in rule form) but not Capture (in either form). What we want is at least (rule) Release for $\mathbb{J}$

» $\mathbb{J}$-Release: $\mathbb{J}(\alpha) \vdash \alpha$

but no Capture:

» No $\mathbb{J}$-Capture: $\alpha \nvdash \mathbb{J}(\alpha)$

In what follows, two options towards such an operator are discussed.

« *Parenthetical remark.* One might wonder why we want an *operator* (something that, syntactically, takes sentences and makes sentences) versus a *predicate* (which, syntactically, takes names or, generally, singular terms and yields sentences). As it turns out, when we enjoy, as we do, a fully transparent truth predicate, the distinction between operators and predicates diminishes in importance. Using *ttruth*, one can always define an operator in terms of a given predicate, and similarly vice versa (a predicate in terms of an operator). For ease of exposition, I simply concentrate on an operator. *End parenthetical.* »

3.5.1   *Available: many 'partial' operators*

One natural idea is to rely on the 'merely linguistic', classical base-language restriction of the current proposal and acknowledge a plurality of notions of *just true*, each tied to a different fragment of the language. For example, let $\mathcal{L}$ be our *ttruth*-free (and, generally, semantic-free) fragment of our language. We can then define a *just true* operator $\mathbb{J}_0$ as α *is ttrue and in the given fragment* $\mathcal{L}$. Since anything that's both ttrue and in $\mathcal{L}$ is ttrue, we have Release:

$$\mathbb{J}_0(\alpha) \vdash \alpha$$

Moreover, as desired, Capture fails:

$$\alpha \nvdash \mathbb{J}_0(\alpha)$$

That Capture fails is clear: just consider a ttrue α that is not in $\mathcal{L}$.

The given approach goes some way towards a non-vacuous account of 'just true', but it is at best partial. An obvious limitation is that, for all that's been said, $\mathbb{J}_0$ is not ttrue of any 'ttrue'-ful sentence, since such sentences are not in the given fragment.

There may be smoother fixes, but the current idea is that we simply use more and more such operators: $\mathbb{J}_1$, $\mathbb{J}_2$, and so on, each $\mathbb{J}_i$ being tied to the relevant fragment of our language. For example, let $\mathcal{L}_1$ comprise all base-language sentences and the sentences that result from substituting $Tr(\ulcorner\beta\urcorner)$ for any occurrence of β in α, where β and α are themselves base-language. Then $\mathbb{J}_1$ is tied to $\mathcal{L}_1$ along the lines of $\mathbb{J}_0$ and $\mathcal{L}$. In turn, we let $\mathbb{J}_2$ be tied to $\mathcal{L}_2$ (understood as per $\mathcal{L}_1$), and $\mathbb{J}_3$ be tied to $\mathcal{L}_3$, and so on.

This sort of approach goes only so far, but it yields the appropriate Release feature and avoids the relevant Capture feature. While I think that the approach is viable (notwithstanding details), I set further discussion aside. It is clear that, given the account advanced in Chapters 1 and 2, we have such (limited) notions of 'just true' if we need them. For now, I turn to one other (fairly speculative) approach.

3.5.2 *Speculative: another 'not'*

On my theory, negation is exhaustive but not exclusive; it satisfies E1 but not E2. If, unlike the suggestion in §3.5.1, we have a *single* notion of 'just true' that is stronger than ttruth, in the sense of satisfying Release but not Capture, it is unlikely to be definable in terms of negation and ttruth. Assuming—only for brief exploration—that we do have such a (single) notion, how might it be understood? That's the question.

A natural idea, I think, is to acknowledge a usage of 'not' distinct from negation, a usage that, in concert with ttruth, gives us our (supposed) single notion of *just true*. Let 'NoT' be the relevant term, although in English it is presumably spelled 'not'.

The role of *NoT*, on the going suggestion, is to serve as a 'commentary device' on *non-gluts*. The given usage is at work in our claims that α is a non-glut, that α is ttrue but NoT tfalse (or tfalse but NoT ttrue). Letting $\flat$ be *NoT*, its role is to serve as a non-vacuous way of expressing, for example, that α is a non-glutty ttruth (or, similarly, non-glutty tfalsehood).

$$\alpha \wedge \flat(\alpha \wedge \neg\alpha)$$

Clearly, negation does not do the NoT-ting trick. After all, if α is ttrue, then

$$\alpha \wedge \neg(\alpha \wedge \neg\alpha)$$

is ttrue, for *all* ttruths—gluts included. So, negation will not play the role of $\flat$; it will not serve as our supposed 'commentary device' on non-gluts. (Negation does not NoT, as one might say.)

How, then, is $\flat$ to be understood? Though I have no proof, my conjecture is that any purely 'extensional' operator will be inadequate. (I do have strong inductive evidence, but as yet no proof.) One might, as we do with negation, go 'intensional', invoking 'worlds' or the like, but a different approach might be more natural.

Instead of taking $\flat$ to be an ordinary operator, either extensional or intensional, we take $\flat$ to be a 'partially defined' connective. In particular, $\flat$ has only a *sufficient condition* for its application, in addition to a few other guiding principles. Indeed, as suggested below, the natural idea here is to follow the lead of da Costa and Alves (1977), where 'negation' is quite non-compositional.[7] The difference, on the present account, is that what we're specifying is *not* negation; rather, it is a usage of 'not' developed for one purpose—namely, to 'comment' on the non-gluts. Were it not for the given role, $\flat$ would be utterly superfluous, an otherwise terribly weak and uninteresting connective.

What we might want is a necessary and sufficient condition for the ttruth and, in turn, tfalsity of $\flat$-claims; however, it's not clear that we need as much—or, for that matter, can have as much in any simple fashion. The idea is modest. With da Costa and Alves, we recognize only a sufficient condition for $\flat$. In particular, where $\flat$ is our device, we give the following *sufficient* condition for the truth of $\flat$-claims.

N. If $w \not\models \alpha$ then $w \models \flat\alpha$

Notice that N is compatible with negation itself. Indeed, restricting to 'normal worlds' or, for simplicity, base worlds @, we already have it that if @ $\not\models \alpha$ then @ $\models \neg\alpha$, but, as with $\flat$, we do not have the converse. (See Chapter 1.) The difference is that *only* the minimal condition N governs $\flat$, leaving it very, very weak but adequate for its (supposed) 'commentary' role.

One clear desideratum of a commentary-on-non-gluts device is the failure of 'Non-Contradiction' in at least the following form.

$$\flat(\alpha \wedge \neg\alpha)$$

Call this 'LNC1' (only for a convenient tag). That LNC1 should fail is clear from the chief role of *NoT*, namely, to (non-vacuously) characterize α as being a *nonglut*, a sentence such that $\alpha \wedge \neg\alpha$ is NoT ttrue. If LNC1 held for all α, as its *negation* correlate does (i.e., replace $\flat$ with $\neg$), then *NoT* would fail to serve as a non-vacuous 'commentary device' on non-gluts. That LNC1 *does* fail is clear. In the formal picture, a relevant case is one in which @ $\models \alpha\wedge\neg\alpha$ but @ $\not\models \flat(\alpha\wedge\neg\alpha)$. Because $\flat$ is governed only by N, and N does not require anything of $\flat\alpha$ when α is true, such countermodels are ubiquitous.

NoT, so understood, is clearly very, very weak. Typical de Morgan principles fail, as does much (perhaps most) familiar 'negation-like' behavior, such as Double Negation features (in both directions). With respect to the latter, one could

---

[7]Actually, the *tradition* behind or around da Costa and Alves' work might be in tension with some of my proposal. The point is that the proposal joins da Costa and Alves in advancing only a relatively modest and, in effect, non-compositional account of the device.

follow da Costa and Alves and stipulate that if $w \models \flat\flat\alpha$ then so too $w \models \alpha$, thereby achieving at least Double Negation Elimation (DNE). (This still fails to ensure the converse, which, in fact, fails.) I see no obvious reason why DNE, let alone equivalence, should hold for the device, which, as above, is not our *negation* but rather a usage of 'not' that serves only to 'comment on non-gluts'. The given role of *NoT* requires a great deal of latitude and, ultimately, a very weak logic.

« *Parenthetical remark.* This isn't to say, of course, that, with further details in place, *NoT* couldn't collapse into negation over a suitable proper fragment of our language. Indeed, in previous work (Beall, 2005*a*) I have advocated a Diderik Batens-inspired 'adaptive' approach to the theory of *NoT*, wherein *NoT* is ultimately to be understood via a non-monotonic logic such that, for much of the language, *NoT* behaves in perfectly familiar ways but, when it comes to 'commentary work' (on non-gluts), *NoT*'s very weak logic takes over. I do not go into this approach here, mainly because I've since come to think that, as earlier in this chapter, we needn't recognize a notion of *just true* beyond *ttruth*, except perhaps for the ones—as in §3.5.1—already at hand. *End parenthetical.* »

Notice that, despite its weakness, *NoT* does exhibit some familiar behavior. In particular, as with negation, $\flat$ is exhaustive, that is, 'Excluded Middle' for $\flat$ holds.

$$\vdash \alpha \vee \flat\alpha$$

One notable difference is that, *unlike negation*, which is forced to take a 'holiday' in the face of gluts (i.e., negation can sometimes yield 'gaps' at abnormal worlds), *NoT* is exhaustive at *all* worlds—normal or abnormal. Let $w \in \mathcal{W}$. If $w \models \alpha$, then so too $w \models \alpha \vee \flat\alpha$. If $w \not\models \alpha$, principle N gives us that $w \models \flat\alpha$, and hence $w \models \alpha \vee \flat\alpha$.

That $\flat$, unlike negation, is 'everywhere exhaustive' (taking no holidays) requires that it not be 'explosive'. (Think of E1 and E2 discussed above in §3.2.) Not surprisingly, given its exhaustive behavior, $\flat$-ful spandrels of *ttruth*, like a sentence λ equivalent to $\flat Tr(\ulcorner\lambda\urcorner)$, wind up glutty, by familiar reasoning. As such, 'Explosion' fails for $\flat$.

$$\alpha, \flat\alpha \nvdash \beta$$

In the formal account, a model such that $@ \models \alpha$ and $@ \models \flat\alpha$ and $@ \models \neg\alpha$ but $@ \not\models \beta$ does the trick.

Spandrels aside, that *NoT* is exhaustive raises a question. One might wonder why we should recognize both negation and our 'loose' connective *NoT*. While I do not officially endorse *NoT*, a few comments on this issue are in order.

The main reason for rejecting that *NoT* is our only 'negation-like' device is that *negation* seems to enjoy a recognizably independent usage. For example, typical de Morgan behavior, or double-negation behavior seems to be at work in at least one common usage of 'not', namely, what I take to be *negation*. Admittedly, such appearances might arise from *NoT* behaving as such over some suitably proper fragment of our language, one on which our 'intuitions' of 'negation' are built. As such, the given appearances mightn't be ultimately decisive. In the end, it may be that the strongest reason to recognize negation (as I've construed it) as something different from *NoT*—if the latter is ultimately recognized—is that *NoT* is fairly wildly non-compositional. While I am very open to the idea of enjoying a non-compositional usage of 'not', I find it hard to accept that there's no compositional usage at all. For this reason, it strikes me that if *NoT* were recognized—invoked for purposes of cashing out a stronger notion of *just true* than what I've advanced—we should nonetheless see it as something other than negation. But I admit that the issue is not easy.

More might be said about the *NoT* approach to 'just true', but the basic idea is clear enough. The idea, in short, is that when we say that α is *just true*, we're using *ttruth* combined with a special (and especially weak) connective *NoT*. As above, one could very easily define a unary 'just true' connective $\mathbb{J}$ (it is just true that...) in terms of *ttruth* and *NoT*, namely,

$$\mathbb{J}\alpha =_{df} \alpha \wedge \flat(\alpha \wedge \neg\alpha)$$

This, in turn, will yield Release in at least rule form (RR) but, as desired, not Capture.

» $\mathbb{J}\alpha \vdash \alpha$. This follows from the basic features of Conjunction (namely, Simplification).
» $\alpha \nvdash \mathbb{J}\alpha$.

Whether the *NoT* approach is ultimately viable or, contrary to what I've suggested, even needed is for debate to tell. While I find the proposal to be interesting, I do not ultimately endorse the idea. The chief reason, as discussed above, is that I'm not convinced that the apparent notion of *just true* requires as much.

Summary

The apparent problem of *just true* is that it cannot be accommodated in a dialetheic framework. Whether this is correct depends on what *just true* amounts to. As in §3.1, it cannot be an operator that yields both E1 and E2, assuming, as I am, that we enjoy F1 and F2, namely, Capture and Release (in at least unrestricted rule form) and DP. What, then, is it?

In this chapter, I've argued that, aside from more limited (or speculative) notions discussed in §3.5, *just true* is just *ttruth*. This account respects the surface of 'just true', which appears to be either 'true and not false' or 'true and not a glut'. As discussed (see §3.3), both of these are equivalent to *ttruth*, at least if, as I assume, 'true' in 'just true' is just *ttruth*.

If one wants more from a notion of *just true* than *ttruth*, one at least has the various $\mathbb{J}_i$ operators discussed in §3.5.1, and perhaps—details notwithstanding—something along the *NoT* approach. But, again, pending some argument to the contrary, the need for more remains unclear.

CHAPTER THREE APPENDIX: ANOTHER APPROACH

This appendix briefly notes another approach to *just true* already available in BXTT (and, indeed, the basic star-simplified framework for *BX*). (I noticed the idea late, when this book was days away from press, at which point only two pages could be added.) Like the other avenues discussed in Chapter 3, this approach is not intended to capture *everything* that *everyone* wants;[8] however, it's arguably as much as one should reasonably demand.

Desiderata of a 'just true' operator $\mathbb{J}$

D1. Release (at least rule): $\mathbb{J}\alpha \vdash \alpha$.
   Rationale. if α is *just true*, then surely it's true.
D2. No Capture: $\alpha \nvdash \mathbb{J}\alpha$.
   Rationale. α may be a glut.
D3. Explosive: $\neg\alpha, \mathbb{J}\alpha \vdash \beta$.
   Rationale. α's being *just true* should 'rule out' its being false.
D4. Not Exhaustive: $\nvdash \mathbb{J}\alpha \vee \mathbb{J}\neg\alpha$.
   Rationale. we don't want that all α are just true or just false.
D5. Ensuring Detachment (etc.): $\mathbb{J}\alpha, \alpha \wedge (\alpha \supset \beta) \vdash \beta$.
   Rationale. we want our 'consistent truth' or 'just truth' operator to do work validity-wise. (MMP is but one among many such 'inferences' at issue.)
D6. Non-triviality: not only do we want $\mathbb{J}$ to not yield triviality; we want a proof that it doesn't.

The idea

Our focus is *BX* and the star-simplified semantics (see Chapters 1–2), where truth in a model is truth at @ (with @ normal). To see the idea, let τ be any just-true sentence in an arbitrary (non-trivial) *BX* model: $@ \models \tau$ and $@^\star \models \tau$. I claim that

$$\tau \to \alpha$$

is a plausible *just true* operator in the D1–D6 sense.[9] Our key proposition is this:

Proposition *(Forcing Consistency: FC) Consider any non-trivial BX model, and let τ be a just-true sentence in the model. If $@ \models \tau \to \alpha$ then $@ \nvDash \alpha \wedge \neg\alpha$.*

Proof of FC. Assume $@ \models \alpha \wedge \neg\alpha$, in which case $@ \models \alpha$ and $@ \models \neg\alpha$. Since $@ \models \neg\alpha$ we have $@^\star \nvDash \alpha$. But $@^\star \models \tau$. Hence, there's a point (viz., $@^\star$) at which τ is true but α not. As @ is normal, we have: $@ \nvDash \tau \to \alpha$.

---

[8]In fact, there's a sort of essential 'incompleteness' (of predictable sort) that remains.
[9]Once the idea is seen, it's obvious that many sentences will do the trick. I've picked the simplest.

The desiderata D1–D6

Note, first, that the trivial model is inessential to the logic BX.[10] Hence, we can restrict our class of models to the non-trivial ones, and we thereby ensure at least one just-true sentence—a sentence that plays the role of τ. Letting $\mathbb{J}\alpha$ be $\tau \to \alpha$, the desiderata, in turn, are achieved.

D1. $\mathbb{J}\alpha \vdash \alpha$. *Proof.* Since @ $\models \tau$ and @ $\models \tau \to \alpha$, we have @ $\models \alpha$.

D2. $\alpha \nvdash \mathbb{J}\alpha$. *Proof.* Let @ $\models \alpha \wedge \neg\alpha$, in which case FC gives @ $\nvDash \tau \to \alpha$.

D3. $\neg\alpha, \mathbb{J}\alpha \vdash \beta$. *Proof.* This follows from D1 and FC.

D4. $\nvdash \mathbb{J}\alpha \vee \mathbb{J}\neg\alpha$. *Proof.* Let @ $\models \alpha \wedge \neg\alpha$, in which case FC gives @ $\nvDash \tau \to \alpha$ *and,* letting α be $\neg\alpha$ in FC, @ $\nvDash \tau \to \neg\alpha$.

D5. $\mathbb{J}\alpha, \alpha \wedge (\alpha \supset \beta) \vdash \beta$. *Proof.* Given @ $\models \mathbb{J}\alpha$, FC delivers @ $\nvDash \neg\alpha$, in which case we have to have @ $\models \beta$ since we have @ $\models \neg\alpha \vee \beta$.

D6. Non-triviality? The non-triviality proof in Chapter 2 Appendix covers BX and, in particular, the theory BXTT. $\mathbb{J}$, as here given, adds nothing that isn't already available in the theory. [Indeed, we can make the point stronger by adding a constant $\top$ axiomatized $\alpha \vdash \top$ and $\neg\top \vdash \alpha$. This is covered by a non-triviality construction along the lines of Chapter 2 Appendix, wherein 'truth-value' constants are added. See Brady 1989. Chapter 5 contains related discussion.]

A few remarks

As Chapter 3 makes plain (see 'incoherent operators'), there are essential limits on any plausible candidate for a (coherent) 'just true' operator. Our $\mathbb{J}\alpha$, as $\tau \to \alpha$, is no different. One might think that if α is neither ttrue nor tfalse, then it ought count as just true or just false. Along these lines, one might want to impose

$$\neg(\alpha \wedge \neg\alpha) \vdash \mathbb{J}\alpha \vee \mathbb{J}\neg\alpha$$

as another desideratum; however, quick reflection shows that this is asking to transcend the limits—asking for incoherence. After all, according to BXTT, *every* sentence α is such that $\neg(\alpha \wedge \neg\alpha)$ is true. But now consider predictable sentences like some ζ equivalent to $\mathbb{J}\neg\zeta$. On the going account, ζ has the form $\tau \to \neg\zeta$, saying in effect 'I am just false'. Pushing the going desideratum clearly pushes to incoherence: since we have $\neg(\zeta \wedge \neg\zeta)$, we would get $\mathbb{J}\zeta \vee \mathbb{J}\neg\zeta$, which—as is straightforward to check—implies triviality.

The current account of *just true* need not be seen as replacing the other approaches discussed in Chapter 3. The point of this appendix is to note the rather surprising fact that, in effect, BX already contains a plausible 'just true' operator. Certainly, the features of $\tau \to \alpha$ canvassed here are available in BXTT, for which we enjoy a non-triviality proof.

---

[10]The trivial model cannot invalidate anything that isn't already invalidated. (Whether particular BX-ish *theories* need—for some reason—to acknowledge the trivial model is another matter. BXTT, as advanced in this book, shuns a trivial model.)

4

A LOOK AT THE FIELD

Chapters 1–3 have laid out the basic theory and driving philosophical account. Before turning to objections (Chapter 5), it is worth discussing alternative approaches to transparent truth. That's the aim of this chapter.

As it turns out, there aren't many theorists who've specified an account of how, in the face of the paradoxes, we can enjoy a transparent truth device. In fact, until very recently, the main account was that of Kripke (1975), who offered a non-paraconsistent, 'paracomplete' account—an account for which Excluded Middle fails. Kripke's account, however, faces fairly conspicuous shortcomings. In very recent work, Hartry Field (2008) has provided an account that, like Kripke's, is paracomplete (and non-paraconsistent) but nonetheless overcomes the salient shortcomings of Kripke's proposal. My focus, in this chapter, is on these two leading alternatives to my (paraconsistent, non-paracomplete) theory, namely, Kripke's and Field's.

« *Parenthetical remark.* Martin and Woodruff (1975) also gave an account of transparent truth, as did Woodruff (1984), whose four-valued account is both paraconsistent and paracomplete. (See also Visser 1984.) In the end, though, all such accounts suffer from the same basic shortcomings involved in Kripke's account (see below). For direct discussion of Woodruff's four-valued account, see Priest 1984, with whose discussion I'm in large agreement. I should also note that, while his theory is not a transparent truth theory, Priest's early discussion (Priest, 1987; Priest, 2006b) paves much of the way for the theory that I have advanced in this book. (I discuss some of Priest's views in Chapter 5.) *End parenthetical.* »

The plan, then, is to first sketch Kripke's account, focusing on the 'formal picture' which is presupposed in Field's account, and then sketch Field's account. By way of framing the discussion, I begin with a brief background note on general, guiding projects. I close the chapter by discussing points of agreement and disagreement between Field's account and my own, and briefly discussing how one might adjudicate between the two approaches.[1]

4.1 Broad background projects

A typical Liar is a sentence that says—or may be used to say—of itself only that it is false (or, equivalently in the case of ttruth, not true). An example is the

---

[1] I should note that much of this chapter is from Beall 2006b, which essay actually drew from early drafts of this book.

first displayed sentence in §1.3 of this book. Two related but distinct projects
dominate the Liar literature and work on semantic paradoxes in general, at least
among philosophical logicians concerned with modeling truth itself.

NTP.   *Non-Triviality Project*: explain how, despite having a truth predicate (in
        our language, for our language) and Liar-sentences, our language is non-
        trivial.[2]

ECP.   *Exhaustive Characterization Project*:[3] explain how, if at all, we can truly
        characterize—specify the 'semantic status' of—all sentences of our lan-
        guage (in our language).

These projects reflect the core appearances that give rise to the Liar paradox
(and its ilk). Semantic paradoxes arise, at least in part, from the appearance
that we can 'exhaustively characterize' all sentences of our language in terms of
'semantically significant' predicates, and truly do as much in our language.

   Consider the classical picture according to which our semantically significant
predicates are 'true' and 'false'. Our exhaustive characterization takes the form
of bivalence.

CEC.   *Classical*: Every sentence is either true or false.

Given such a characterization—one that purports to be truly expressible in our
language and likewise exhaustive—the non-triviality of our truth predicate (and,
hence, our language, in general) is immediately in question in the face of Liars—
the first displayed sentence in §1.3 or some such spandrel.

   The classical picture, of course, is just a special case of the Liar phenomenon. At bottom, there is a tension between the apparent non-triviality of our
truth predicate and our language's apparent capacity to achieve (true) exhaustive characterization.

EC.   *Exhaustive Characterization*: Every sentence is either True, False, or *Other*.

Here, 'Other' is a stand-in for the remaining 'semantically significant predicates'.[4]
For present purposes, one can focus on the 'problem cases' and think of the
semantically significant predicates as those that are invoked to classify such cases
(e.g., Liars and the like). For example, if one wishes to classify all Liars (etc.)
as *defective in some sense or other*, then 'defective in some sense or other' is
semantically significant and thereby stands among one's *Others* in EC.

---

[2]As in Ch. 1, a *trivial language* (or, better, theory) is one according to which everything is
true. A *non-trivial language* is one that isn't trivial. While most theorists—including Kripke
and Field—are in fact concerned with *consistency* (and, hence, non-triviality), paraconsistent
theorists, in general, are concerned with (reasonable) non-trivial but (negation-) inconsistent
languages/theories, and so 'non-triviality' is a more general term.

[3]In his Grim 1991, Patrick Grim uses 'complete' in the target sense of 'exhaustive'. Were
it not for the already too many notions of 'complete' in logical literature, Grim's terminology
would be quite appropriate here.

[4]I assume throughout that 'true' and 'false' are among our 'semantically significant predicates'. Of course, since I also assume (throughout) that falsity is truth of negation (i.e., that
α is false exactly if $\neg\alpha$ is true), one might better put EC just as True($\ulcorner\alpha\urcorner$) $\vee$ Other($\ulcorner\alpha\urcorner$), with
'Other' as a stand-in, as above. But I will set this aside.

The Liar paradox makes it difficult to see how we can have both EC and a non-trivial—let alone (negation-) consistent—truth predicate. In this book, our focus is on *ttruth*, an entirely see-through device $Tr(x)$ such that full intersubstitutability holds (see Chapter 1). NTP and EC jointly ask how we enjoy—as we appear to enjoy—a non-trivial ttruth predicate (in our language, for our language) and also achieve exhaustive characterization.

With respect to *ttruth*, there are two chief approaches: *paracomplete* and *paraconsistent*. In this book, I have championed the latter sort of approach—indeed, a dialetheic (so-called *strong paraconsistent*) approach. In this chapter, I present and discuss the two most prominent 'paracomplete' (and non-paraconsistent) approaches to *ttruth* (viz., those of Kripke and Field).

« *Parenthetical remark.* Another very recent approach, which I do not discuss, is proposed by Alan Weir (2005), which advocates a restriction on the so-called (substructural) 'cut' rule, according to which we infer $\alpha \vdash \beta$ from the facts that $\alpha, \gamma \vdash \beta$ and $\alpha \vdash \gamma$. In effect, then, Weir advocates a rejection of the general transitivity of implication. While Weir 2005 does not present a transparent truth theory (in the sense of TP), the framework should provide as much with various tweaks to Weir's conditional. Regrettably, I have little by way of strong—or even interesting—objection against Weir's suggested course (assuming that TP-transparency is achieved), but I find it less prima facie plausible than either of the standard paracomplete accounts (discussed in this chapter) or my own account. *End parenthetical.* »

Paracomplete accounts are the dominant approaches towards *ttruth*. 'Para' in 'paracomplete' comes from the Greek for *beyond* (or, perhaps, *beside*). The classical picture is one in which every instance of LEM (Excluded Middle) is true. Paracomplete theorists, by contrast, reject LEM, and see it as the main principle that paradoxes call into question.

« *Parenthetical remark.* The terminology of 'paracomplete', as far as I can tell, is from Achillé Varzi (1999), also used by Dominic Hyde (1997), but my usage is somewhat looser than theirs. (The related terminology of 'gaps' and 'gluts', used throughout, was introduced by Kit Fine (1975).) Paracomplete accounts are often called 'partiality accounts' or 'partial-predicate accounts'. See McGee 1991, Reinhardt 1986, and Soames 1999. *End parenthetical.* »

4.2 Kripke: basic paracomplete

For present purposes, I focus on what is known as Kripke's 'least fixed-point' model (with empty ground model), using the Strong Kleene scheme (discussed below). Given the chiefly philosophical aims of this book, I leave proofs to cited works (all of which are readily available), and try to say just enough to see how the formal picture goes.

For purposes of discussing Field's account (after Kripke's), I present the Kripkean formal picture in a slightly different way than in earlier chapters (including appendices), but a way that is entirely standard. The idea is as follows.

« *(Long) Parenthetical remark.* I should note that we can give a 'star seman-tics', as in Chapter 1, for K_3 (the Strong Kleene logic). In particular, instead of imposing our 'exhaustive' constraint, namely,

$$w \models \alpha \text{ or } w^\star \not\models \alpha \text{ for all } w \in \mathcal{N}$$

we *instead* impose

K-star: for all $w \in \mathcal{N}$, if $w \models \alpha$ then $w^\star \models \alpha$.

This allows for 'gaps' in the sense that, for some sentence α (and some model), @ $\not\models \alpha$ and @ $\not\models \neg\alpha$. This, in turn, requires 'abnormal gluts' in the sense that @$^\star \models \alpha$ and @$^\star \models \neg\alpha$, where @$^\star \in \mathcal{W} - \mathcal{N}$ (i.e., @* is abnormal). As a result, we lose LEM, and indeed have no logical truths, but we reinstate EFQ (explosion) since validity remains defined only over normal points. (Suppose @ $\models \alpha$. Then, by K-star, @$^\star \models \alpha$, in which case @ $\not\models \neg\alpha$. Hence, for any α, no model verifies both α and $\neg\alpha$, and so EFQ vacuously holds.) That K-star, combined with the setup in Chapter 1 (minus the 'exhaustive' constraint on normal worlds above), suffices for K_3 is something the proof of which I here omit.

Despite the availability of a star semantics for K_3, I follow the more standard many-valued approach in this chapter, which is employed by Kripke, Field, and Kleene himself. *I should also note that, for ease of readability (particularly for those unfamiliar with the basic constructions), I do not presuppose familiarity with the Chapter 1 or 2 appendices*, and so lay out the basic Strong Kleene Kripke construction without relying on the given appendices. (The K_3 construction is basically the same as that for *LP*, sketched in the Chapter 1 appendix. The difference is that our ground model is 'empty' rather than 'overstuffed'. The many-valued semantics for K_3 is just like that of *LP* except that the middle value is undesignated in the former.) *End (long) parenthetical.* »

Think of an *interpreted language* $\mathcal{L}$ as a triple $\langle \mathrm{L}, \mathcal{M}, \sigma \rangle$, where L is the syntax (the relevant syntactical information), $\mathcal{M}$ is an 'interpretation' or 'model' that provides interpretations to the non-logical constants (names, function symbols, predicates), and σ is a 'semantic scheme' or 'valuation scheme' that, in effect, provides interpretations—semantic values—to compound sentences. For present purposes, a semantic scheme or valuation scheme σ is simply some general defi-nition of *truth (falsity) in a model*. (For a more involved discussion of semantic schemes, see Gupta and Belnap 1993.)

Consider, for example, familiar classical languages, where the set $\mathcal{V}$ of 'seman-tic values' is $\{1, 0\}$, and designated value 1. In classical languages, $\mathcal{M} = \langle \mathcal{D}, I \rangle$, with $\mathcal{D}$ our non-empty set of objects (i.e., domain) and I an 'interpretation func-tion' that assigns to each name an element of $\mathcal{D}$ (the denotation of the name), assigns to each n-ary function symbol an element of $\mathcal{D}^n \longrightarrow \mathcal{D}$, that is, assigns an n-ary function from $\mathcal{D}^n$ into $\mathcal{D}$, and assigns to each n-ary predicate an el-ement of $\mathcal{D}^n \longrightarrow \mathcal{V}$, a function—sometimes thought of as the *intension* of the predicate—taking n-tuples of $\mathcal{D}$ and yielding a 'semantic value'. The *extension* of an n-ary predicate φ (intuitively, the set of things of which φ is true) contains all n-tuples $\langle a_1, \ldots, a_n \rangle$ of $\mathcal{D}$ such that $I(\varphi)(\langle a_1, \ldots, a_n \rangle) = 1$. The classical valuation scheme τ (for Tarski) is the familiar one according to which a negation is true (in a given model) exactly when its negatum is false (in the given model), a disjunction is true (in a model) iff one of the disjuncts is true (in the model), and existential sentences are treated as generalized disjunctions.[5]

Classical languages (with suitably resourceful L) cannot have their own *transparent* truth predicate. Paracomplete languages, like Kripke's, drop the 'exhaustive' feature implicit in classical languages (and in my own theory): namely, that a sentence or its negation is true, for *all* sentences.

Concentrating on the so-called *Strong Kleene* account (Kleene, 1952), the formal story runs as follows. We expand our classical $\mathcal{V}$, as above, to the broader $\{1, \frac{1}{2}, 0\}$, and so our language $\mathcal{L}_\kappa = \langle \mathrm{L}, \mathcal{M}, \kappa \rangle$ is now a so-called three-valued language (because it uses three semantic values). Our set of designated values, as above, is a subset of our semantic values; in the Strong Kleene case, as in the classical case, there is exactly one designated element, namely 1.

« *Parenthetical remark.* Kripke (1975) made much of emphasizing that 'the third value' is not to be understood as *a third truth value* or anything other than 'undefined' (along the lines of Kleene's original work (1952)). I will not make much of this here, but see Chapter 3 for brief discussion of my 'instrumentalist' take on such values. (Note that if one wants to avoid a three-valued language, one can let $\mathcal{V} = \{1, 0\}$ and proceed to construct a Kleene language either by using *partial functions* (hence the standard terminology 'partial predicates') for interpretations or along the 'star' lines mentioned in a (long) parenthetical remark above. I think that this is ultimately merely terminological, but I won't dwell on the matter here. *End parenthetical.* »

A Strong Kleene model $\mathcal{M} = \langle \mathcal{D}, I \rangle$ is much as before, with I doing exactly what it did in the classical case except that it now assigns to n-ary predicates elements of $\mathcal{D}^n \longrightarrow \{1, \frac{1}{2}, 0\}$, since $\mathcal{V} = \{1, \frac{1}{2}, 0\}$. Accordingly, the 'intensions' of our paracomplete (Strong Kleene) predicates have three options: 1, $\frac{1}{2}$, and 0. What about *extensions*? As above, we want to treat predicates not just in terms of extensions (as in the classical languages) but also anti-extensions. The *extension* of an n-ary predicate φ, just as before, comprises all n-tuples $\langle a_1, \ldots, a_n \rangle$ of $\mathcal{D}$ such that $I(\varphi)(\langle a_1, \ldots, a_n \rangle) = 1$. (Again, intuitively, this remains the set of objects of which φ is true.) The *anti-extension*, in turn, comprises all n-tuples $\langle a_1, \ldots, a_n \rangle$ of $\mathcal{D}$ such that $I(\varphi)(\langle a_1, \ldots, a_n \rangle) = 0$. (Again, intuitively, this is the set of objects of which φ is false.) Of course, as intended, an interpretation might fail to put x in either the extension or anti-extension of φ. In that case, we say (in our 'metalanguage') that, relative to the model, φ is *undefined* for x.

---

[5] I assume familiarity with the basic classical picture, including 'true in $\mathcal{L}$' and so on. For simplicity, I sometimes assume that we've moved to models in which everything in the domain has a name; otherwise I assume familiarity with standard accounts of *satisfies* $\varphi(x)$ *in* $\mathcal{L}$ etc.

« Parenthetical remark. A common way of speaking is to say that, for example, $\varphi(t)$ is 'gappy' with respect to $I(t)$. This terminology is appropriate if one is clear on the relation between one's formal model and the target notions that the model is intended to serve (in one respect or other), but the terminology can also be confusing, since, e.g., in the current Strong Kleene language, one cannot truly assert of any α that α is 'gappy', i.e., $\neg Tr(\ulcorner\alpha\urcorner) \wedge \neg Tr(\ulcorner\neg\alpha\urcorner)$. (I return to this issue, in a different vein, below.) *End parenthetical. »*

Letting φ^+ and φ^- be the extension and anti-extension of φ, respectively, it is easy to see that, as noted above, classical languages are a special case of (Strong Kleene) paracomplete languages. Paracomplete languages typically eschew inconsistency, and so typically demand that $\varphi^+ \cap \varphi^- = \emptyset$, that nothing be in both the extension and anti-extension of any predicate. In this way, paracomplete languages typically agree with classical languages (and, obviously, sharply disagree with paraconsistent ones). Paracomplete languages differ from the classical approach in *not* demanding that $\varphi^+ \cup \varphi^- = \mathcal{D}$ for all predicates φ. On the other hand, paracomplete languages *allow* for such 'exhaustive constraints' (e.g., some models might satisfy the constraint), and in that respect can enjoy classical languages as a special case.

« Parenthetical remark. This is not to say that paraconsistent languages cannot also be paracomplete. One of the most familiar paraconsistent logics, Anderson and Belnap's *FDE* (1975, 1992), is both paraconsistent and paracomplete. Indeed, this is one scheme for which Woodruff (1984) showed the availability of a transparent truth predicate. Still, in this chapter, I consider only the two most prominent paracomplete theories of transparent truth, both of which are non-paraconsistent. *End parenthetical. »*

To see the close relation between classical languages and Strong Kleene, notice that κ, the Strong Kleene valuation scheme, runs as follows (here treating only $\neg$, $\vee$, and $\exists$). Where $\nu_{\mathcal{M}}(\alpha)$ is the semantic value of α in model $\mathcal{M}$, and, for simplicity, letting each object in the domain name itself,

K1. $\nu_{\mathcal{M}}(\neg\alpha) = 1 - \nu_{\mathcal{M}}(\alpha)$.

K2. $\nu_{\mathcal{M}}(\alpha \vee \beta) = \max(\nu_{\mathcal{M}}(\alpha), \nu_{\mathcal{M}}(\beta))$.

K3. $\nu_{\mathcal{M}}(\exists x\, \alpha(x)) = \max\{\nu_{\mathcal{M}}(\alpha(t/x)) :$ for all $t \in \mathcal{D}\}$.

The extent to which classical logic is an extension of a given paracomplete logic depends on the semantic scheme of the language. Since κ, as above, is entirely in keeping with the classical scheme *except* for 'adding an extra possibility', it is clear that every classical interpretation is a Strong Kleene interpretation but not vice versa. (In classical languages, $\nu_{\mathcal{M}}(\alpha) \in \{1, 0\}$ for any α, and the familiar classical clauses on connectives are simply K1–K3.)

Let us say that an interpretation *verifies* a sentence α iff α is assigned 1 on that interpretation, and that an interpretation verifies a set of sentences Σ iff it verifies every element of Σ. We define *semantic consequence* in familiar terms:

α is a consequence of Σ iff every interpretation that verifies Σ also verifies α. I shall use '$\vdash_{SK}$' for the Strong Kleene consequence relation, so understood.

Let us say that a sentence α is logically true in $\mathcal{L}_{SK}$ exactly if $\emptyset \vdash_{SK} \alpha$, that is, iff α is assigned 1 in every model. A notable feature of $\mathcal{L}_{SK}$ is that there are no logical truths. To see this, just consider an interpretation that assigns $\frac{1}{2}$ to every atomic, in which case, as an induction will show, every sentence is assigned $\frac{1}{2}$ on that interpretation. Hence, there's some interpretation in which no sentence is designated, and hence no sentence designated on all interpretations. A fortiori, LEM fails in Strong Kleene languages.

« *Parenthetical remark.* This is not to say, of course, that one can't have a Strong Kleene—or, in general, paracomplete—language some proper fragment of which is such that $\alpha \vee \neg\alpha$ holds for all α *in the proper fragment*! One might, for example, stipulate that arithmetic is such that $\alpha \vee \neg\alpha$ holds. *End parenthetical.* »

An answer to one guiding question becomes apparent. What we want is an account of how our language can be non-trivial (indeed, in Kripke's case, consistent) while containing both a transparent truth predicate and Liar-like sentences. In large part, the answer is that our language is (in relevant respects) along Strong Kleene lines, that the logic is weaker than classical logic. Such a language, as Kripke showed, can contain its own ttruth predicate.

The formal Kripke construction—which is also essential for discussing Field's account—runs as follows. For simplicity, let $\mathcal{L}_\kappa$ be a classical (but nonetheless Strong Kleene) language such that L (the basic syntax, etc.) is free of semantic terms but has the resources to describe its given syntax—including, among other things, having a name $\ulcorner\alpha\urcorner$ for each sentence α. (By a 'classical but Strong Kleene language' I mean that the language is a 'Strong Kleene' language that happens also to be classical: I assigns to each n-ary predicate an element of $\mathcal{D}^n \longrightarrow \{1,0\}$, even though the values $\mathcal{V}$ of $\mathcal{L}_\kappa$ also contain $\frac{1}{2}$.) What we want to do is move to a richer language the syntax L^t of which contains $Tr(x)$, a unary predicate intended to be a transparent truth predicate for the enriched language. For simplicity, assume that the domain $\mathcal{D}$ of $\mathcal{L}_\kappa$ contains all sentences of L^t.[6]

The aim, intuitively, is to keep moving through richer and richer languages in the sense that each 'new' language expands the previous language's account of what's true. The idea, more precisely, is that each successive language contains a fuller account of what's true (and, derivatively, false) than the previous language's account. In terms of extensions and anti-extensions, successive languages expand the extension and anti-extension of $Tr(x)$. The goal, of course, is to find a language at which we finally have a 'fixed point', one at which anything true in the language is fully recorded in the given language, so that one needn't go further.

Returning to the construction, we have our given 'ground language' $\mathcal{L}_\kappa$ and expand to $\mathcal{L}_\kappa^t$, the syntax of which includes that of $\mathcal{L}_\kappa$ but also has $Tr(x)$ and the

---

[6]This is usually put (more precisely) as that the domain contains the Gödel codes of all such sentences, but for present purposes I skip the full mathematical details.

resulting sentences formable therefrom. We want the new language to 'expand' the ground language, and we want the former to have a model that differs from the latter only in that it assigns an interpretation to $Tr(x)$. For present purposes, we let I^t, the interpretation function in $\mathcal{L}^t_\kappa$, assign $\langle \emptyset, \emptyset \rangle$ to $Tr(x)$, where $\langle \emptyset, \emptyset \rangle$ is the function that assigns $\frac{1}{2}$ to each element of $\mathcal{D}^t$, the domain of $\mathcal{L}^t_\kappa$. (Hence, the extension and anti-extension of $Tr(x)$ in $\mathcal{L}^t_\kappa$ are both empty.)

« *Parenthetical remark.* While, in this chapter, I try to avoid presupposing familiarity with the appendices of Chapters 1 and 2, it is worth noting that the construction here is just like that in the Chapter 1 appendix (and presupposed in the Brady construction in the Chapter 2 appendix). The main difference is that in the LP scheme employed in the Chapter 1 appendix, the middle value is designated. As a result, the relevant LP ground model is 'overstuffed', while the K_3 ground model—at issue in this chapter—is absolutely 'under-stuffed' (as above, empty extension and anti-extension of $Tr(x)$). While this difference makes a big difference, the basic construction is roughly the same. *End parenthetical.* »

The crucial question concerns *expansion*. How do we expand the interpretation of $Tr(x)$? How, in other words, do we move to richer languages (richer with respect to the truth predicate)? How, in short, do we eventually reach a language in which we have a transparent truth predicate for the whole given language? This is the role of Kripke's 'jump operator'. What we want are 'increasingly informative' interpretations $\langle \mathcal{T}_i^+, \mathcal{T}_i^- \rangle$ of $Tr(x)$, but interpretations that not only 'expand' the previous interpretations but also *preserve* what has already been interpreted. If α is true at a 'level' i, then we want as much preserved: that α remain true at the next level $i+1$. This is the role of the 'jump operator', a role that is achievable given the so-called *monotonicity* of Strong Kleene valuation scheme κ.

« *Parenthetical (slightly technical) remark.* Monotonicity is the crucial ingredient in Kripke's (similarly, Martin and Woodruff's) general result. Let $\mathcal{M}$ and $\mathcal{M}'$ be paracomplete (partial) models for (uninterpreted) L. Let φ_M^+ be the extension of φ in $\mathcal{M}$, and similarly $\varphi_{M'}^+$ for $\mathcal{M}'$. (Similarly for anti-extension.) Then $\mathcal{M}'$ *extends* $\mathcal{M}$ iff the models have the same domain, agree on interpretations of names and function signs, and $\varphi_M^+ \subseteq \varphi_{M'}^+$ and $\varphi_M^- \subseteq \varphi_{M'}^-$ for all predicates φ that M and M' interpret. (In other words, $\mathcal{M}'$ doesn't change $\mathcal{M}$'s interpretation; it simply interprets whatever, if anything, $\mathcal{M}$ left uninterpreted.) MONOTONICITY PROPERTY: A semantic (valuation) scheme σ is *monotone* iff for any α that is interpreted by both models, α's being designated in $\mathcal{M}$ implies its being designated in $\mathcal{M}'$ whenever $\mathcal{M}'$ extends $\mathcal{M}$. So, the monotonicity property of a scheme ensures that it 'preserves truth (falsity)' of 'prior interpretations' in the desired fashion. (The interested reader might benefit from comparing this account of 'monotonicity' with that in the Chapter 1 appendix.) *End parenthetical.* »

The role of the jump operator is to eventually 'jump' through successive interpretations $I_i(Tr)$ and land on one that serves the role of transparent truth—serves as a transparent interpretation of $Tr(x)$. In other words, the role of the jump operator is to jump through languages until we reach one that enjoys a *ttruth* predicate. As above, letting $I_i(Tr)$ be a function $\langle \mathcal{T}_i^+, \mathcal{T}_i^- \rangle$ yielding the extension and anti-extension of $Tr(x)$ at level i, the goal is to eventually 'jump' upon an interpretation $\langle \mathcal{T}_i^+, \mathcal{T}_i^- \rangle$ such that $\langle \mathcal{T}_i^+, \mathcal{T}_i^- \rangle = \langle \mathcal{T}_{i+1}^+, \mathcal{T}_{i+1}^- \rangle$.

Focusing on the 'least such point' in the Strong Kleene setting, Kripke's construction proceeds as above. We begin at stage 0 at which $Tr(x)$ is interpreted as $\langle \emptyset, \emptyset \rangle$, and we define a 'jump operator' on such interpretations:[7] $Tr(x)$ is interpreted as $\langle \mathcal{T}_{i+1}^+, \mathcal{T}_{i+1}^- \rangle$ at stage $i + 1$ if interpreted as $\langle \mathcal{T}_i^+, \mathcal{T}_i^- \rangle$ at the preceding stage i, where, note well, $\mathcal{T}_{i+1}^+$ comprises the sentences that are true (designated) at the preceding stage (language) i, and $\mathcal{T}_{i+1}^-$ the false sentences (and, for simplicity, non-sentences) at i. Accordingly, we define the 'jump operator' J_{SK} as follows. (Kripke's definition applies to *any* monotone scheme σ. I relativize the operator to SK just to remind that we are focusing on the Strong Kleene case.)

$$J_{SK}(\langle \mathcal{T}_i^+, \mathcal{T}_i^- \rangle) = \langle \mathcal{T}_{i+1}^+, \mathcal{T}_{i+1}^- \rangle$$

The jump operator yields a sequence of richer and richer interpretations that 'preserve prior information' (given monotonicity), a process that can be extended into the transfinite to yield a sequence

$$\langle \mathcal{T}_0^+, \mathcal{T}_0^- \rangle, \langle \mathcal{T}_1^+, \mathcal{T}_1^- \rangle, \ldots, \langle \mathcal{T}_j^+, \mathcal{T}_j^- \rangle, \ldots$$

defined (via transfinite recursion) thus:[8]

Jb. Base. $(\langle \mathcal{T}_0^+, \mathcal{T}_0^- \rangle) = \langle \emptyset, \emptyset \rangle$.

Js. Successor. $\langle \mathcal{T}_{j+1}^+, \mathcal{T}_{j+1}^- \rangle = J_{SK}(\langle \mathcal{T}_j^+, \mathcal{T}_j^- \rangle)$.

Jl. Limit. For limit stages l, we collect up by unionizing the prior stages:

$$\langle \mathcal{T}_l^+, \mathcal{T}_l^- \rangle = \left\langle \bigcup_{i<l} \mathcal{T}_i^+, \bigcup_{i<l} \mathcal{T}_i^- \right\rangle$$

What Kripke showed—for *any* monotone scheme, a fortiori for Strong Kleene—is that the transfinite sequence reaches a stage at which the desired transparent truth predicate is found, a 'fixed point' of the jump operator such that we obtain

$$\langle \mathcal{T}_j^+, \mathcal{T}_j^- \rangle = \langle \mathcal{T}_{j+1}^+, \mathcal{T}_{j+1}^- \rangle = J_{SK}(\langle \mathcal{T}_j^+, \mathcal{T}_j^- \rangle)$$

The upshot is that language j is such that $\mathcal{T}_j^+$ and $\mathcal{T}_j^-$ comprise all of the true (respectively, false) sentences of $\mathcal{L}_\kappa^j$, the Strong Kleene language at j, which is to say that $\mathcal{L}_\kappa^j$ contains its own transparent truth predicate.

---

[7]So, our operator operates on the set of all (admissible) functions from $\mathcal{D}$ into $\{1, \frac{1}{2}, 0\}$, where $\mathcal{D}$ is in our given 'ground language'.

[8]Transfinite recursion is much like ordinary recursive definitions except for requiring an extra clause for so-called 'limit ordinals'. (One can find a discussion of transfinite recursion in most standard set theory books or metatheory textbooks. Additionally, McGee 1991 and Smullyan 1993 are very useful, with the former especially useful for the present applications.)

The *proof* of Kripke's result is left to other (widely available) work. For now, I turn to a few comments on the corresponding philosophical picture.

« *Parenthetical remark.* Kripke's own proof is elegant, bringing in mathematically important and interesting results of recursion theory and inductive definitions; it is also perhaps more philosophically informative than a popular algebraic proof, especially with respect to the least fixed point (on which I've focused here). Still, as mentioned in Chapter 1 appendix, if one simply wants *a* proof of the given result (e.g., existence of least fixed point), a straightforward algebraic proof is available, due to Visser (2004) and Fitting (1986), and discussed in a general, user-friendly fashion by Gupta and Belnap (1993). *End parenthetical.* »

4.2.1 *Comments*

In this section I briefly mention a few issues concerning the philosophical application of Kripke's paracomplete account, concentrating on the noted projects NTP and ECP. I leave much of the discussion to cited sources, especially with respect to what I call 'interpretation issues'.

Interpretation issues.   Three salient interpetation-related issues have emerged with respect to Kripke's proposal(s).[9] Since they are not of chief concern in this discussion, I simply mention the issues here, pointing to cited works for further discussion. The three interpretation-related issues are as follows.

Ik1. Which fixed point?

Ik2. Supervenience or Transparency?

Ik3. Classical or non-classical theory?

I shall very briefly discuss each issue in turn.

Ik1: Take any monotonic semantic (valuation) scheme σ.[10] Kripke showed that the (suitably defined) 'jump operator' over σ-interpretations has a fixed point that can serve as an interpretation of a ttruth predicate (for the given language). But while we've narrowly focused on one particular interpretation (the least fixed point), there are in fact many fixed points (as Kripke noted), and there's some controversy about which of the many fixed points best model the ttruth predicate. For discussion of the issue see Gupta and Belnap 1993.

Ik2: This issue is related to Ik1. Michael Kremer (1988) argues that the so-called 'supervenience' and 'transparency' ideas about ttruth are in conflict in Kripke's proposal. The former is the idea that once the non-semantic 'facts' are fixed, then so too is the interpretation of 'ttrue'. The latter idea is as indicated throughout: that 'ttrue' is entirely transparent, that it, unlike the former idea,

---

[9]Despite my talk of *Kripke's proposal* or the like, I should note that Kripke himself abstained from endorsing any of the particular accounts in Kripke 1975.

[10]Kripke (1975) explicitly discusses two other well-known schemes, viz., the Weak Kleene scheme (which is Bochvar's 'internal' scheme) and van Fraassen's 1966 *supervaluational* scheme. Martin and Woodruff (1975) proved the existence of the 'maximal fixed point' with respect to the Weak Kleene scheme.

dictates no particular interpretation other than one that affords its essential intersubstitutability. A related issue—concerning the philosophical significance of fixed-point constructions, generally—is discussed by Philip Kremer (2000). (My own position, as discussed, bucks the supervenience idea, an idea that strikes me as ignoring the potential for spandrels to generate 'un-supervening' ttruths. See Chapter 1.)

Ik3: This is a slightly more technical issue. In presenting Kripke's account, I've focused entirely on κ-based languages, the Strong Kleene, least fixed-point proposal. Moreover, I've focused entirely on a *non-classical reading* of that proposal—one for which the resulting logic is non-classical (and, indeed, Strong Kleene). As it turns out, a related, *classical* reading is also available, a reading (and resulting classical truth theory) proposed by Solomon Feferman (1984). This reading is standardly called 'KF' (for Kripke–Feferman). While the proposal is interesting, it is not an account of *ttruth*, since it gives up the essential intersubstitutability of $Tr(\ulcorner \alpha \urcorner)$ and α. (That it gives up on ttruth is plain from the fact that Feferman was after a consistent, classical theory, something with which ttruth is incompatible, at least given usual syntactic resources. One conspicuous example of the departure from ttruth is in KF's commitment to instances of $\alpha \wedge \neg Tr(\ulcorner \alpha \urcorner)$, something that would be inconsistent if $Tr(x)$ were fully transparent.) See Reinhardt 1986 for further discussion, and Maudlin 2004 for an interesting philosophical account of (non-transparent) truth along such lines. Also see McGee 1989 and Halbach and Horsten 2006 for related considerations.

Non-triviality (consistency) project. Recall that NTP, the non-triviality project, is to explain how we can enjoy a non-trivial language that has both a transparent truth predicate and paradoxical sentences. In Kripke's case, the project is to show how we can enjoy a *consistent* such language. What Kripke aimed to do—and succeeded in doing—is prove that, provided the language had various features (and lacked various features), we could have a consistent language with transparent truth.

Some standardly object that Kripke's account doesn't answer NTP, the reason being that certain notions used in the metalanguage are not expressible in the object- or 'model language'. Though a dominant objection, this is the same issue discussed in Chapter 3, and the reply, at least by my lights, is the same.

Briefly, let $\mathcal{L}_\kappa$ be such a (fixed-point) language constructed via the κ-scheme. (The point applies to any of the given languages.) In constructing $\mathcal{L}_\kappa$, we use—in our (classical) metalanguage—classical set theory, and we proceed to define *truth-in-$\mathcal{L}_\kappa$* (in effect, designation, as above). In turn, as in Chapter 3, if—as I'm assuming—our 'model language' $\mathcal{L}_\kappa$ does not include the language of set theory (but rather arithmetic), then such *truth-in-$\mathcal{L}_\kappa$* is not expressible in $\mathcal{L}_\kappa$ for the dull reason that arithmetic isn't able to do the job. Moreover, if set theory is used (as the base language), then the notion is expressible but, via the argument employed in §3.4.2, doesn't play the role that the objection assumes it to play. As discussed in Chapter 3, the standard sort of 'revenge' arguments at best seem to conflate model-dependent notions with the model-independent (or absolute) notions that the former purport to illuminate. So long as one takes a sufficiently 'instrumentalist' view of the given formal construction, the given sort of revenge objection—popular as it is—need not undermine the Kripkean proposal.

On the other hand, there is something correct in the objection, at least with respect to Kripke's account. In particular, the objection points to an apparent and perhaps serious expressive poverty. This issue, however, has less to do with NTP than with ECP, to which I now briefly turn.

Exhaustive characterization project.   ECP is the project of explaining how, if at all, we can achieve 'exhaustive characterization' in a language with its own truth predicate (in the language) and Liar-like sentences. While 'exhaustive characterization' remains imprecise, the intuitive import is clear: a language in which we have various 'semantically significant predicates' that may be used to *exhaustively* and correctly (semantically) categorize all sentences of the language.

One way of thinking about 'exhaustive characterization', as here intended, is as follows. Suppose that our semantic-free fragment $\mathcal{L}_0$ is exhaustively characterized *classically*, in which case we have it that, where CEC is the 'classical exhaustive characterization',

CEC. Every sentence of $\mathcal{L}_0$ is either ttrue or tfalse.

Now, what Kripke showed—and paracomplete theorists, in general, advance—is that we can enjoy a consistent *ttruth* device (the predicate 'ttrue') if our language goes beyond the classical—opens up the 'semantically significant options' for sentences. While CEC may suffice for $\mathcal{L}_0$, a genuinely *exhaustive* characterization requires another category, given spandrels.

EC. Every sentence (in the language) is either ttrue, tfalse, or *Other.*

The question is: how shall *other* be understood?

One way that 'Other' should *not* be understood, at least on the Kleene approach, is as implying *not ttrue* or, hence, *neither ttrue nor tfalse.* Suppose, for example, that 'other' in EC is cashed out such that $Other(\ulcorner\alpha\urcorner)$ implies $\neg Tr(\ulcorner\alpha\urcorner)$, and hence—given intersubstitutability—implies $\neg\alpha$. One reason for introducing $Other(x)$ into the language is to *correctly characterize* Liars—for example, the first displayed sentence in §1.3. Let α be a sentence that says of itself (only) that it's not ttrue, that is, a sentence equivalent to $\neg Tr(\ulcorner\alpha\urcorner)$ and, hence, $\neg\alpha$. If $Other(x)$ is to play the role for which it was introduced—namely, to correctly characterize, perhaps among other things, Liars—then one would want $Other(\ulcorner\alpha\urcorner)$ to be ttrue. But if, as supposed, $Other(\ulcorner\alpha\urcorner)$ implies $\neg Tr(\ulcorner\alpha\urcorner)$ and, hence, implies $\neg\alpha$, then inconsistency abounds: from the fact that α is *Other*, it follows that α is *not ttrue*, in which case, since that is precisely what α says, α is also ttrue, by the essential intersubstitutability of *ttruth.*

In general, then, it is not difficult to see that 'Other' in EC cannot be consistently understood as implying *not ttrue*, at least if, as above, negation is along

Kleene lines.[11] The point applies in particular to the Strong Kleene proposal of Kripke: it makes no sense to say of Liars that they are neither ttrue nor tfalse.

« *Parenthetical remark.* Recall, from Chapter 3, the difference between the *model language* and the *real language*, and in particular the difference between *model-dependent*—ultimately, merely instrumental—notions and the 'real notions' intended to be modeled. It makes perfect sense, *standing squarely and only in the classical fragment (metalanguage)*, to say of sentences in the 'model language' that they're neither true-in-the-model language nor false-in-the-model language. But such model-dependent notions aren't at issue here. *End parenthetical.* »

In the end, while his account provides a (paracomplete) response to NTP, Kripke's Strong Kleene proposal affords no answer to ECP. As a result, there's no predicate that is introduced—in the given language (as opposed to model-dependent metalanguage terms)—for purposes of correctly classifying Liars, at least on Kripke's paracomplete account. In short, Kripke gives us nothing at all to (ttruly) say about Liars or other such spandrels.

« *Parenthetical remark.* In fact, one might take some of Kripke's remarks to suggest that, by his lights, there's no escaping a 'Tarskian' or 'hierarchical' approach to ECP. (See the famous passage about Tarski's ghost (Kripke, 1975).) But I will not dwell on the exegetical issue here. [Note that one might take the 'classical reading' of Kripke, formulated by Feferman's KF, as having an answer to ECP, and in many respects that's correct. (One can truly say, e.g., that Liars are not true.) But, again, KF gives up ttruth (and, so, NTP with respect to ttruth).] *End parenthetical.* »

Tr-biconditionals and Curry. While perhaps not falling under either NTP or ECP, one other salient feature of Kripke's account concerns a suitable conditional. As discussed in Chapter 2, biconditionals of the form $Tr(\ulcorner \alpha \urcorner) \leftrightarrow \alpha$, have long been thought to be an essential feature of truth, something at least essential to 'the' so-called naïve theory of truth.[12] But what about *ttruth*? As in Chapter 2, what is essential to *ttruth* is its transparency, its intersubstitutability. Whether all instances of $Tr(\ulcorner \alpha \urcorner) \leftrightarrow \alpha$ hold depends entirely on the sort of conditional one has, whether, for example, one's conditional $\rightarrow$ is such that $\alpha \rightarrow \alpha$ is valid. If $\alpha \rightarrow \alpha$ is valid in the language, then the Tr-biconditionals will thereby hold (assuming, as I do, that $\leftrightarrow$ is defined as usual).

Whether an acceptable theory of ttruth must validate all Tr-biconditionals is not something for which I have a strong argument. For present purposes,

---

[11] Deviating from *ttruth*, of course, affords more options, and in many ways is what—or, more accurately, what may have—motivated approaches like Feferman 1984, McGee 1989, Halbach and Horsten 2006, Maudlin 2004, and so on.

[12] I generally refrain from using 'naïve theory of truth', since I'm not sure what it is supposed to be. Sometimes, it seems as if 'the' so-called naïve theory of truth is 'the' theory that takes all T-biconditionals to be basic; however, as McGee (1992) showed, even if one restricts oneself to 'maximally consistent' sets of T-biconditionals, there are uncountably many such theories (compatible with, say, Peano Arithmetic). I refrain from using the term again.

as in Chapter 2, I assume—without argument—that, other things being equal, an account of *ttruth* that validates all such biconditionals is prima facie more attractive than an account that fails to do so. Accordingly, an account of ttruth for which we have the validity of $\alpha \to \alpha$ is prima facie more attractive than an account for which $\alpha \to \alpha$ isn't valid, at least other things being equal.[13]

That $\alpha \to \alpha$ is not valid in Kripke's Strong Kleene proposal is clear, since $\to$, in Strong Kleene, is simply the material conditional, which is defined $\neg\alpha \vee \beta$, that is, our hook $\alpha \supset \beta$. But, then, $\alpha \supset \alpha$ is valid only if $\neg\alpha \vee \alpha$ is valid, that is, only if LEM (Excluded Middle) is valid. But LEM isn't valid in Strong Kleene, as noted above. Indeed, the heart of paracomplete proposals is the rejection of LEM.

While Kripke's proposal seems to show how we can have a non-trivial (indeed, consistent) ttruth predicate despite the existence of paradoxical sentences, it fails to show how we can achieve as much in a language for which the Tr-biconditionals hold.

One might think it an easy fix to add a conditional. After all, Łukasiewicz's (pronounced 'woo-kush-YE-vitch') three-valued language differs from the Strong Kleene language only in that it adds a conditional for which $\alpha \to \alpha$ is valid. (One can retain the hook, of course, so as to have two conditionals, $\to$ and $\supset$. This is no surprise given that, as noted above, $\alpha \supset \beta$ simply is $\neg\alpha \vee \beta$.) Łukasiewicz's conditional is defined as follows.

$\to_3$	1	$\frac{1}{2}$	0
1	1	$\frac{1}{2}$	0
$\frac{1}{2}$	1	1	$\frac{1}{2}$
0	1	1	1

As one can see, $\alpha \to_3 \alpha$ is always designated in the Łukasiewicz semantics, and hence, given the essential intersubstitutability of ttruth, $Tr(\ulcorner\alpha\urcorner) \leftrightarrow_3 \alpha$ is always designated (with $\leftrightarrow_3$ defined as usual via conjunction).

The *trouble*, however, is that this proposal will not work in the sort of paracomplete, fixed-point languages at issue. One way to see this is to consider a version of Curry's paradox (see Chapter 2). Without getting into the technical details, a simple way to see the problem is via an informal Curry-like situation. Assume a Strong Kleene (fixed-point) language augmented with the Łukasiewicz conditional above. Let α be a sentence that says $Tr(\ulcorner\alpha\urcorner) \leftrightarrow_3 \bot$, where $\bot$ is some false sentence in the semantic-free fragment, say, '$1 = 0$'. Let γ be a (Curry) sentence that says $Tr(\ulcorner\gamma\urcorner) \leftrightarrow_3 Tr(\ulcorner\alpha\urcorner)$. A paracomplete theorist wants to say that α is to receive value $\frac{1}{2}$ (or modeled as such). Suppose that γ receives the value $\frac{1}{2}$. Then the values of γ and α are the same, in which case γ gets the value 1. Contradiction. Similarly, a contradiction arises if γ receives 0 or, obviously, 1.

---

[13]One natural route towards an *argument* is given by Feferman (1984), who argues that without the validity of $\alpha \to \alpha$, at least for some conditional $\to$, 'ordinary reasoning' is crippled; however, despite endorsing the validity of $\alpha \to \alpha$ for our 'suitable conditional', I am far from clear that this is right in general.

Hence, there's no obvious way to add Łukasiewicz's conditional to the Strong Kleene (fixed point) language.

« *Parenthetical remark.* As briefly mentioned in Chapter 2, one might think that, while his three-valued conditional won't work, the full continuum-valued language $\mathcal{L}_\infty$ of Łukasiewicz, which, except for more values, retains the K1–K3 clauses for standard connectives (see above), might do the trick. In particular, $\rightarrow_\infty$, the conditional in $\mathcal{L}_\infty$, satisfies none of the given contraction principles from Chapter 2 but nicely satisfies Identity. [More promising yet, perhaps, is that 'semantical property theory', sometimes called 'naïve set theory', is consistent in $\mathcal{L}_\infty$. See White 1979. (I briefly discuss 'semantical property theory' in Chapter 5.)] Unfortunately, the proposal won't work, as Greg Restall (1992) and, more generally, Hájek, Paris and Shepherdson 2000 show: the resulting theory will be ω-inconsistent. For details, see Restall 1992, which is very user-friendly, and, in turn, the more general results in Hájek, Paris and Shepherdson 2000. *End parenthetical.* »

Of course, there's nothing barring one from adding something along the lines of our abnormal-worlds conditional, from Chapter 2, to the Kripke framework. In fact, in some sense, Field's proposal is along just such lines, although his conditional is different from what would result from adding the simple, abnormal-worlds conditional of Chapter 2. It is to Field's proposal that I now turn.

4.3   Field: advanced paracomplete

The upshot of the foregoing comments is that while Kripke's paracomplete proposal shows that, despite having Liars in the language, we can have a non-trivial (indeed, consistent) ttruth predicate (in the language, for the language), it nonetheless exhibits two apparent inadequacies.

I1. The proposal fails to answer NTP for a language in which all of the Tr-biconditionals hold.

I2. The proposal fails to answer ECP in any fashion.

As in Chapter 2, Curry's paradox puts constraints on adding a genuine conditional for which $\alpha \rightarrow \alpha$ is valid (and, hence, for which the Tr-biconditionals all hold). Answering ECP, in turn, likewise requires care, since 'strengthened Liars' (paradoxical spandrels of one's characterization tools) are ever ready to emerge.

Hartry Field (2008) advances the Kripkean paracomplete proposal by attempting to overcome I1 and I2, the two notable inadequacies of Kripke's own proposal. Field maintains the basic paracomplete line that paradoxes—perhaps among other phenomena—teach us that LEM is to be rejected, that some instances of $\alpha \vee \neg\alpha$ are to be rejected.

« *Parenthetical remark.* This is not to say that there aren't significant (proper) fragments of the language for which LEM holds. Just as I maintain that, e.g., EFQ holds over certain proper fragments (see Chapter 1), one might maintain, in a paracomplete theory, that LEM holds over certain proper fragments—the arithmetical fragment of our language, or physics, or so on. Indeed, Field (2003) explicitly agrees with this, maintaining that LEM holds for mathematics and the like, in general. *End parenthetical.* »

By recognizing a (novel) suitable conditional, Field contributes an answer to NTP for a (consistent) language in which all Tr-biconditionals hold and, in turn, an answer to ECP.

In what follows, I provide a sketch of (the basic idea of) Field's conditional and, in turn, his approach towards characterization. Before doing so, I first sketch the background philosophical picture, and then turn to the formal account.

4.3.1   *Philosophical picture: stronger truth*

An inadequacy of Kripke's proposal is that we're left with nothing to truly say about Liar-like sentences, at least not *in our language* (the language that enjoys its own ttruth predicate). Intuitively, a paracomplete theorist thinks that, for purposes of truly characterizing or 'classifying' Liar-like sentences, we need to acknowledge an additional category beyond ttruth (and tfalsity). But how shall this 'other' category be understood?

As discussed above, there's no clear sense in saying that Liars are *neither ttrue nor tfalse*, at least if 'neither' and 'nor' are cashed out in terms of the proposed (Kleene) negation. Still, one might think that there's *some* sense in which Liars are 'not true' or 'not false'. This thought motivates Field's proposal.

« *Parenthetical remark.* The thought likewise seems to motivate a related (and well-known) earlier proposal by Vann McGee (1991). McGee's work precedes that of Field's, but the two are related. Since McGee's theory ultimately loses full transparency (and, hence, isn't a theory of *ttruth*), I do not go into it here. *End parenthetical.* »

The paracomplete theorist rejects that Liars are ttrue or not ttrue (or, equivalently, tfalse or not). But perhaps one can recognize a stronger notion of 'truth' according to which Liars and their negations are *not true*. Let $\mathbb{T}(x)$ be our 'stronger truth predicate', stronger than our transparent $Tr(x)$. Being a stronger notion than ttruth, one might have it that while both forms of Release hold, namely,

st1. $\vdash \mathbb{T}(\ulcorner \alpha \urcorner) \to \alpha$, for all α (and for some suitable conditional!)
st2. $\mathbb{T}(\ulcorner \alpha \urcorner) \vdash \alpha$, for all α

one or another of the Capture principles—the converse of either st1 or st2—fails. Such failure need not get in the way of expressing the generalizations for which *ttruth* was constructed, since *ttruth* remains as before: full intersubstitutability holds. Indeed, *ttruth* remains our expressive—entirely see-through—device. The new predicate $\mathbb{T}(x)$ is brought in to do a job that *ttruth* was never intended to do: namely, *fail to be transparent*! In particular, we want to use $\mathbb{T}(x)$ to ttruly 'classify' Liars, sentences like the first displayed sentence in §1.3 or the like. For by-now-familiar reasons, we can't (consistently) classify such sentences as ttrue or tfalse; however, with our stronger notion of truth, we may be able to classify such sentences as *not strongly true*. That is the idea.

Care, of course, must be taken. On pain of 'strengthened paradox' (in general, paradoxical spandrels of one's characterization tools), $\mathbb{T}(x)$, however it is spelled out, must be such as to resist Excluded Middle, resist having $\mathbb{T}(\ulcorner\alpha\urcorner) \vee \neg\mathbb{T}(\ulcorner\alpha\urcorner)$ for all α, at least if one aims—as Field does—to avoid gluts. To see the issue, just consider an inevitable spandrel of $\mathbb{T}$, for example, a sentence α equivalent to $\neg\mathbb{T}(\ulcorner\alpha\urcorner)$. Given normal Boolean connectives and normal quantifiers (as is the case with Field's proposal) and DP (i.e., our 'Disjunctive Principle' from Chapter 3), and the given Excluded Middle for $\mathbb{T}(x)$, we quickly get inconsistency. From $\mathbb{T}(\ulcorner\alpha\urcorner)$, Release yields $\neg\mathbb{T}(\ulcorner\alpha\urcorner)$. Since $\neg\mathbb{T}(\ulcorner\alpha\urcorner)$ implies itself, principle DP yields that $\mathbb{T}(\ulcorner\alpha\urcorner) \vee \neg\mathbb{T}(\ulcorner\alpha\urcorner)$ implies $\neg\mathbb{T}(\ulcorner\alpha\urcorner)$. Since, by assumption, the former is ttrue, so too is the latter. But, then, Capture—in either form (i.e., rule form or the conditional)—yields $\mathbb{T}(\ulcorner\alpha\urcorner)$. Hence, $\neg\mathbb{T}(\ulcorner\alpha\urcorner)$ is ttrue, and so is $\mathbb{T}(\ulcorner\alpha\urcorner)$. This yields triviality in a non-paraconsistent language. As such, Excluded Middle for $\mathbb{T}(x)$ must be rejected. (Actually, there are many options, but not many if one wants to keep normal Boolean connectives—that is, conjunction, disjunction, negation—and DP, as is the case with Field's account.)

But now an apparent tension arises. The reason that we want a stronger notion of truth is that we want to be able to ttruly classify Liar-like sentences, 'characterize' them as being *in some sense* 'not true'. Towards doing as much, we bring in $\mathbb{T}(x)$, and we want to say for any Liar-like sentence α in the $\mathbb{T}$-free fragment that α is not strongly true; we want to assert $\neg\mathbb{T}(\ulcorner\alpha\urcorner)$. This much is not difficult, provided we're restricting ourselves to αs in the $\mathbb{T}$-free fragment. The *trouble*, of course, is that we want to talk about *any* sentence in the *full* language, including any $\mathbb{T}$-ful sentences—sentences that use $\mathbb{T}$. But, then, we want to be able to say of $\mathbb{T}$-ful Liars that they are not strongly true. And that's the problem. Inevitably, there will be $\mathbb{T}$-ful sentences α such that, were either $\mathbb{T}(\ulcorner\alpha\urcorner)$ or $\neg\mathbb{T}(\ulcorner\alpha\urcorner)$ to hold, inconsistency would follow. Avoiding such inconsistency requires, as above, the rejection of (the equivalent of) Excluded Middle for $\mathbb{T}$ (assuming that we want DP, normal Boolean connectives, etc.). But, now, there would seem to be $\mathbb{T}$-ful sentences that fail to be 'correctly classified' by $\mathbb{T}(x)$, and hence that $\mathbb{T}(x)$ fails to do its job.

The apparent tension is the usual one, but it is worth making it explicit. For simplicity, assume, as on Field's account, Strong Kleene for the basic Boolean connectives. We *begin* with a transparent expressive device $Tr(x)$, which, when introduced into the language (to play its transparency role), gives rise to Tr-ful Liar-like sentences (viz., spandrels of the device). The paracomplete theorist maintains that such sentences are not problematic if we reject LEM, and in particular (at least) the Liar instances of LEM. So, we can keep our (consistent) transparency device $Tr(x)$ despite its inevitable Liars. One problem solved. But, *next*, we want to be able to ttruly 'classify' or 'characterize' the given Liars. Towards that end, we introduce a stronger notion of truth, $\mathbb{T}(x)$. And now we can use $\mathbb{T}(x)$ to ttruly classify all Tr-ful Liars. Another problem solved. But, *now again*, to avoid inconsistency, we must likewise reject Excluded Middle for $\mathbb{T}(x)$, and in particular reject $\mathbb{T}$-ful Liar instances of Excluded Middle. We now seem to require *yet another* 'even stronger truth' to ttruly classify the given $\mathbb{T}$-ful Liar-sentences, ones remaining 'unclassified' on pain of inconsistency. And so on ad infinitum.

The tension is clear. Suppose that we have some *'unified' predicate*—say, $Other(x)$—that characterizes all Liar-like sentences, so that we have the following, where, as throughout, $F(\ulcorner \alpha \urcorner)$ is just $Tr(\ulcorner \neg \alpha \urcorner)$.

EC. $\vdash Tr(\ulcorner \alpha \urcorner) \vee F(\ulcorner \alpha \urcorner) \vee Other(\ulcorner \alpha \urcorner)$

Given as much, we seem to be stuck in inconsistency, at least assuming (as we are) normal behavior for the extensional connectives.[14] After all, consider a sentence α (in effect, a spandrel of 'Other') that says $\neg \alpha \vee Other(\ulcorner \alpha \urcorner)$. By EC, α is either ttrue, its negation ttrue, or it is Other. If ttrue, then α is tfalse or Other. If tfalse or Other, then α is ttrue. If, then, the given categories are exhaustive and exclusive (i.e., exhaust the domain and there's no overlap among extensions), then inconsistency arises.

What the picture of infinitely many 'stronger truth predicates' requires is the absence of any such 'unified' predicate in terms of which all Liar-like sentences are to be classified.[15] The given picture must be accompanied by a rejection of anything yielding something along the lines of EC.

Perhaps the rejection of EC—the rejection of a 'unified' predicate in terms of which all Liar-like sentences are classified—is not unnatural. After all, the heart of standard paracomplete accounts is a rejection of LEM *all the way through*. In broadest—though, admittedly, somewhat vague—terms, the rejection of LEM might be seen as a basic rejection of an 'exhaustive characterization' in terms of unified 'semantic' predicates.

The basic tension, in the end, is one arising from a common aim: the aim of ttruly classifying (within one's language) all Liar-like sentences in one's given language. (Of course, we're talking about languages that have their own, non-trivial—indeed, in this chapter, consistent—ttruth predicate.) Intuitively, the aim is to achieve such exhaustive characterization along the lines of EC. Another route, however, is available: namely, classifying any given Liar via infinitely many 'stronger and stronger' truth predicates, none of which afford a 'unified predicate' that, as it were, serves as a 'unionizer' of all such predicates. While Field does not achieve the former, he nonetheless provides a powerful approach along the latter lines.

---

[14]See Appendix A for another option, one that I find interesting but do not discuss beyond Appendix A.

[15]Note that this immediately requires rejecting the coherence of 'quantifying over the hierarchy' of such predicates in the—otherwise intuitive—sense of, e.g., *true in some sense or other of 'strongly true'* or the like. For the technical details of this point, see Field 2008.

4.3.2 *Formal sketch: conditional and determinacy*

As above, Field aims to retain a consistent ttruth predicate but, going beyond Kripke, also to have all Tr-biconditionals *and* a way of 'classifying' any given Liar-like sentence in the language. Field shows how to add a suitable conditional to the Kripkean Strong Kleene framework, and then defines 'stronger truth' or, as Field says, 'determinate truth', in terms of the given conditional. Given that, as in §4.3.1, any such 'stronger truth' predicate (or operator) must resist Excluded Middle, Field's aim of 'characterizing' Liars requires infinitely many such 'stronger truth' devices. One notable feature of Field's framework is that the requisite infinite stock of (stronger and stronger) truth devices falls out of his constructed conditional.

This section presents only a sketch of Field's basic idea for introducing a suitable conditional into a paracomplete—and otherwise merely Strong Kleene—language with a (consistent) ttruth predicate. I first present an initial sketch of (the basic idea of) how to extend Kripke's initial construction with a suitable conditional—what Field calls a *restricted semantics*. In turn, I sketch a more general setting (what Field calls 'General semantics') for the conditional.

« *Parenthetical remark.* I should note that, in many respects, Field's conditional is constructed along the lines of the Brady construction sketched in the Chapter 2 appendix—though with K_3, not LP, as the underlying scheme. This is not to say that the constructions are the same. They're not. Moreover, unlike my use of the given Brady construction—which is merely to give a non-triviality proof for the given theory—Field uses his construction to define his given conditional (or, at least, to give it a formal 'semantics'), and so there are various novelties involved in Field's construction that are not involved in the Brady construction. That said, the following presentation skirts many of the technicalities, and simply tries to present the basic idea. (Because I am not presupposing the appendices of Chapter 1 or 2, I herein follow Field's notation for the most part.) *End parenthetical.* »

Restricted semantics.   Let K_3 be the Strong Kleene logic. Field's aim is to give an extension of K_3 that, in addition to containing a consistent ttruth predicate, validates all Tr-biconditionals in such a way that Curry paradox is avoided. The basic proposal is a novel combination of ideas from Kripke (1975) and *revision theorists* (Herzberger, 1982; Gupta and Belnap, 1993).

We start with a (first-order) syntax supplemented with $Tr(x)$ and a primitive two-place connective $\rightarrow$ which I'll call *the conditional*. (Any sentence the main connective of which is the conditional will be called a *conditional*.) With respect to the conditional-free fragment, the language is interpreted exactly along the lines of Kripke (as in §4.2). The challenge is to interpret all sentences, including all conditionals, in such a way as to retain a (consistent) ttruth predicate—and, so, achieve full intersubstitutability even with respect to (and 'inside of') conditionals—and validate all Tr-biconditionals. The aim, in short, is to get TP (on which see Chapter 2).

Field's proposal is to interpret the language via a transfinite sequence of

Kripkean (Strong Kleene) fixed points $\mathcal{P}^k$ (for 'point k', with k an ordinal),[16] where each such fixed point is 'built from' an initial *starting valuation* $\mathcal{S}_k$ (for 'start k'), which assigns elements of $\{1, \frac{1}{2}, 0\}$ to *all and only conditionals*. Beginning with such 'start points', Kripke's construction (see §4.2) yields a value for every sentence in the language in such a way that ttruth (transparency, intersubstitutability) is preserved. With respect to such start points $\mathcal{S}_k$, and in particular how any given $\mathcal{S}_k$ is determined on the basis of 'prior' Kripkean $\mathcal{P}^j$, Field proposes the following recipe. (For ease, I write '$\mathcal{S}_k(\alpha)$' to abbreviate *the value of α in the start point $\mathcal{S}_k$*.)

Fb. Base (Zero). $\mathcal{S}_0(\alpha \rightarrow \beta) = \frac{1}{2}$ for all α and β.

Fs. Successor. At successor points (or stages), we look back at the prior Kripkean fixed point.

$$\mathcal{S}_{k+1}(\alpha \rightarrow \beta) = \begin{cases} 1 \text{ if } \mathcal{P}^k(\alpha) \leq \mathcal{P}^k(\beta) \\ 0 \text{ otherwise.} \end{cases}$$

Fl. Limit. At limit points (stages), we look backwards at *all* prior Kripkean fixed points.

$$\mathcal{S}_l(\alpha \rightarrow \beta) = \begin{cases} 1 \text{ if } \mathcal{P}^i(\alpha) \leq \mathcal{P}^i(\beta) \text{ for some } j < l \text{ and any } i \text{ st } j < i < l \\ 0 \text{ if } \mathcal{P}^i(\alpha) > \mathcal{P}^i(\beta) \text{ for some } j < l \text{ and any } i \text{ st } j < i < l \\ \frac{1}{2} \text{ otherwise.} \end{cases}$$

So goes the construction of 'start points' from the 'prior' Kripkean fixed points. As above, the latter—the Kripkean fixed points—are the points that yield the 'ultimate values' in terms of which all sentences eventually stabilize into a language with both ttruth and all Tr-biconditionals. The various $\mathcal{P}^k$, as above, are determined entirely by the $\mathcal{S}_k$ (which give values to the conditionals) and the Strong Kleene (minimal) fixed point construction—the various clauses for compounds, K1–K3. (Again, see §4.2.)

Brief reflection on Fb–Fl indicates that values assigned to (at least typically paradoxical) sentences at the various $\mathcal{S}_k$ and, in turn, $\mathcal{P}^k$, fluctuate quite a bit; such sentences exhibit jumpy instability. By way of settling on 'ultimate values', by way of bringing about order to such apparent chaos, Field takes a leaf from revision theory (Herzberger, 1982; Gupta and Belnap, 1993). In particular, Field defines the *ultimate value of α*, say $|\alpha|$, as follows.

$$|\alpha| = \begin{cases} \lim_j \mathcal{P}^j(\alpha) \text{ if the limit exists} \\ \frac{1}{2} \quad\quad\quad\quad \text{ otherwise.} \end{cases}$$

In other words, suppose that, for some point k, we have it that $\mathcal{P}^j(\alpha)$ is 1 for any $j \geq k$. In that case, $|\alpha| = 1$. Similarly for 0. In general, where $n \in \{1, 0\}$, the idea is that if α is eventually forevermore assigned n, then n is α's ultimate

---

[16]Note that these are fixed points of Kripke's 'jump operator' from §4.2, which will henceforth be left as implicit.

value. But, of course, there may be no such point beyond which the value of α 'stabilizes' at either 1 or 0, in which case $|\alpha| = \frac{1}{2}$. More precisely, $|\alpha| = \frac{1}{2}$ if either α is never eventually forevermore assigned anything or there's some point k such that, for any $j \geq k$, we have it that $\mathcal{P}^j(\alpha) = \frac{1}{2}$ (i.e., we have it that α is eventually forevermore assigned $\frac{1}{2}$).

Field (2003) proves that such 'ultimate values' obey the K_3-rules for extensional connectives, that is, for all connectives except the non-extensional $\rightarrow$, the conditional. (More technically, Field's 'Fundamental Theorem' shows that there are ordinals i such that, for any non-zero j, the value of any sentence α at $i \cdot j$ is just $|\alpha|$.) Moreover, the construction validates all Tr-biconditionals.[17]

I discuss the virtues of Field's proposed conditional, and its role with respect to 'stronger truth', in §4.3.3. For now, I turn to a more general, and perhaps philosophically more 'intuitive', account of the conditional.

General semantics. In Chapter 2, I endorsed a common 'worlds' approach to a suitable conditional (an abnormal-worlds approach, but a 'worlds' approach nonetheless). Field's conditional may likewise be cast in a 'worlds' setting (what Field calls the 'general semantics'), though the intended philosophical interpretation, as Field (2003) remarks, is better thought of as 'possible assignments relative to actual conditions or constraints'. In this (sub-) section I simply sketch the construction, leaving comments to §4.3.3.

« *Parenthetical remark.* A few caveats are in order: first, the 'general semantics' was motivated largely by a 'unified solution' to both semantical and soritical (vagueness-) paradoxes. I do not discuss the latter here, though the issue of 'unsettledness' and vagueness, with respect to my own theory, is briefly discussed in Chapter 5. Second, I do not give all of the constraints that Field proposes for purposes of achieving various desirable features of the conditional; I simply sketch the basic idea. *End parenthetical.* »

The aim, once again, is to give an extension of K_3 (i.e., give a 'stronger' logic and corresponding ttruth theory), but in this case we work with a 'modalized' K_3 (first-order) language, where, as above (throughout), we can stipulate that the 'semantic-free' fragment is entirely classical, and the ttruth predicate is achieved along Kripkean lines, as above. (As noted, the framework is motivated by not only semantic paradox but also soritical paradox. As a result, if we were concentrating on vagueness, we wouldn't stipulate an entirely classical 'semantic-free' language, but the stipulation simplifies for present purposes.) The difference, now, is that we expand our interpretations with a non-empty set $\mathcal{W}$ of 'worlds' and, in turn, assign values to sentences relative to such worlds, where the values remain either 1, 0, or $\frac{1}{2}$. This much is standard. The task is to tweak

---

[17]Field also shows that the Tr-biconditionals are validated in a stronger sense that he dubs 'conservative', the idea being (roughly) that the resulting theory is consistent *with any arithmetically standard starting model*. For discussion, see Hartry Field 2003.

such interpretations in such a way as to give the target conditional its desired features.

Field's proposal is a novel variation on so-called 'neighborhood semantics' (a type of semantics, sometimes called *Montague-Scott* semantics, that generalizes standard Kripke semantics; see Chellas 1980). We let $\mathcal{W}$ be an infinite set of worlds at which sentences are assigned an element of $\{1, \frac{1}{2}, 0\}$, letting @ be a (unique) distinguished element of $\mathcal{W}$, the 'actual world'. In turn, we impose a 'similarity relation' on $\mathcal{W}$ in such a way that each $w \in \mathcal{W}$ comes equipped with a set of 'sufficiently similar worlds' (a so-called 'neighborhood' of w), worlds that satisfy some condition of similarity with respect to w. Specifically, Field proposes that each $w \in \mathcal{W}$ be assigned a (possibly empty) *directed* family $\mathcal{F}_w$ that comprises non-empty elements of $\wp(\mathcal{W})$, non-empty subsets of $\mathcal{W}$. The *directedness* of $\mathcal{F}_w$, which amounts to

$$(\forall w \in \mathcal{W})(\forall \mathcal{X}, \mathcal{Y} \in \mathcal{F}_w)(\exists \mathcal{Z} \in \mathcal{F}_w)\, \mathcal{Z} \subseteq \mathcal{X} \cap \mathcal{Y}$$

allows for 'incomparability', that is, that the relation of similarity needn't be linear.[18]

With an eye towards semantic paradox, a few other tweaks are required. (Actually, achieving all of Field's desired features requires other constraints on interpretations, but for present purposes I skip over them here, as noted above.) Define, for any $w \in \mathcal{W}$, the following features.

Normality. w is *normal* iff $w \in \mathcal{X}$ for all $\mathcal{X} \in \mathcal{F}_w$.

Non-normality. w is *non-normal* iff it is not normal.

Loneliness. w is *lonely* iff $\{w\} \in \mathcal{F}_w$.

Happiness. w is *happy* iff it is not lonely.

Field stipulates that @ be both normal and happy on any interpretation, but otherwise worlds may be non-normal and lonely. Accordingly, every interpretation is such that, per normality, $@ \in \mathcal{X}$ for all $\mathcal{X} \in \mathcal{F}_@$ and, per happiness, $\{@\} \notin \mathcal{F}_@$. Hence, @ is 'sufficiently similar' to itself on all interpretations, and @ is also 'sufficiently similar' to some $w \neq @$ on all interpretations.

As is standard, sentences are now assigned a value at each world. With respect to the conditional-free fragment, the valuations simply follow the Strong Kleene rules; K1–K3, in effect, are modified only with respect to being relativized to worlds, even though reference to worlds in the clauses for extensional connectives makes no essential difference. (In other words, where α is conditional-free, the value of α at w depends only on the values of α's constituent parts at w. One needn't 'look at other worlds' to figure out the value of purely extensional sentences.) The worlds come into play with conditionals.[19]

---

[18] Field (2003) notes that one could, without radical deviation from the basic proposal, simply impose a linear ordering via $\subseteq$.

[19] I shall continue to use the bar notation, e.g. $|\alpha|$, to abbreviate 'the value of α'. (This follows Field's notation, and ties in the earlier discussion of 'ultimate values'.) The difference, of course, is that values are now relative to worlds, and so, e.g., $|\alpha|_w$ is the value of α at w.

$$|\alpha \to \beta|_w = \begin{cases} 1 \text{ if } |\alpha|_{w'} \leq |\beta|_{w'} \text{ for some } \mathcal{X} \in \mathcal{F}_w \text{ and any } w' \in \mathcal{X} \\ 0 \text{ if } |\alpha|_{w'} > |\beta|_{w'} \text{ for some } \mathcal{X} \in \mathcal{F}_w \text{ and any } w' \in \mathcal{X} \\ \frac{1}{2} \text{ otherwise.} \end{cases}$$

With valuation-conditions in hand, the (semantic) consequence relation $\vdash$ may be defined. Towards that end, let us say that, relative to an interpretation, a sentence α is *actually verified* iff $|\alpha|_{@} = 1$ (in the given interpretation). Similarly, a set Σ of sentences is *actually verified* iff β is actually verified, for each $\beta \in \Sigma$. Then the (semantic) *validity* relation $\vdash$ is defined thus:

$$\Sigma \vdash \alpha \text{ iff any interpretation that actually verifies } \Sigma \text{ actually verifies } \alpha$$

with *valid sentences* being consequences of $\emptyset$. Given the existence of non-normal and lonely worlds (or the existence of interpretations containing as much), other notions of validity may be introduced, but, for present purposes, I focus just on the given notion.

« *Parenthetical remark.* In standard 'abnormal-worlds' semantics, wherein one has different 'types' of worlds (e.g., in Chapter 2), broader notions of validity are standardly introduced by various restrictions on the 'types' of worlds invoked in one's definition. Field's neighborhood account is similar, and Field 2003 introduces 'universal validity' (quantifying over all worlds of all interpretations) and 'strongly valid' (all normal worlds of all interpretations). For present purposes, I concentrate only on the account of validity of above. *End parenthetical.* »

4.3.3 *Remarks: suitable conditional and strong truth*

So goes the basic framework. While, for simplicity, I have left out various details, there is enough in the foregoing to turn to philosophical discussion.[20] In the following discussion, I concentrate on the 'general' or 'world' semantics for Field's conditional.

Suitable conditional. To begin, notice that Field's conditional gives us Conditional Identity.

$$\vdash \alpha \to \alpha$$

Hence, given the intersubstitutability of $Tr(x)$, which is preserved in *all* (non-opaque) contexts, all Tr-biconditionals are similarly valid. Moreover, since Field (2003) gives a consistency proof for the resulting language (and ttruth theory), this virtue amounts to a remarkable step forward in (consistent) paracomplete accounts of ttruth. Kripke provided an answer—a paracomplete answer—to NTP for a language in which not all Tr-biconditionals hold. What Field's conditional

---

[20]One thing that I have not indicated is that Field's 'restricted semantics' may be seen as a special case of the 'general semantics'. To achieve this, one allows for 'normal ordinals' (analogous to 'normal worlds') in the former, and modifies the account of validity in the latter in terms of a distinguished such 'normal ordinal' (something guaranteed by Field's Fundamental Theorem). For discussion see Field 2003; Field 2008.

has given us is an answer—a paracomplete answer—to NTP for a language in which all Tr-biconditionals hold, an answer that preserves the insights of Kripke but goes further, properly extending the resulting logic.

But there's more. Not only does the conditional give us Identity, it also exhibits various familiar features.[21]

$$\alpha, \alpha \to \beta \vdash \beta \qquad\qquad\qquad\qquad \alpha, \neg\beta \vdash \neg(\alpha \to \beta)$$
$$\vdash \neg\neg\alpha \to \alpha \qquad\qquad\qquad\qquad\qquad \vdash \alpha \wedge \beta \to \alpha$$
$$\vdash \neg(\alpha \to \beta) \to (\alpha \vee \neg\beta) \qquad\qquad \vdash (\alpha \to \neg\beta) \to (\beta \to \neg\alpha)$$
$$\vdash \forall x\alpha \to \alpha(t/x) \text{ (for proper substitution)}$$

Indeed, in general, in addition to other features that are here omitted, Field's conditional exhibits a notable relation with the hook: $\to$ behaves just like $\supset$ when LEM is assumed. Accordingly, we have, for example,

$$\alpha \supset \beta \vdash \alpha \to \beta$$

and, indeed,

$$\alpha \vee \neg\alpha, \beta \vee \neg\beta \vdash (\alpha \supset \beta) \leftrightarrow (\alpha \to \beta)$$

« *Parenthetical remark.* The given connection between the hook and Field's suitable conditional serves as a notable difference from the suitable conditional advanced in Chapter 2. In particular, the following fail in BX.

1. $\alpha, \neg\beta \vdash \neg(\alpha \to \beta)$
2. $\alpha \supset \beta \vdash \alpha \to \beta$
3. $\alpha \vee \neg\alpha, \beta \vee \neg\beta \vdash (\alpha \supset \beta) \leftrightarrow (\alpha \to \beta)$

With respect to (1), consider a simple model where β just is α. Let $\mathcal{W} = \{@, @^\star\}$ with $@^\star \in \mathcal{W} - \mathcal{N}$ (i.e., abnormal). Let α be glutty, that is, $@ \models \alpha$ and $@ \models \neg\alpha$, and so $@^\star \not\models \alpha$ and $@^\star \not\models \neg\alpha$. Now, let $R = \emptyset$, in which case, vacuously, $@^\star \models \alpha \to \alpha$, and so $@ \not\models \neg(\alpha \to \alpha)$, and so (1) fails. With respect to (2) and (3), a countermodel is as per (1), but let $@ \not\models \beta$ and, as in (1), α glutty.

Whether these 'failures' count as a defect of my BX theory is an issue that I take up in Chapter 5. *End parenthetical.* »

As discussed in Chapter 2, a conditional needs to lack certain features if Curry's paradox is to be avoided. That Field's conditional avoids the problematic features is established by his consistency proof (Hartry Field, 2003), but it is worth at least very briefly touching on the issue—and so I will, but only very briefly.

The key point is that the conditional avoids problematic Contraction principles. As such, arguments towards Curry paradox are blocked as invalid. By

---

[21] For a list of other notable features see Hartry Field 2003; Field 2003; Field 2005c, and for a very illuminating discussion see Yablo 2003.

way of illustration, consider a counterexample to some of the invalid principles. In particular, consider the principle PMP (see Chapter 2).

$$\alpha \wedge (\alpha \rightarrow \beta) \rightarrow \beta$$

Field's demand that @ be happy provides an immediate counterexample to PMP: just consider an interpretation in which $\mathcal{F}_@ = \{\{@, w\}\}$ and, for simplicity, let $\mathcal{F}_w = \emptyset$. Let $|\alpha|_@ = |\beta|_w = |\alpha|_w = \frac{1}{2}$ and $|\beta|_@ = 0$. Then $|\alpha \rightarrow \beta|_@ = \frac{1}{2}$ and, hence, $|\alpha \wedge (\alpha \rightarrow \beta)|_@ = \frac{1}{2}$, and so $|\alpha \wedge (\alpha \rightarrow \beta)|_@ > |\beta|_@$. But most importantly, since not every world in the (unique) @-neighborhood is such that $|\alpha \wedge (\alpha \rightarrow \beta) \rightarrow \beta| \leq |\beta|$ or $|\alpha \wedge (\alpha \rightarrow \beta) \rightarrow \beta| > |\beta|$, we have what paracomplete theorists naturally want with respect to Curry instances of PMP, namely, that $|\alpha \wedge (\alpha \rightarrow \beta) \rightarrow \beta|_@ = \frac{1}{2}$. And since $\frac{1}{2}$ is not designated, PMP is invalid. Similar counterexamples are available for the other Contraction principles.

Characterization: Strong truth, determinacy.   As discussed above, Field's aim is not only to validate all Tr-biconditionals but also to go beyond the silence of the Kripkean framework with respect to characterizing Liar-like sentences. Towards that end, Field proposes to recognize a stronger notion of truth than our see-through device *ttruth*.

As mentioned in §4.3.1, there is always a risk of introducing more 'truth-like' devices (predicates, operators): paradoxical sentences are always ready to spring up. This is where Field's consistency proof (2003) for the full conditional-ful, Tr-ful language comes into play.

Field's consistency proof shows that the conditional doesn't introduce any further paradoxes that aren't already resolved by the guiding, paracomplete rejection of LEM. And that is the key. Field wants to characterize all Liar sentences via 'stronger and stronger truth', and do so without bringing about yet further paradox. Given the consistency proof, it is natural to seek an account of such 'strong truth' that *invokes only the resources of the language at hand*, the language for which we have Field's consistency proof. A remarkable feature of Field's framework is that he enjoys just such an account: he defines infinitely many 'determinately' operators—these amount to 'stronger and stronger truth'—*out of the conditional*. For present purposes, there are two items that need to be explained:

» What is the definition of 'determinately' in terms of the conditional?

» Why infinitely many?

I very briefly sketch the answer to each question, leaving details to Field's work (cited throughout).

Determinately. Where $\top$ is any logical truth, Field proposes to 'introduce' a *determinately* operator $\mathbb{D}$ thus:

$$\mathbb{D}\alpha =_{df} (\top \rightarrow \alpha) \wedge \alpha$$

This immediately gives standard behavior for 'determinately' operators, in particular, Capture and Release in *rule* form, and Release but not Capture in *conditional* form. (See Chapter 2 for 'Release' and 'Capture' terminology.)

d1. RC for $\mathbb{D}$. $\alpha \vdash \mathbb{D}\alpha$

d2. RR for $\mathbb{D}$. $\mathbb{D}\alpha \vdash \alpha$

d3. CR for $\mathbb{D}$. $\vdash \mathbb{D}\alpha \rightarrow \alpha$

d4. *No* CC for $\mathbb{D}$. $\nvdash \alpha \rightarrow \mathbb{D}\alpha$

That Conditional Capture fails for $\mathbb{D}$ (see d4) may be seen by considering an interpretation in which $|\alpha|_@ = \frac{1}{2}$, in which case $|\top \rightarrow \alpha|_@$ is not designated, regardless of $\mathcal{F}_@$.

With $\mathbb{D}$ at hand, one can now classify $\mathbb{D}$-free Liars as proposed: neither they nor their negations are *determinately* true. For any such sentence α, we have the ttruth of $\neg \mathbb{D}\,Tr(\ulcorner\alpha\urcorner) \wedge \neg \mathbb{D}\neg Tr(\ulcorner\alpha\urcorner)$ or, equivalently (given transparency), $\neg \mathbb{D}\alpha \wedge \neg \mathbb{D}\neg\alpha$.

So, Field's conditional provides a way of characterizing basic spandrels of *ttruth*, like the first displayed sentence in §1.3. Such sentences are characterized in terms of $\mathbb{D}$, which, as above, is defined via the conditional. With this, we have an improvement over the (silent) Kripkean account.

Infinitely many. The question concerns the inevitable spandrels of $\mathbb{D}$ itself. Now that we have $\mathbb{D}$ in the language, we inevitably get $\mathbb{D}$-ful Liars—for example, sentences that say of themselves (only) that they're not determinately true, or not determinately determinately true, or so on. Such sentences call for 'stronger and stronger truth'. Nicely, Field's construction already yields as much.

The point is fairly obvious. Consider a Liar λ that says $\neg \mathbb{D}\lambda$. That Field's construction handles λ, so understood, follows from his consistency proof: such a sentence receives an interpretation in the language, namely, $\frac{1}{2}$. Of course, given d1–d3, one cannot ttruly classify λ as being not determinately ttrue. What one can do is generalize Field's proposal in a natural way: one can ttruly classify λ as *not determinately determinately ttrue*, that is, one may ttruly assert $\neg \mathbb{D}\mathbb{D}\lambda$.

What is critical here is the failure of so-called Idempotence of $\mathbb{D}$, namely, that iterations of $\mathbb{D}$ are distinct operators; they do not collapse on iteration—unlike, for example, the familiar 'necessity' operator in the normal modal logic $S5$. One might have the 'intuition' that $\mathbb{D}\mathbb{D}\alpha$ ought to 'say the same thing' as $\mathbb{D}\alpha$, and similarly for any iteration of $\mathbb{D}$. Maybe so, but one would thereby lose the resources to characterize more than a few basic Liars in terms of 'determinately'.

In general,[22] Field's operator may be iterated into the transfinite: for some suitable ordinal notation that yields σ, we have an operator $\mathbb{D}^\sigma$, the σ-many iteration of $\mathbb{D}$. And for each such 'determinately' operator, there are (increasingly weaker) $\mathbb{D}^\sigma$-ful Liars, each of which gets 'correctly characterized' by a stronger

---

[22]I warn that this paragraph presupposes some technical background that I leave to cited works. For present purposes, one may simply think of $\mathbb{D}^\sigma$ as σ-many iterations of $\mathbb{D}$, where there may be constraints on how 'big' or, in effect, on what σ might be.

operator $\mathbb{D}^{\sigma+1}$ (provided the ordinal notation cooperates). (For limit ordinals, one mimics infinite conjunctions via *ttruth* and a suitable ordinal notation.)

What is central to the proposal is its thoroughgoing paracompleteness. Excluded Middle does not hold even for 'determinate truth'. Consistency is purchased by such thoroughgoing paracompleteness: for any $\mathbb{D}^{\sigma}$-ful Liar λ_{σ} (for suitable σ), the failure of $\mathbb{D}^{\sigma}\lambda_{\sigma} \vee \neg\mathbb{D}^{\sigma}\lambda_{\sigma}$ will arise. Of course, as mentioned in §4.3.1, the failure of Excluded Middle for one's level-σ 'strong truth device' requires having an even stronger device if one wants to classify level-σ Liars. But the point is that Field's basic construction provides as much. For any Liar constructible in the language (or, at least, the hierarchy of determinately operators), there's a 'strong' or 'determinate' device that classifies the sentence.

And to repeat: there is no threat of 'determinately'-ful Liars wreaking havoc, since all such Liars are constructible only in a language (the full conditional-ful language) that enjoys a consistency proof. Needless to say, this is a significant improvement on the Kripkean picture.

4.3.4 *Comments:* NTP *and* ECP

How does Field's proposal fare with respect to the projects NTP and ECP?

NTP. Field's answer to NTP is a thoroughgoing paracomplete answer. We enjoy a non-trivial—indeed, according to Field, a consistent—*ttruth* device in virtue of the 'failure' of Excluded Middle. What separates Field's answer from the basic Kripkean answer is that it applies to a language in which we have a suitable conditional, a language in which all of Tr-biconditionals are ttrue. In this respect, Field's answer to NTP is a fuller answer than the basic Kripkean one. As above, what Kripke's account tells us, at least with respect to NTP, is that we can enjoy a *ttruth* device in (and for) our language if our language is devoid of a suitable conditional. (This is not to suggest that Kripke tells us the inverse, of course.) While this is an important lesson to learn, it does not really answer NTP if our language does enjoy a suitable conditional. Inasmuch as Field's account applies to a language with a suitable conditional, Field's answer to NTP, as said, is a fuller and, in general, a better answer than the basic Kripkean one.

Another virtue of Field's answer to NTP, in contrast to the basic Kripkean one, is related to the topic of 'characterization' (on which topic more below). Both paracomplete theorists—namely, Kripke and Field—answer NTP along the basic, paracomplete lines. But what is that answer?

The NTP question is how, despite paradoxical spandrels, we achieve a non-trivial (indeed, here, consistent) transparent truth predicate in our language. How, in other words, does *ttruth* avoid inconsistency despite its Liar-like spandrels? The paracomplete answer, one wants to say, is as above: namely, that *ttruth* avoids inconsistency in virtue of the *failure* of some instances of $\alpha \vee \neg\alpha$ (LEM). But what is meant by *a failure of some* LEM *instance*? The basic Kripke story has little, if anything, to say here. In the Kripke framework, one cannot ttruly say that there's some α such that $\alpha \vee \neg\alpha$ is not ttrue. (The formal model is useful here. Let $\nu(\alpha) = \frac{1}{2}$, in which case the negation of $\alpha \vee \neg\alpha$ is similarly $\frac{1}{2}$, and hence undesignated.) What, then, does 'a failure of LEM' amount to? Without an account of what a 'failure of LEM' amounts to, the given answer to NTP seems to be incomplete (at best) or a non-answer (at worst).

In Field's account, we do not have this problem (though see the discussion of ECP below). If we ask the NTP question about simple Liars in the $\rightarrow$-free fragment, the Field answer is clear: *ttruth* avoids inconsistency in virtue of the *failure* of some LEM instances, where a *failure* of such instances amounts to their being *not determinately true*. This answer is what one expects from a paracomplete theorist, and it's an answer that Field, unlike Kripke, provides. In turn, one might ask about the $\mathbb{D}$-ful Liars, and how *ttruth* escapes inconsistency from those sentences. Again, Field provides an answer, as discussed above: *ttruth* avoids inconsistency in virtue of a failure of the relevant LEM instances, where *failure* now amounts to such instances being *not determinately determinately true* (or whathaveyou, depending on the given Liar).

The point, with respect to NTP, is that while Field joins Kripke in embracing a paracomplete answer, there's a significant sense in which only Field actually gives a paracomplete answer. Pending some account of what 'failure of LEM' amounts to, the Kripkean answer seems to be just that: pending. Of course, one might say that Kripke's answer to NTP is straightforward: we *reject* LEM, and in particular Liar instances of LEM. This, though, is not an answer to NTP. As above, NTP asks the question of how *ttruth* avoids inconsistency in the face of its paradoxical spandrels. While one's position regarding such sentences may well be—and, for paracomplete theorists, is—rejection, the answer to NTP, presumably, has nothing to do with whether Kripke (or Field, or you, or I) *rejects* such and so sentences. Instead, the paracomplete answer has to do with the status of such sentences. Field, as emphasized above, gives an answer: namely, such sentences are not 'determinately true' (or 'determinately determinately true', or etc.). Kripke's answer, as emphasized, is at best pending.

ECP.   How, if at all, are Liar-like sentences to be ttruly classified? More clearly, what, if anything, is the 'semantic status' of such sentences? One would think that Kripke's answer is that such sentences, *in some sense*, are 'neither true nor false'. As above, however, Kripke gives no account of how such sentences are to be classified; the account, as above, fails to clearly answer the 'exhaustive characterization project' (ECP).

The question now concerns Field's account. Here, the issue is delicate. What Field provides is a way of consistently classifying all Liar-like sentences (would-be paradoxical sentences) definable in the 'hierarchy of determinately operators'. Unlike Kripke's account, we have it that, for example, $\mathbb{D}$-free Liars are simply not 'determinately true' or 'determinately false'. In turn, $\mathbb{D}$-ful Liars similarly get classified: they're not determinately determinately true or determinately determinately false. In turn, $\mathbb{DD}$-ful Liars similarly get classified. And so on.

Accordingly, inasmuch as ECP calls only for an account of how, if at all, we can ttruly characterize (or classify) the 'semantic status' of any (definable) Liar-like sentences, Field has provided an answer to ECP. It is hard to ask for much more.

On the other hand, one might wonder whether Field has achieved 'exhaustive characterization' in the target—albeit admittedly imprecise—sense. In particular, using terminology from above, it seems that Field's position—in the spirit of any paracomplete position—recognizes ttrue sentences, tfalse sentences, and some *Others*. For example, there are sentences (say, simple $\mathbb{D}$-free Liars) for which Field will reject that they're ttrue or tfalse; however, Field will accept that they're not *determinately true* and not *determinately false*. Indeed, if one were to give an elementary, intuitive account of Field's basic proposal, one would first note that, in addition to the ttruths and tfalsehoods, we have an infinity of 'determinately' operators that yield increasingly stronger notions of truth and falsehood; and such stronger notions of truth (falsehood) are employed to characterize Liar-like sentences (or paradoxical sentences, in general). In turn, one would be inclined to say that the gist of Field's proposal—at least with respect to characterization or classification—is the following.

FEC. Every sentence is ttrue, tfalse, or not determinately true or determinately false *in some sense or other of 'determinately'*.

If this were right, then there would be no question that Field has achieved 'exhaustive characterization' in the intuitive, target sense (imprecise as it is). But this is not right. What FEC presupposes is the existence of some absolute, 'coverall' determinacy operator, some overarching notion of *determinacy* that implies all of the others. Such a thing does not exist in Field's proposed framework. If there were, we'd have inconsistency from typical spandrels such as

√ The ticked sentence in §4.3.3 is tfalse or determinately false *in some sense or other of 'determinately'*.

Given FEC, we have it that the given sentence is ttrue, tfalse, or not determinately true or determinately false in some sense or other of 'determinately'. Familiar reasoning reveals the would-be inconsistency. But such inconsistency is merely would-be inconsistency; it doesn't in fact arise given that we don't have FEC in Field's framework. We don't have FEC in Field's framework because, as above, we have no 'coverall' notion of *determinate truth*, one that implies all others.

« *Parenthetical remark.* This is not to say that one couldn't adjust Field's official framework to (consistently) add such a thing, though I have not worked out the details. Provided that one is willing to accept 'overlap without inconsistency', one could impose a 'coverall' notion of *determinacy* 'on top' of Field's framework. For a simple, related but non-Fieldian example, see Appendix A. (Field 2003 provides very brief comments on how one might do this in his basic framework.) *End parenthetical.* »

That Field's proposal lacks 'exhaustive characterization' in the given sense (e.g., FEC) might be seen as a clear defect. There is a strong, 'intuitive' sense that we ought (in some sense!) to be able to ttruly say something like FEC if Field's proposal is correct—that we 'ought', to put it slightly differently, be able to quantify over all of Field's 'determinately' operators to get such a 'coverall' sense.

Is the given absence of a 'coverall' notion of 'determinacy' a defect of Field's position? Alas, I am not sure. One might, as discussed in Chapter 3, charge that my position faces an analogous defect. In particular, one might insist that we have an explosive and exhaustive notion of 'just true' if my proposal is correct. Specifically, one might say that if the given dialetheic proposal is correct, then we have something like the following.

BEC. Every sentence is ttrue, tfalse, both, or *just true* or *just false, in an explosive sense of 'just true'.*

An 'explosive sense' of 'just true' is supposed to be one according to which triviality follows from any α's being both *just true* (in the alleged sense) and also *tfalse*. Of course, for reasons discussed in Chapter 3 (see §3.1), there simply is no such notion on my account.

Insisting, then, that Field's proposed lack of a 'coverall' notion of *determinacy* is a clear defect is directly analogous to insisting that there's some explosive notion of 'just true' (or 'just false' or etc.). As such, I do not so insist.

While I strongly accept that our language enjoys 'exhaustive characterization' in the target (but, admittedly, imprecise) sense, I have no clear, non-question-begging arguments for such a feature. Pending such an argument, I remain neutral on whether Field's lack of a 'coverall' notion of *determinacy* is a clear defect.

4.4   Choosing among rivals?

In Chapters 1–3, I presented the paraconsistent account of transparent truth and paradox that I endorse. In this chapter, I have presented two prominent paracomplete (and non-paraconsistent) approaches. Given that Field's approach considerably extends Kripke's, there's no question that Field's account is the chief alternative. The question, in the end, is how to choose between the two given accounts—my account and that of Field's. The short answer, of course, is that we should choose the right account. The trouble, though, is that, while I reject Field's proposal and endorse the simple account I've laid out in this book, I find myself in the dubious position of enjoying precious little by way of strong objections against Field's position. As such, I ultimately—though with genuine regret—leave the matter open for future debate. The chief aim of this section is to briefly and very broadly compare the two accounts, and suggest a few—alas, far from conclusive—reasons for preferring my account to Field's. Various related issues, particularly objections to my account, are taken up in Chapter 5.

4.4.1   *Unity*

There is significant agreement between Field and me on various key points. (In part, this may be the reason why choosing between the accounts is considerably difficult.) The chief points of agreement concern *ttruth*, valid *Tr*-biconditionals, validity and 'truth preservation', and a proper classical fragment (e.g., mathematics). I simply list the points of agreement.

Transparent truth. We are both at least 'methodological deflationists' about truth (and cognate notions). While Field may not fully embrace the 'constructed device' picture of *ttruth*, he is nonetheless committed to a fully see-through—fully intersubstitutable—truth predicate. We agree about the basic role and rules of such a see-through predicate. Our respective accounts both aim to be accounts of the same transparent truth predicate and its spandrels.

Valid Tr-biconditionals. We both agree that our language enjoys valid Tr-biconditionals, where the conditional involved is a suitable conditional, a detachable conditional for which $\alpha \rightarrow \alpha$ is valid—from which the validity of Tr-conditionals derives via intersubstitutability—and Curry-driven triviality is avoided.

Validity and truth preservation. We both reject that all valid arguments are truth-preserving, at least where such truth preservation is expressed using our respective suitable conditionals. (As in Chapter 2, I think that there's a clear sense in which all valid arguments are truth-preserving, when such 'truth preservation' is expressed using the hook; however, this is not a terribly useful account of truth preservation, given that the hook, on my account, fails to detach in general. Field must reject that valid arguments are truth-preserving in even the hook sense.)

Classical proper fragment. Field and I accept that our language enjoys a proper, classical fragment, though we differ on the 'size' of that fragment. (See §4.4.2, 'Negation and unsettledness'.) We both agree that, at the very least, arithmetic—and, by both of our lights, mathematics, in general—is classical.

4.4.2 *Division*

The salient points of disagreement between Field's account and mine are as follows. (There are also differences in the behavior of our respective 'suitable conditionals', but I set this aside here, returning to the issue in Chapter 5.)

Inconsistency. One salient difference between the accounts is that Field's theory is consistent, mine inconsistent. Field thinks that our constructed device *ttruth* avoids gluts; I think that it yields gluts. This difference ultimately turns on another difference concerning negation.

Negation and unsettledness. While I maintain that negation is essentially 'exhaustive', that every sentence is ttrue or not, Field rejects as much. With me, Field recognizes a significant fragment of our language for which LEM holds (e.g., mathematics); however, it is but a proper fragment. Indeed, Field maintains that our *base language*—free of *ttruth* and similar notions—is such that LEM fails, that some sentences in the base language are, as Field would say, neither 'determinately true' nor 'determinately false'. The paradoxical spandrels of *ttruth*, in turn, are just more of the same phenomenon: 'unsettledness' or (non-epistemic) 'indeterminacy'.

4.4.3 *A few reasons against the Field*

So go some of the salient similarities (see §4.4.1) and salient differences (see §4.4.2) between Field's account and my own. While I firmly endorse my own account, I nonetheless (regrettably) find it difficult to muster strong reasons against Field's account. Still, there are a few reasons that might count against Field's account and in favor of mine. In this section, I flag two such reasons, but leave further discussion, and discussion of related issues, to Chapter 5.

Exhaustive negation. On the surface, there seems to be an exhaustive notion of negation—that α is ttrue or *not*, for all α. Such an appearance, I think, is strong, but it is not clearly telling. Field, for example, may explain the appearance as one that conflates 'determinate falsity' with tfalsity. I admit that, on the surface, this is a viable explanation of what's going on—namely, that we're not using an *exhaustive negation* (which, according to Field, doesn't exist), but rather using a non-exhaustive negation and some stronger notion of truth than ttruth. On the other hand, the viability of such an account turns on the viability of the posited notion of 'determinacy', something that is not altogether clear. (See 'Non-epistemic determinacy' below.)

The question, in the end, is why we should reject the appearance of an exhaustive negation, why we should seek to explain the appearance in terms of something else—Field's 'determinately' operators or the like. One might argue that *ttruth*, due to its spandrels, is inconsistent if negation is exhaustive (and the logical connectives are otherwise fairly normal), and an inconsistent *ttruth* device is bad. This is not terribly telling for reasons partly sketched in Chapter 1 but also taken up in Chapter 5. One might, instead, point to vagueness and the appearance of 'unsettledness' involved in vague expressions, arguing that such appearances tell against an exhaustive negation. This issue (viz., vagueness) is too big for the present discussion, but I admit that, given the prevalence of such thinking, there's a burden on those who accept LEM to explain—or explain away—the given appearance. This burden is briefly taken up in Chapter 5.

« *Parenthetical remark.* One might think that the best position is a compromise: an account according to which we have two negations (or negation-like connectives), one that's exhaustive (as I think) and one that's not (as Field thinks). In this way, one might have 'unsettledness' with the one (less than exhaustive) negation, but also some gluts with the other (exhaustive) negation. I set this aside here, but briefly take it up in Chapter 5. *End parenthetical.* »

Non-epistemic determinacy. One might, with me, be wary of a non-epistemic notion of 'determinacy' or, more to the point, 'indeterminacy'. We have a familiar epistemic sense of determinacy, but this is not the relevant notion(s) involved in Field's account (or other 'determinacy' accounts like, e.g., McGee 1991). The question, then, is what Field's notion of *determinacy* amounts to. What does it mean to say that α is 'indeterminate' or, equivalently, 'not determinately true'? Except for pointing to the logic, there is little in Field's account that answers this question. Of course, with respect to my account, wherein negation is exhaustive and we needn't recognize (non-epistemic) 'determinacy' operators, one might ask what *negation* amounts to. Beyond pointing to the logic of negation, little can be said. But this is to be expected of negation, and few would demand more. A notion like *determinacy*, even if—as for Field—treated as a mere logical operator, *seems* to be different. Why speak of 'determinacy' at all? What's the difference between a determinately true sentence and one that's neither determinately true nor determinately false? On the surface, it seems that an answer ought to be forthcoming, one that goes beyond merely pointing to the logic of $\mathbb{D}$ (as it were).

While I think that there's a genuine issue here, I'm not sure how telling it is in the end. On Field's account, we aren't introducing some new 'determinacy' operator into the language, but rather are making use of already available *logical* resources—principally, his conditional. Maybe, in the end, $\mathbb{D}$ (and so on) shouldn't be called 'determinately operator', but perhaps just some other notion of truth—*struth* or the like. This would get around the worry that the use of 'determinate' is misleading or such. While one might, in turn, press for what 'struth' amounts to, such pressing is probably not productive. After all, in the end, we can forget about calling it 'determinacy' or 'struth' altogether, and just 'classify' the target sentences in primitive form—e.g., $\alpha \wedge (\top \rightarrow \alpha)$. Put in primitive form, none of these worries about what 'determinacy' or 'struth' amounts to seem to arise, just as they don't arise for negation itself. So, as said, while there seems to be an issue, at least on the surface, about what Field's 'determinacy' talk amounts to, it is not obvious that serious problems are involved.

4.5 Summary and closing remarks

In this chapter, I discussed the most prominent alternatives to my theory, namely, the paracomplete theories of Kripke and Field (with Field's the clear frontrunner). As §4.4 makes plain, I do not have strong arguments against Field's theory. What need to be addressed are objections to my own dialetheic approach. I turn to those in the final chapter.

5

OBJECTIONS AND REPLIES

The aim of this chapter is to address various objections to the proposed position. In general, my aim is to take up those objections—and, more broadly, issues—that help to further illuminate the overall position (or, in some cases, openly acknowledge where further work needs to be done); I do not try to cover everything. Given that some of the objections are closely related, there is some overlap among some of the replies.

The objections are loosely categorized into four different topics, although not all objections fit neatly into just one (if any) category.

» Dialetheism, in general: addresses some objections to dialetheism in general.

» Negation, gaps, and unsettledness: addresses a few issues concerning the 'exhaustive' nature of negation.

» Truth, mathematics, and metaphysics: addresses scattered objections concerning truth, one or two about mathematics, and a few metaphysical issues.

» Base-language gluts: covers a few arguments against the 'merely semantic' aspect of my position.

The final section—§5.5—of this chapter is intended for those who are not familiar with Graham Priest's (pioneering) work, or whose familiarity stops at the idea of 'true contradictions'. I do not aim to present Priest's overall theory, either logical or philosophical; I simply try to highlight a few salient points.

« *Parenthetical remark.* With respect to style, I present the objections as if directed towards me, and hence 'you', in the given objections, generally picks out me. *End parenthetical.* »

5.1 Dialetheism, in general

While many of the objections to dialetheism, in general, have been sufficiently answered by Graham Priest (2006*a*, 2006*b*), some of them may be worth rehearsing here—though only some. In places where I fully endorse Priest's reply, I say as much. In places where we differ—or, at least, there's something peculiar to my own reply—I say as much.

Objection: truth abhors a contradiction. The very nature of truth makes it incoherent that there be true falsehoods.

Reply. The first reply is that, on my account, such an objection is entirely misplaced. In short, my claim is only that there are *ttrue tfalsehoods*—sentences that are *transparently true and transparently false*. Transparent truth has no interesting 'nature' at all, and hence no nature to 'conflict' with true falsehoods. It might be that the 'nature' of truth—whatever, if any, such 'nature' might be—abhors contradictions, but it is neither surprising nor abhorrent that our constructed see-through device should bring about inconsistency.

The second reply is that, as Priest (2000*b*) makes plain, most standard accounts of the 'nature' of truth—coherence, correspondence, whathaveyou (e.g., see Lynch 2001)—in no way conflict with true falsehoods. One might, of course, ad hocly impose the constraint that truth's 'nature' is such that triviality abounds in the face of true falsehoods, but the constraint would at best be ad hoc. With respect to correspondence, the ideas of van Fraassen (1969) and, more recently, Barwise and Perry (1983, 1989) provide all of the resources for 'correspondence-true correspondence-falsehoods' (as it were). And that coherence, short of an ad hoc ban, naturally accommodates (negation-) inconsistency is plain. See Priest 2000*b* for full discussion.

As above, though, the main reply is that, at least with respect to my account, any objection from 'truth's nature' is at best misplaced.

Objection: negation abhors a (true) contradiction. A related objection is that nature abhors 'realizing' both the truth of α and the truth of $\neg\alpha$. In other words, whatever makes it the case that α is true thereby makes it the case that α is incompatible with it being the case that $\neg\alpha$ is true.

Reply. The reply is much the same. To begin, all that there is to the 'realization of the truth' of α is that α be ttrue. So, this objection seems to be little more than the previous objection. On the other hand, suppose that, as assumed in the current (version of the previous) objection, $\neg\alpha$ is *incompatible* with α. I am happy to grant as much, but it is not clear how this objection is supposed to be problematic. If the given incompatibility principle is correct, then there are some *ttrue but incompatible* sentences—for example, spandrels such as the Liar and its negation—but this seems not to be problematic. Of course, if 'incompatibility' is supposed to involve explosion (i.e., that arbitrary α and $\neg\alpha$ jointly imply arbitrary β), then it is problematic—indeed, incoherent—to hold that incompatible sentences are both ttrue; however, this supposition would be conspicuously question-begging, taking us back to the first objection about abhorring contradictions. Either way, the objection seems not to be problematic.

Objection: false theory. You are accepting a false theory! This is not rational.

Reply. Again, Priest (1998, 2006*a*) has sufficiently answered this question: that the theory is false doesn't take away from its truth. One might insist that any trace of falsity removes the rational acceptability of a theory, even if the theory is also true; however, such a claim either begs the question or requires substantial argument.

While the above reply is sufficient, it is worth noting that, at least in my case (i.e., on my account), the given 'inconsistency', and hence the given falsity, of the overall theory is merely the *ttruth*-driven sort—merely the spandrels of *ttruth* (or related notions). While the given sentences are 'true falsehoods', and hence false, they are merely transparently true falsehoods—sentences that are *transparently* true (i.e., ttrue) and have transparently true negations. Why should rationality care whether our constructed device of generalization (viz., ttruth) has spandrels that wind up counting as ttrue and tfalse? As far as I can see, there's no strong reason to think that rationality cares.

Objection: inconsistency as prima facie badness.   That inconsistency, in general, is a deal-breaker may be question-begging or, at the very least, requires argument. On the other hand, one might put forth a weaker principle according to which inconsistency is at least a prima facie mark against a theory. This is directly relevant to the issue in Chapter 4 on choosing between your account and Field's (consistent) alternative. What do you say?

Reply.   I think that we need to be slightly more careful in stating the principle in question. In particular, I accept that, with respect to the *base language* (free of 'ttrue' and similar devices), inconsistency is prima facie bad. But why think that this should be so with respect to the full language in which, as we know, *ttruth*-ful spandrels arise? By my lights, if the only inconsistency is driven by *ttruth* (or, perhaps, similar expressions definable therefrom), then there simply isn't any prima facie badness. As in Chapter 1, it strikes me as an initially surprising, certainly unexpected—and unintended—side effect of our see-through device that some sentences are ttrue and tfalse. But such side effects are prima facie bad only if they carry genuinely bad effects. The current objection presupposes that the inconsistency of our see-through device is badness itself; however, this presupposition requires argument. I agree that if the given inconsistency results in some serious, theoretical or practical disadvantage, then badness has surfaced and we need to seek an alternative route towards our see-through device. What I as yet don't see is an argument that such serious, theoretical or practical disadvantage has transpired.

Objection: rejection and the like.   You accept some sentences of the form $\alpha \wedge \neg\alpha$ while also accepting LEM. This clashes with classical probability theory and its role in guiding (or, at least, modeling) acceptance and rejection. So, either you need a deviant account of acceptance and rejection, or you have to reject classical probability theory.

Reply.   While nobody accepts and rejects something at the same time, acceptance and rejection are properly modeled non-classically, not in terms of classical probability. In short, since some claims of the form $\alpha \wedge \neg\alpha$ are ttrue, the 'law' according to which $Pr(\alpha) + Pr(\neg\alpha) = 1$ is to be rejected; instead, we need to allow that $Pr(\alpha) + Pr(\neg\alpha)$ may exceed 1. See Priest 2006*b* for further discussion.

What should be emphasized is that a non-classical approach to probability—and acceptance/rejection—is not peculiar to dialetheic theorists. Indeed, theories of *ttruth*, in general, will normally require a non-classical probability theory. Field's paracomplete approach (see Chapter 4), for example, is no exception. Since the paracomplete theorist rejects some instances of LEM, she will naturally adjust the classical account of probability to allow $Pr(\alpha) + Pr(\neg\alpha)$ to be less than 1. See Field 2008 for further discussion.

5.2   Negation, gaps, and unsettledness

Objection: (non-) contradiction.   One would think that, qua one who accepts that there are ttrue tfalsehoods, you would reject the law of non-contradiction. But you don't, since on your account, $\neg\,(Tr(\ulcorner\alpha\urcorner) \wedge Tr(\ulcorner\neg\alpha\urcorner))$ is valid. This is at least peculiar.

Reply.   'The' so-called law of (non-) contradiction is not one but many. One version that I reject is the following.

>   » Rationality LNC (RLNC): it is irrational (or rationally incoherent, or rationally absurd, or etc.) to knowingly accept that a sentence and its negation are ttrue.

But why think, as the current objection suggests, that there's an oddity in the validity of 'the' non-contradiction principle for *negation*?

$$\text{NLNC.}\quad \neg\,(Tr(\ulcorner\alpha\urcorner) \wedge Tr(\ulcorner\neg\alpha\urcorner))$$

or, given transparency, simply

$$\neg(\alpha \wedge \neg\alpha)$$

My conjecture is that one is conflating features of negation with something along the lines of RLNC, or perhaps resting on 'intuitions' that were built on a spandrel-free diet.

In the end, when truth is merely transparent (a see-through device), we leave it up to the language or world to dictate what's ttrue or tfalse or otherwise. Given the spandrels of *ttruth*, we learn that, in addition to being logically true, NLNC and its equivalents are also tfalse. I take Liar-like sentences *not* to undermine NLNC or its equivalents; such sentences indicate only that the law (so given) is also tfalse.

'Objection': argument for LEM.   This is not so much an objection as a question. In Chapter 4, you refrain from endorsing any arguments for LEM, for 'exhaustive negation'. Priest and Sylvan (1989) and Priest (2006*a*) give an argument for LEM from tradition. If nothing's wrong with it, why not bolster your theory with the

given argument for exhaustive negation? The question is: what is wrong with the following argument for LEM?

Tradition itself is for LEM, in particular, the tradition according to which negation is a *contradictory-forming operator*, where, traditionally, this is taken to involve the exhaustiveness of negation. In short, a contradictory-forming operator $\odot$ is one such that at least one of α and $\odot\alpha$ is true but not both; more precisely, $\odot$ is a contradictory-forming operator if $\alpha \vee \odot\alpha$ is logically true and $\alpha \wedge \odot\alpha$ logically false. (This assumes normal disjunction, which is not at issue.) Priest and Sylvan (1989) and Priest (2006a) argue that, at least traditionally, *negation* is taken to be a contradictory-forming operator in the given sense. But, then, if negation is a contradictory-forming operator in the given sense, it requires exhaustiveness, and hence satisfies LEM.

Reply. The question at hand is whether the given argument establishes as much. While I grant that, traditionally, negation is thought to be a contradictory-forming operator in the given sense, putting much weight on tradition seems to me to be unreasonable. Without additional reason to think that tradition is *right* about the matter, the argument from tradition seems to pull little weight against a paracomplete theorist who rejects that negation is exhaustive.

This is not to say that there's nothing at all to the Priest–Sylvan argument. That tradition typically characterizes negation as a contradictory-forming operator (at least in the given sense) may be *some* evidence of some such 'exhaustive', negation-like connective in the language. While the given evidence mightn't be conclusive, it may require at least some reply from those who reject the existence of such a connective (paracomplete theorists). In this respect, there is value in the given argument. Still, as above, the argument itself does not seem to establish that negation is exhaustive, which is what was sought.

'Objection': aim of assertion. Again, this is not so much an objection but a question. In addition to the argument from tradition, Priest (2006a, 2006b) advances a stronger argument against paracomplete theories—theories for which LEM fails to hold (and fails for any negation-like connective in the language). The argument revolves about the 'aim of assertion'. As he puts it,

> Essentially, the argument is to the effect that, since assertion is a one-player game, anything less than truth is falsity: there is no middle ground—such as drawing, in a two-player game. (Priest, 2006b, p. 267)

If there's 'no middle ground' between truth and falsity, then every sentence is true or false, and this is close enough to having an exhaustive negation. Surely you accept that there's no middle ground between truth and falsity (in virtue of accepting that negation is exhaustive and falsity is truth of negation). The question, then, is the same as the previous one: why not invoke the aim-of-assertion argument for LEM (thereby strengthening your overall position with more arguments)?

Reply. The problem with the argument is that it relies on a notion of truth that goes beyond mere *transparent truth*. The argument turns on a Dummettian 'teleological theory of truth' (1978), which is that truth just is the *telos* of assertion— the aim of a certain linguistic activity. Now, such an account mightn't involve a terribly 'inflated' notion of truth; however, it is clear that it goes beyond the target transparent truth. After all, our see-through device is indeed brought into the language to serve assertion activities; however, it was not brought in to name or otherwise express some 'telos of assertion'. Indeed, it is not at all clear that 'the telos of assertion' would even afford full transparency; in fact, I think it doubtful. Even if it does, the argument presupposes too much beyond mere *ttruth* to serve as an argument that I can endorse for LEM.

« Parenthetical remark. It is also worth noting that if the given notion of truth fails to be fully intersubstitutable—in the sense that $\text{True}(\ulcorner \alpha \urcorner)$ and α are intersubstitutable in all non-opaque contexts—then it's not obvious how one gets from 'bivalence' (which I take 'no middle ground' to be)

$$\text{True}(\ulcorner \alpha \urcorner) \lor \text{True}(\ulcorner \neg \alpha \urcorner)$$

to LEM. But I shall leave this aside, since I've already noted that, regardless of its potential merits, the argument is not available to me.

I should also mention that a related argument for 'exhaustive negation', for LEM, is given by Michael Glanzberg (2003). While Glanzberg's argument is substantially more involved than Priest's argument above, it ultimately shares the same defect. Details aside, Glanzberg's argument presupposes a non-transparent notion of truth, specifically an intricate, essentially 'contextual' truth predicate, one for which (for example) RC fails in certain contexts (Glanzberg, 2001; Glanzberg, 2004). As such, Glanzberg's argument, like Priest's, relies on a notion of truth that goes well beyond our target see-through notion. *End parenthetical. »*

Objection: compromise. The paracomplete theorist says that there's no exhaustive negation (or negation-like connective) in the language. You say that negation is essentially exhaustive. Why not consider a compromise? In particular, suppose that, as per the paracomplete theorist, one negation (say, *choice*) is not exhaustive, while the other negation (call it *exhaustive*) is exhaustive. This might allow for the apparent 'unsettledness' that paracomplete theorists recognize while nonetheless bringing about gluts (via exhaustive negation) that you recognize. Why not go this route?

Reply. This sort of idea is intriguing, and I'm not against it in general. The trouble is that it's hard to see how to make it work in a language for which we have transparent truth. The most natural 'compromise' framework between (e.g.) Field's approach and mine is FDE (Anderson and Belnap, 1975; Anderson, Belnap and Dunn, 1992; Dunn, 1969), at least for the conditional-free fragment.

« Parenthetical remark. A basic many-valued (propositional) semantics for FDE takes the set of values to be $\mathcal{V} = \{1, \mathsf{b}, \mathsf{n}, 0\}$, with $\{1, \mathsf{b}\}$ as designated values. In

turn, $\mathcal{V}$ is ordered as a 'diamond lattice' with 1 on top, 0 on bottom, and b and n incomparable. Conjunction and disjunction, in turn, are interpreted as infimum and supremum, respectively. Negation, finally, toggles 1 and 0, is fixed at b and n. Validity is defined in terms of designated values: any model that designates all premises designates the conclusion.

(I should note that a 'star' semantics, similar to that discussed in Chapters 1 and 2, is available for FDE. Indeed, this was the original motivation for such 'star semantics'. See works cited in Chapter 1.) *End parenthetical.* »

This logic is paracomplete and paraconsistent, in the sense that LEM fails and EFQ fails too. While Woodruff (1984) and Visser (1984) showed that one can enjoy a transparent truth theory with FDE as the logic, one isn't logically forced to recognize gluts, since there's no exhaustive negation that forces such gluts. The current, 'compromise' idea is to add an exhaustive negation on top of FDE. What this requires, in effect, is an operator η that takes all undesignated values to designated values. However one does this, there are going to be problems. In the most natural way of doing it, where η toggles 1 and 0, is fixed at b and takes n to 1, there's a serious problem: the only 'transparent models' (models for which WT holds) are free of sentences that take value n! For example, suppose that we have a transparent model in which $\nu(\alpha) = $ n. Then we can't have a sentence β that 'says', for example, $\eta(\beta \vee \alpha)$, since it will have no interpretation in the FDE scheme. If β is 0 or n, then $\beta \vee \alpha$ is n and, so, $\eta(\beta \vee \alpha)$ is 1. If β is b or 1, then $\beta \vee \alpha$ is 0, and either way $\eta(\beta \vee \alpha)$ is 0. Hence, there's no interpretation that yields WT. Since the languages we care about have sentences like the given β, this is a serious obstacle to the most natural approach to the given sort of FDE 'compromise'.

One might try a base scheme different from FDE, and I think it worth trying, but I am not sure what will work. (On experimentation, the more promising the schemes are with respect to accommodating transparent truth, the more philosophically strange—if not downright implausible—the schemes become.) An alternative might be to keep the base scheme as FDE but add a da Costa-like exhaustive negation on top (see, e.g., the discussion of 'NoT' in Chapter 3), but I am not sure how this would work.

However a 'compromise' might go, there is a glaring philosophical issue that arises. If we succeed in having an exhaustive negation with *ttruth*, why do we also need a non-exhaustive negation? On the surface, I think that motivation for a non-exhaustive negation, in addition to an exhaustive negation, is hard to come by. The one consideration that might push for recognizing a non-exhaustive negation in addition to an exhaustive one is the appearance of 'unsettledness' in our language. I take this up separately. (See 'Objection: unsettledness' below.)

Objection: gaps and gluts.   You claim to be a glut theorist about transparent truth: that *ttruth* gives rise to gluts, sentences that are ttrue and have a ttrue negation. But, given the logic of your ttruth theory, you are committed to *gaps*! A *gap theorist* claims that some sentences are neither true nor false, and you're committed to as much. After all, let α be any glut. Given your logic, and the transparency of truth, you're committed to $\neg Tr(\ulcorner \alpha \urcorner) \wedge \neg Tr(\ulcorner \neg \alpha \urcorner)$, and this is just the claim that α is gappy—not ttrue and not tfalse. That you're committed to as much follows from the transparency of $Tr(x)$ and the equivalence of $\alpha \wedge \neg \alpha$ and $\neg \alpha \wedge \neg\neg \alpha$ in your theory.

« *Parenthetical remark.* Hartry Field (2005*a*) raises this objection against Priest's dialetheic theory. It is not obvious to me that the point goes through for Priest's less than transparent truth predicate, but the point certainly goes through in my case. *End parenthetical.* »

Reply. The point is correct. Any glut is also a gap, *so understood*. Of course, traditional 'gap theorists', whatever else they might (or might not) say about 'gaps', are those who *reject* (what they want to call) 'gaps'. The gaps in my theory are ones that I fully embrace: they're ttrue and tfalse. While this might seem puzzling initially, the puzzle seems to dissolve quickly on reflection. As the objection (rightly) states, $\alpha \wedge \neg \alpha$ is equivalent to $\neg \alpha \wedge \neg\neg \alpha$ in my theory. Hence, if we have a glutty spandrel α, we can call it either a glut or a gap, in the given sense; but we are calling it ttrue (and tfalse) whatever we say. So go the spandrels: they're peculiar.

Objection: gaps, gluts, and 'abnormal' worlds. The star mate of our world is a gap world. In general, and at least for the conditional-free fragment, $w^\star$ and w are alike except that they switch gaps and gluts. If α is glutty at w then it's gappy at $w^\star$, and if gappy at w then glutty at $w^\star$, and so on. This raises two questions.

1Q. Why can't there be a world with both gaps and gluts?
2Q. Why think that the actual world is what you call 'normal', having gluts but no gaps rather than the reverse?

Reply. I take each question in turn.

» *On 1Q.* This objection is related in various ways to the 'Compromise' objection above, but something else can be said. If the question is simply asking whether one can add 'worlds' with both gaps and gluts and preserve the basic (conditional-free) logic, the answer is affirmative, at least so long as these worlds are abnormal. If, on the other hand, the question is whether there can be normal worlds with both gaps and gluts, the answer is negative, at least if negation is to remain exhaustive. But perhaps this is the thrust of the question: that we should acknowledge that, in concert with *ttruth* (or similar 'semantic' devices), negation affords both gaps and gluts.[1] My reply to this is to request further argument. After all, negation seems to be exhaustive, and I've assumed as much throughout.

---

[1] As in the reply to 'Objection: gaps and gluts' (above), there's a straightforward sense in which negation does afford gaps simply by yielding gluts, but I take the current objection to be using 'gap' in a way that rationality demands the rejection of gaps (which is not the situation involved in 'glutty gaps' discussed in the previous objection).

The objection, on the current reading, now seems like it is simply rejecting the exhaustiveness of negation (since accepting 'normal worlds' at which there are gaps is simply rejecting that negation is exhaustive). But, then, the objection requires further argument. While this point is a sufficient reply to the objection, one more point is worth noting. If, as the objection seems to suggest, we become paracomplete theorists and reject that negation is exhaustive, the motivation for gluts is significantly diminished. It seems to me that the motivation is diminished without something like an exhaustive negation-like connective. Moreover, adding an exhaustive, negation-like connective in addition to one's non-exhaustive one raises the issue discussed in reply to 'Objection: compromise' (above): why the non-exhaustive one if we've got an exhaustive one? Answers to these questions would need to be provided in addition to arguments for rejecting the apparent exhaustiveness of negation.

» *On 2Q.* The answer to 2Q has been said throughout. Negation, I think, is exhaustive; there's a strong appearance that every sentence is either ttrue or not. Hence, the actual world is gapless (in the relevant sense of 'gap'), and hence its 'star world' gappy—at least on this star-way of thinking about things. As I've conceded throughout, I do not have a non-question-begging argument for the exhaustiveness of negation, and hence have no non-question-begging argument for the thesis that the actual world is gapless (in the relevant sense of 'gap').

What the objection may be suggesting is that the star-way of thinking about our Boolean framework (i.e., our Boolean connectives) requires the existence of gaps at some world—namely, at the star mate of any glutty world—and thereby suggests a 'gappy' (or, generally, paracomplete) theory of ttruth as a live option. In other words, it may well be that there's no non-question-begging argument for the exhaustiveness of negation, but if we're forced to have worlds where negation is not exhaustive, then why not see them as candidates for actuality (as it were) rather than the glutty ones? (Of course, the objection goes either way too. On a paracomplete and non-paraconsistent setting, e.g., Strong Kleene, one takes normal worlds to be gappy and abnormal worlds to be glutty. Objection 2Q then emerges: why take the actual world to be 'normal' instead of taking the glutty worlds to be normal? I concentrate on the glutty side.)

I think that there are a number of replies that are relevant. One is that the star setup need not be taken in any 'realist' fashion; one may concentrate only on the given BXTT logic. This reply aside, another one deserves mention. Suppose that we broaden the objection and consider our (suitable) conditional. Just like negation, our conditional is a logical expression that exhibits different behavior at different types of worlds. In particular, the conditional fails to detach at abnormal worlds: there are abnormal worlds w such that, for some α and β, we have $w \models \alpha$ and $w \models \alpha \rightarrow \beta$ but $w \not\models \beta$. (One key example involves a Curry α equivalent to $\alpha \rightarrow \bot$, for unsatisfiable $\bot$.) So, a slight variant of 2Q, now pointed at our conditional rather than at negation, is simply the question

2Q*. Why think that the actual world is what you call 'normal', exhibiting detachment rather than a failure of detachment?

In other words, why not see detachment-failing worlds (i.e., worlds where the conditional fails to detach for some sentences) as candidates for actuality? The answer, as with negation, is that our (suitable) conditional is essentially detaching; hence, it detaches at all normal points. This is not a non-question-begging answer, but such (non-question-begging) answers are not clearly available at this level. (I should note that one might say that it's a priori that our conditional detaches and equally a priori that negation is exhaustive. This might avoid being question-begging, but the reply is unavailable to me; I have no sufficiently illuminating—or ultimately non-question-begging—account of the a priori that may be offered along these lines.)

Objection: unsettledness. A challenge that confronts those, like yourself, who endorse LEM and take truth to be *ttruth* is the apparent 'unsettledness' of our language.[2] Such unsettledness is usually thought to require the failure of LEM. In particular, for the appropriate predicate $\varphi(x)$, there are objects y such that we should reject both $\varphi(y)$ and $\neg\varphi(y)$.

Vagueness is one of the driving phenomena behind the appearance of such 'unsettledness'. Let R^φ be a 'tolerance relation' for (vague) predicate $\varphi(x)$, so that $R^\varphi x, y$ only if x and y are relevantly similar. Various plausible assumptions, coupled with your logic, has the (prima facie untoward) consequence of 'sharp cutoffs' for $\varphi(x)$, namely,

SC. $\exists x \exists y (R^\varphi(x, y) \land \varphi(x) \land \neg\varphi(y))$

But philosophical intuition rails against such cutoffs. That there's a moment t such that at t you're a person but, for i as small as you like, at $t - i$ you're *not* a person strikes many philosophers as absurd, or at least too hard to believe. Our usage, one is inclined to think, is simply not that sharp. Accordingly, unless you can accommodate the appearance of 'unsettledness', we should reject LEM and, hence, reject your account of *ttruth*—and perhaps go paracomplete with Field (see Chapter 4).

Reply. This issue is too big to address fully here. Moreover, I do not have a fully worked out account of such 'unsettledness'. Still, I do think that the issue is serious, that it bears on my proposed account of *ttruth*, and that it deserves *some* comment here. By way of reply, then, I suggest the direction of my response.

To begin, there are already a few well-known proposals that purport to accommodate apparent unsettledness in classical languages. In particular, classical *epistemicist* proposals, such as Sorensen 2001 and Williamson 1994, firmly accept—as I do—that our language is bivalent but nonetheless enjoys 'gaps' of some sort. The 'gaps', on such accounts, are *epistemic gaps*, gaps in our knowledge, as opposed to 'gaps' between truth and falsity (whatever, in the end, that might come to when it doesn't come to a glut). On these approaches, SC is an

---

[2]This objection and the corresponding reply is an only very slightly revised rehearsal of ideas sketched in Beall 2009.

inevitable consequence of the exhaustive nature of negation and the logical behavior of our other connectives. While I do not accept such *epistemic* accounts
of 'unsettledness', there is a point of agreement: SC is inevitable given the logic
of our language—in my case, not classical logic, but a logic 'classical enough' to
give SC. Inasmuch as negation is *supposed to cut sharp boundaries*, as I think
that it is, the appearance of 'unsettledness' must be explained another way. The
appearance is neither essentially epistemic nor one that involves the failure of
SC or LEM; it is something else. I suggest that the real unsettledness—the real
'gaps', as it were—arises at the atomic level. Let me briefly explain.

To simplify matters, suppose that $\mathcal{L}$ is devoid of 'semantic' terms like 'true'
and the like. (This isn't ultimately necessary, but I will not go into the matter
here.) Suppose that, for every 'positive atomic' predicate $\varphi(x)$ in $\mathcal{L}$, there is an
'overline mate' $\overline{\varphi}(x)$, which—for simplicity—is also an *atomic* predicate, though
not a 'positive' one.[3] Now, suppose that the relation between our positive atomics
and their overline mates is *exclusive* but *not* necessarily *exhaustive*, in the sense
that, where $\varphi(x)^+$ is the extension of $\varphi(x)$, for all x,

EXC. $\varphi(x)^+ \cap \overline{\varphi}(x)^+ = \emptyset$

but, where $\mathcal{D}$ is our domain, we *need not* have

EXH. $\varphi(x)^+ \cup \overline{\varphi}(x)^+ = \mathcal{D}$

In other words, while we never have some b of which both $\varphi(x)$ and $\overline{\varphi}(x)$ are
true, we might have some b of which neither $\varphi(x)$ nor $\overline{\varphi}(x)$ is true.

Notice that, given the behavior of negation on my account, EXC will yield

$$\overline{\varphi}(x) \vdash \neg\varphi(x)$$

but we will *not* get the converse, since $\overline{\varphi}(x)$ is simply an atomic governed only
by the minimal constraints above—in effect, only EXC.

The idea, in abstract, may be put succinctly: for every 'positive atomic' $\varphi(x)$
in the language, there is an atomic *contrary*.

« *Parenthetical remark.* I should note that it's not obvious that one must treat
the given 'overline mates' as *atomic predicates*, but I do so for simplicity. If
one were to treat the overline as some sort of connective, the story would be
rather complicated. One route might be along da Costa's 'negation' lines, wherein
overline is interpreted in a *non-compositional* fashion (da Costa and Alves, 1977).
Ultimately, though, the end result will have to be such that $\overline{\varphi}(x)$ is, in effect,
atomic, and so I simply treat it as such. *End parenthetical.* »

---

   [3]I leave the notion of a 'positive predicate' at an intuitive level. For present purposes,
predicates like 'is a book', 'is bald', 'is sad', and so on are one and all positive atomics. (I
should also note that, for readability's sake, I put the overline only over 'φ' versus over '$\varphi(x)$'.
The line is intended only to mark the 'overline mate' of predicate $\varphi(x)$.)

Of course, given that $\neg\alpha$ is the contradictory of α for all α, in the sense that $\vdash \alpha \vee \neg\alpha$ and $\vdash \neg(\alpha \wedge \neg\alpha)$, we have

$$\overline{\varphi}(x) \vee \neg\overline{\varphi}(x)$$

for all given 'overline mates'. But this is simply the result of negation doing its exhaustive job. As for our 'mates' themselves, while we have it that

$$\varphi(x) \wedge \overline{\varphi}(x)$$

is *logically false* for all x and all $\varphi(x)$, we—importantly—do *not*, as mentioned above, have that, for all x, the following holds.

$$\varphi(x) \vee \overline{\varphi}(x)$$

In other words, given standard assumptions of validity, we will have

$$\vdash \neg(\varphi(x) \wedge \overline{\varphi}(x))$$

for any x, but, notably,

$$\nvdash \varphi(x) \vee \overline{\varphi}(x)$$

This latter feature, I suggest, points to at least one natural sort of 'unsettledness' or 'gaps', however modest it may be.

The proposal, in short, is that our own language has such 'overline mates'. While our language is bivalent—in the sense that every sentence is ttrue or tfalse—there is also unsettledness in a non-epistemic sense; there are 'gaps' in the sense that, for some b and vague $\varphi(x)$, we have the following.

$$\neg\varphi(b) \wedge \neg\overline{\varphi}(b)$$

In other words, b falls into the 'gap' between $\varphi(x)$ and $\overline{\varphi}(x)$, though—given bivalence—obviously not the (non-existent) gap between $\varphi(x)$ and $\neg\varphi(x)$.

What plays the role of 'overline mates' in our language? My suggestion is that something along the lines of (some usage of) 'non-$\varphi(x)$' does the work. (There might also be some usage of 'not' at play too, though not qua negation or connective, but rather some atomic construct spelled with 'not'.) In short, there are (at least in effect) *atomic* predicates 'non-$\varphi(x)$' that are contraries of basic atomics.

How are these introduced? On this, I think that Soames (1999) was on the right track. In particular, setting our 'overline mates' aside for the moment, I shall adopt the idea, made explicit by Soames, that 'vague' or 'unsettled' predicates are those for which our practice has established only a sufficient condition for satisfaction.[4] The idea, in short, is that our (vague) positive atomics $\varphi(x)$ enjoy

---

[4]NB: Soames's (contextual) development of the idea is not something to which I'm subscribing, but rather only his initial setup—or, at least, part of his setup.

only some sufficient satisfaction condition $\psi(x)$, so that we have only something of the following sort governing $\varphi(x)$.

$$\psi(x) \rightarrow \varphi(x)$$

The natural suggestion for our 'overline mates', which are similarly 'vague', is the same: we have only some sufficient condition for $\overline{\varphi}(x)$.

$$\mu(x) \rightarrow \overline{\varphi}(x)$$

In turn, so long as we do not have $\psi(x) \vee \mu(x)$, we need not have $\varphi(x) \vee \overline{\varphi}(x)$. In cases—perhaps 'precise' ones—in which we *do* have $\psi(x) \vee \mu(x)$, then we'll have $\varphi(x) \vee \overline{\varphi}(x)$. But, again, there's no reason to think that we'd have such 'overline exhaustion' (i.e., 'overline excluded middle') for all such predicates.

The proposal, in short, is that we can understand the apparent 'unsettledness' of our (bivalent) language along 'overline' lines. Given bivalence (and other logical features of the language), we do not have 'gaps' in the standard sense. Still, our practice, governing 'vague' predicates, leaves lots of 'overline gaps' (as it were); for many (vague) predicates $\varphi(x)$, there are objects y such that neither $\varphi(x)$ nor $\overline{\varphi}(x)$ is true of y. This, I think, is a modest way in which 'unsettledness' arises in our (bivalent) language.

« *Parenthetical remark.* On a technical point: I should note that, at least without imposing other constraints on the 'overline mates', we enjoy a non-triviality proof for the resulting 'overline-mates' theory in virtue of the fact that $\alpha \rightarrow \perp$ is a contrary-forming connective in the BXTT theory, and the Chapter 2 (appendix) construction covers this connective. Hence, letting $\overline{\alpha}$ be interpreted as (say) $\alpha \rightarrow \perp$ shows that the resulting theory is non-trivial. (Of course, if further constraints beyond merely being a contrary-forming connective are imposed on overline mates, then this argument for non-triviality may well fail. I do not impose further constraints on the overline mates.) *End parenthetical.* »

5.3   Truth, mathematics, and metaphysics

Objection: beyond ttruth.   What if, contrary to your theory, there turns out to be more to truth than *ttruth*? What if, for either theoretical or practical ends, we need to acknowledge some substantive property of truth. Won't this undermine the overall position, which proceeds on the assumption that *ttruth* is all there is to truth in general? Won't the modesty of having at most only *transparently true (transparent) falsehoods* inflate into a prima facie more troubling 'robust inconsistency', or at least inconsistency involving 'substantive' truth?

Reply.   One point to emphasize is that, regardless of whether we need to recognize a notion of truth beyond *ttruth*, we'd still want the practical, expressive services of *ttruth*. So, the main position, at least with respect to *ttruth*, remains intact. (If the supposed 'substantive' property of truth were fully see-through, then, obviously, there would be some question as to why we're calling it a 'substantive' account.) The objection, as I see it, does not call this point into question.

As far as the objection's explicit question goes, the short reply is the expected one: the matter depends on the supposed 'substantive' theory of truth. As in §5.1, and notably Priest 2000*b*, most 'substantive' accounts of truth are compatible with dialetheism. Of course, as the objection notes, it would certainly be a prima facie less 'modest' sort of inconsistency if the relevant account of truth involved some substantive property. But, again, the matter depends on the given account.

Another point of reply is that it is unclear whether a 'substantive' account of truth would provide the resources for gluts. Many philosophers concerned with the 'nature' of truth take it to be obvious that, whatever truth may be, it plays both Capture and Release—usually in both 'rule' and 'conditional' forms (see Chapter 2). But why think this if truth is some property 'out there', especially if it's supposed to be a *natural* property.[5] Why think, for example, that the (natural) relation of *correspondence to facts*—whatever, in the end, this (natural) property may be—is such that α's having that property implies α (i.e., Release) or vice versa (i.e., Capture)? Yes, many philosophers *say* as much, and often merely assume as much; however, if this is a genuine (especially natural) property in the world, such an assumption presumably requires argument. Similarly, why think that α's *cohering in the right way* implies α or vice versa, if such 'coherence' is a genuinely natural property? The answers to these questions, as far as I can see, are not obvious. What's notable, and relevant to the current objection, is that if, according to the proffered 'substantive' account, truth (a substantive, natural property) fails to Capture and Release in the right way, the typical paradoxes do not obviously arise—even with the resources of exhaustive negation in the language. So, again, pending details, it is far from clear whether 'immodest inconsistency' (as it were) would result from the need to recognize a substantive notion of truth, in addition to *ttruth*.

« *Parenthetical remark.* On the question of Capture and Release for notions of truth beyond *ttruth*: it is worth observing that the situation is quite different with our constructed, see-through device *ttruth*. This is a tool brought in to do a particular, practical job, and its Release and Capture behavior is stipulated into its construction. As such, the question of whether *ttruth* plays Capture and Release in the relevant ways does not arise in the way that it does when truth is taken to be some substantive—especially natural—property. I briefly return to this point in §5.5. *End parenthetical.* »

Objection: inconsistent maths? It is one thing to acknowledge inconsistencies arising from spandrels of *ttruth* (or related notions); it's quite another matter if we need to acknowledge that arithmetic—or mathematics, generally—is inconsistent. Do we?

---

[5] I owe this observation to Lionel Shapiro, though should emphasize that he is not responsible for my presentation.

Reply.   No, as Chapters 1 and 2 make clear. While there are interesting, so-called 'inconsistent mathematics' (Mortensen, 1995), all of which may be understood classically (i.e., classically constructing models of inconsistent arithmetics), we needn't—and I don't—see arithmetic as anything more than classical. What is important to remember is that, on my account—as on other standard accounts of *ttruth*—we may enjoy a perfectly classical proper fragment of the language. As in Chapter 3, nothing in my account rules out endorsing classical theories, where such theories are written in some suitably proper fragment of the language.

Objection: Russell's paradox and maths.   Russell's paradox is often thought to be the set-theoretic counterpart of the Liar. The naïve comprehension scheme, according to which, for any open sentence $\varphi(x)$, there is a set $\mathcal{Y}$ such that $o \in \mathcal{Y}$ iff $\varphi(x)$ is ttrue of o, for any object o. Russell's paradox invokes the predicate $x \notin x$. By the comprehension scheme, we have some set $\mathcal{R}$ containing all and only the objects that are not self-membered, that is, the objects satisfying $x \notin x$. But, then, $\mathcal{R} \in \mathcal{R}$ iff $\mathcal{R} \notin \mathcal{R}$.

The trouble for you is that standard—say, type-theoretic or otherwise— classical solutions to Russell's paradox are in tension with your dialetheic approach to Liars. In short, you can't have a classical mathematics without an ad hoc solution to Russell's paradox.

Reply.   What should be noted is that, in effect, *Russell's paradox* amounts to two paradoxes, one for *set theory*, and one for *semantics*. By my lights, mathematics is free simply to axiomatize away its version of Russell's paradox, as is standardly done. Sets were introduced within and for mathematics, a role that need not be constrained by our 'intuitions' about natural language. So long as the given role is sufficiently served by axiomatically harnessed sets, then so be it. Of course, mathematicians generally seek the most natural or 'beautiful' route in their endeavors, and perhaps standard axiomatized approaches towards sets are not as natural as one might like. But that is a separate issue. The main goal, at least for *set* theory, is to find entities that play the given mathematical role.

Semantics, on the other hand, seems to be a different matter. What semantics, at least in practice, seems to need are (what I will call) *semantical properties*. Semantical properties are entities that play a particular semantic role, in particular, those entities corresponding to each meaningful predicate in the (given) language.

« *Parenthetical remark.* I used to use the term 'semantical extensions' for what I am now calling 'semantical properties', but Hartry Field (in conversation) convinced me that 'extensions' is apt to mislead, perhaps suggesting that the target entities are *extensional*. Field (2004) and I are largely in agreement on the import of Russell's paradox, though our positions differ in expected ways—one being paraconsistent, the other non-paraconsistent. I should also note that, interestingly, at least according to Myhill (1975), Kurt Gödel took a similar view of Russell's paradox—seeing it as a paradox not for *sets* so much as for (what I'm calling) semantical properties. *End parenthetical.* »

The role of semantical properties is essentially given by the naïve semantical schema, namely,

SP. For any object o and predicate $\varphi(x)$, there is a semantical property $\mathcal{Y}$ such that o exemplifies $\mathcal{Y}$ iff $\varphi(x)$ is ttrue of o.

This principle confronts Russell's paradox for *semantics*, in particular, the instance invoking x *does not exemplify* x.

Perhaps one reason that the two paradoxes are not typically distinguished is that semanticists simply borrowed the mathematical sets to play the role of semantical properties, and the history of (at least contemporary, formal) semantics has gone along with the borrowed entities. But why think that the mathematicians' sets will sufficiently play the role of semantical properties? There is no a priori reason to think as much. Indeed, inasmuch as semantics needs its unrestricted naïve semantical schema (above), there is reason to be pessimistic.

As for the current objection, a solution to the Liar, at least by my lights, need not thereby be a solution to *mathematical set*-theoretic paradoxes; those paradoxes may be solved in whatever way suits mathematics. Of course, if mathematics remains classical, then one's proposed 'all-purpose logic' will need to have classical logic as an extension. The point is that Russell's set-theoretic paradox needn't be an issue in one's resolution of the Liar or truth-theoretic paradoxes in general. On the other hand, one's resolution of the Liar is constrained, to some degree, by Russell's semantics-theoretic paradox—the semantical properties paradox. At the very least, solutions to the Liar that require rejecting the unrestricted semantical schema would seem to carry a prima facie blemish. On that point, I agree with the objection (at least so read).

As it turns out, accommodating the unrestricted semantical schema SP usually goes hand in hand with achieving a suitable conditional, one for which $\alpha \to \alpha$ is valid, $\to$ detaches, and Curry problems are avoided. Accordingly, both my account and Field's alternative (see Chapter 4 and Field 2004) naturally afford a solution to Russell's semantical paradox. (Similarly, though he doesn't agree with the distinction between *sets* and semantical properties—and, moreover, doesn't endorse a *ttruth* theory—Priest's position, which long predates my modest, dialetheic alternative as well as Field's recent work, also provides a suitable, paraconsistent approach to semantical properties.)

« *Parenthetical remark.* I should note that the semantical-properties version of Curry paradox is directly analogous to the truth-theoretic version. Let ϵ be the exemplification relation, $[x : \varphi(x)]$ the semantical property corresponding to $\varphi(x)$, and $x\epsilon[y : \varphi(y)] \leftrightarrow \varphi(x)$ the semantical property schema. Curry is generated via the predicate $x\epsilon x \to \bot$, yielding $[x : x\epsilon x \to \bot]$, where $\bot$ is either explosive or plainly false. *End parenthetical.* »

My theory of semantical properties, underwritten by the BX conditional (see Chapter 2), is inconsistent. (But the theory, as Brady 1989 establishes, is non-trivial.) I shall not dwell on this issue, but one philosophical point, with respect to the 'merely semantic' side of my account, is notable. Suppose that, in the end, semantics continues to need semantical properties, and requires them in the unrestricted way discussed above, wherein ϵ (i.e., exemplification) is introduced over the whole resulting language via SP. (This mightn't be the case in the end. Semantics might ultimately take a form that does away with the idea of having every meaningful predicate in correspondence with some entity. But suppose otherwise.) Given the role and rules of ϵ, as in SP, spandrels of 'ϵ' yield gluts. Happily, though, the resulting gluts are more of the 'merely semantic' sort; they are not in the base language, which, on my account, remains classical. The situation, in the end, remains much the same as on the basic picture involving *ttruth* and its spandrels.

« *Parenthetical remark.* I should also note that it's not obvious that semantical-property-driven gluts arise independently of truth-like notions. Let us set the use of *ttrue of* aside, which is definable via *ttruth* in the expected way. (See the following objection concerning 'definability paradoxes'.) Still, in a BX theory of semantical properties, one automatically gets a truth predicate. In particular, as Greg Restall (in conversation) has noted, the resulting truth predicate over 'propositions' is as transparent as the corresponding 'exemplification' axiom. Given

$$x\epsilon[y : \varphi(y)] \leftrightarrow \varphi(x)$$

we define, for any sentence α, the 'proposition' $\langle\alpha\rangle$ as $[x : \alpha]$, and we get

$$x\epsilon\langle\alpha\rangle \leftrightarrow \alpha$$

In turn, define $T(\langle\alpha\rangle)$ as $\langle\alpha\rangle\epsilon\langle\alpha\rangle$, and we get

$$T(\langle\alpha\rangle) \leftrightarrow \alpha$$

Finally, if we get full substitution in the theory (and we do in BX), then α is always everywhere replaceable by $T(\langle\alpha\rangle)$, and so $T(x)$, so understood, is very much 'transparent' over 'propositions'. As such, it is tempting to think that even the gluts involved in semantical property theory are essentially tied to 'truth'. *End parenthetical.* »

Objection: definability paradoxes.   Beyond Russell's paradox are other paradoxes hovering about mathematics, particularly, the paradoxes of definability. The most famous of these are Berry's, König's, and Richard's. And there are others (e.g., Hilbert and Bernays 1939, Priest 1997, Simmons 2003, among others).

Consider Berry's paradox.[6] Let $\mathcal{L}$ be a so-called countable language so that that, like English, there are at most finitely many expressions of length 100,

---

[6]This is slightly more complicated than König's, but it doesn't presuppose familiarity with ordinals, which perhaps makes it somewhat more accessible in general.

where the length of an expression is the number of 'letters' (including spaces if necessary) that make up the expression. Call a unary $\mathcal{L}$ predicate a *century predicate* if it has length 100 or less (i.e., 100 or fewer 'letters'). We say that an object k is $\mathcal{L}$-*definable*$_{100}$ if there's a century predicate true of k. There are natural numbers (i.e., 'counting numbers' $0, 1, 2, 3, \ldots$) that are not $\mathcal{L}$-definable$_{100}$. Hence, assuming the so-called least number principle (or an appropriate version thereof), there is a *least* such not-$\mathcal{L}$-definable$_{100}$ number, say j. Hence, 'x is the least number not $\mathcal{L}$-definable$_{100}$' is true of j. But, then, since 'x is the least number not $\mathcal{L}$-definable$_{100}$' is a century predicate, it $\mathcal{L}$-defines$_{100}$ j.[7] Contradiction.

The question is whether your 'modest', 'simply semantic' dialetheism accepts the apparent inconsistency generated by the definability paradoxes. What is the treatment of these paradoxes in your theory?

Reply. The treatment is as expected: these are more gluts, and indeed ultimately spandrels of 'semantic terms' (e.g., *definable*, *denotes*, etc.). All of these terms are logical devices along the lines of *ttruth*, many of them very tightly tied to *ttruth*. The paradoxes in question rely on 'true' to the extent that they rely on 'definability', which invokes 'true of', which invokes *ttruth*: $\ulcorner\varphi(x)\urcorner$ is true of something k iff $Tr(\ulcorner\varphi(k)\urcorner)$ iff $\varphi(k)$. (The notion of *denotation*, also definable via 'true of', is similar.)

The lesson is that 'definable', and more fundamentally 'true of', yields gluts. (The same lesson is learned via the familiar Grelling's paradox, which, in effect, considers the predicate 'is not true of itself', which predicate is true of itself just if not true of itself.) What should be noted is that the resulting gluts are *not* in the base language; our base language, as throughout, remains classical. It is only the spandrels of the various 'semantic' terms that are gluts. The account of such paradoxes (definability, denotation, etc.) is in line with the basic, 'modest' account of (transparent) truth advanced throughout.

« *Parenthetical remark.* I should note that the technical details of adding descriptions (e.g., 'the least n such that...' etc.) to the language in which we enjoy a denotation predicate requires care for reasons that Priest (1997) discusses—in effect, descriptions like 'the denotation of this term plus 1' can explode, implying $1 = 0$ or the like, in concert with loose description and denotation rules. The difficulty is resolved by adjusting one's denotation rules in light of a fairly straightforward 'negative' free logic (i.e., treating all denotation failures as yielding falsity), which resolution I endorse. For the (negative) free logic, see Priest 1997; Priest 1999. (Note that Priest 2005 and Priest 2006c present an alternative though non-negative-free resolution.) *End parenthetical.* »

Objection: proving consistency of arithmetic. There is an intuitive argument for proving the consistency of arithmetic, which, given Gödel's second incompleteness theorem, must be wrong if—as you hold—mathematics is classical. The

---

[7]If, when fully spelled out, 'x is the least number not $\mathcal{L}$-definable$_{100}$' has more than 100 'letters', we can change the class to millennium predicates or etc.

argument, presented and criticized by Field (2006), runs as follows. (We assume, as Field does, that we're dealing only with sentences.)

1. Each axiom of our theory T is true.

2. Each rule (of 'inference') of T preserves truth.

3. All theorems of T are true.

Unless this breaks down somewhere, you cannot coherently hold that mathematics is consistent—given Gödel's second incompleteness theorem.

Reply.   The short reply is that Field's diagnosis (2006) is accurate in my case. In particular, I reject the second premise, at least on any reading that would actually validate the given argument. As in Chapter 3, my account affords various ways of (ttruly) saying that valid arguments are truth-preserving; however, none of them—as Field (2006) himself discusses—validates the given argument. So, there's no threat from the given argument against the classicality of mathematics.

Objection: stars.   What philosophical sense is to be made of the 'star worlds' that are essential to your account of negation?

Reply.   As in Chapter 3, I'm inclined to think of the 'formal picture' in a fairly instrumental fashion: it helps to navigate about the logic. Accordingly, I'm not sure how much philosophical sense need be given to the star worlds beyond the surface idea: namely, they're simply 'worlds' relevant to the *truth-at-a-point* conditions for negation.

On the other hand, were one to take a more realistic view of the star semantics, I think that there are philosophically sensible accounts to give. For example, for those who put a lot of weight on the unrestricted 'truthmaker thesis', according to which every truth (and, hence, every true negation) requires a truthmaker, the star framework may yield pleasing results. Instead of having to look for 'negative facts' *here*, one can say that 'falsity makers' are *over there* (at the relevant star world). But I'll leave the suggestion there, being disinclined myself towards any 'truthmaker' thesis aside from the minimal 'truthmaker thesis' that resides in *ttruth*-biconditionals. (See Beebee and Dodd 2005 for some of the issues concerning truthmakers, etc.)

There are other stories to give. Perhaps the most plausible philosophical story arises from Dunn's work on negation (1999, 2000), wherein a primitive *compatibility* relation over points is recognized, and negation is defined in terms of such 'compatibility'. As Restall (1999) spells out, the star semantics for negation may be seen as a special case of Dunn's 'compatibility' approach. I leave the details to Dunn and Restall, but the point is that, inasmuch as philosophers are inclined to recognize a primitive notion of compatibility among points, the star semantics has a promising philosophical story.

« *Parenthetical remark.* I should also note that, in unpublished work, Dave Ripley argues that Dunn's framework is very promising with respect to linguistic evidence concerning negation in natural languages. This work is in its early stages, but, should the linguistic evidence hold up, it might well usher in the star semantics as a special case of Dunn's more general framework. *End parenthetical.* »

Objection: ternary relation. The 'access' relation R^2 in standard possible worlds semantics for aletheic modalities has straightforward intuitive sense: viz., relative possibility. No equally clear sense is available for the *ternary* relation R^3 essentially involved in the semantics for your conditional (see Chapter 2). This makes the account suspect, in general.

Reply. First, I should emphasize that, as with the 'stars', I'm happy to treat the given 'semantics' as entirely heuristic, or as an instrumental semantics for navigating one's way about the logic. In that respect, there needn't be anything suspect about the ternary relation or other ingredients of the formal picture. Still, I agree that the formal picture is generally more useful if it carries good, intuitive sense—much like, as the objection indicates, the intuitive sense involved in standard 'access' of aletheic modal operators. Where I disagree is that there's no equally clear sense.

Some philosophers (Urquhart, 1972) have suggested that the ternary relation be understood along informational lines, while others (Restall, 1995; Mares, 1996) have suggested information flow and a link with situation semantics (Barwise and Perry, 1983). I think that such suggestions are worthwhile, and both make good sense. On the other hand, I do not think that such elaborate theorizing is required. It seems to me that the ternary relation can be thought of along the lines of the familiar binary access relation involved in aletheic modalities. If, as the objection has it, the latter is sensible enough, so too, I think, is the former. In particular, as briefly mentioned in Chapter 2, one can think of $Rxyz$ holding just when the pair $\langle y, z \rangle$ is 'accessible' from x. In what sense 'accessible'? As far as I can see, one may think of this along one's favorite lines for cashing out 'aletheic accessibility' (i.e., the binary 'accessibility' involved in aletheic modal frameworks). As far as I know, there's no saying what 'relatively possible' or, *equivalently*, 'accessible' means with respect to R^2, except to say that y is possible with respect to—or, equivalently, accessible from—x just if R^2x, y. There's no reason that I can see that bars talking of 'access' between x and $\langle y, z \rangle$. This, at least by my lights, has as much intuitive sense as is involved in the more familiar R^2. (Indeed, as mentioned in Chapter 2, R^2 can be seen as a special case of R^3, in particular, R^2 is R^3 restricted to 'identity pairs' $\langle y, z \rangle$ such that $y = z$. But even this, I think, isn't required to make as much 'access' sense of R^3 as there is involved in R^2.)

Objection: abnormal-worlds semantics. Such 'abnormal-worlds semantics' is not really an account of one connective at all, but rather of two different connectives.

(An objection along these lines is advanced in Mares 2004*a*, though Mares might have had a slightly different objection in mind.) The meaning of a connective is simply its truth conditions. In the account that you endorse (in Chapter 2), we have different truth conditions at different 'types' of worlds—normal and abnormal. But a difference in truth conditions is a difference in meaning. Hence, we're not really defining a single connective, but rather two different connectives. You might say that Curry teaches us to recognize abnormal worlds, and to recognize a conditional defined over them. Maybe so, but you've succeeded only in defining two different conditionals, one over normal points, one over abnormal points. What's particularly bad, for your purposes, is that we still have the old connective, namely, the one defined only over normal worlds. And this connective falls prey to Curry—and, hence, triviality.

Reply. The main reply is that serious argument is required for the claim that meaning—even meaning of connectives—is 'truth conditions'. Given methodological deflationism, which I've assumed from the outset (see Chapter 1), the claim is out of place for reasons given in Field 1994. If *ttruth* is our fundamental notion of truth, then it doesn't play an explanatory role in 'semantics'. (Of course, deflationists may allow 'truth conditions' in an appropriate sense, namely, the Tr-conditionals; but this, presumably, is not the sort of 'truth conditions' involved in traditional 'truth-conditional semantics'. Alternatively, deflationists may allow 'truth conditions' in an entirely heuristic sense, namely, *truth-in-a-model*, but this too is not likely to sit well with traditional truth-conditional semantics unless, implausibly, one takes there to be a unique model M such that α is true in M just if α is ttrue. But serious argument would be required to demand as much.)

I stand by the first reply, but another reply is available. The second reply is that, even if 'truth conditions' were constitutive of meaning—with such *truth-at-a-point* conditions taken in more than an instrumental fashion—the objection is not strong. After all, giving the 'truth conditions' of a connective is giving the *truth-at-a-point* conditions *for all relevant points whatsoever*. Let $\mathcal{W}$ comprise all points. For simplicity, let $\mathcal{S}$ be a *type* of $\mathcal{W}$-point, for any $\mathcal{S} \subseteq \mathcal{W}$. The aim of 'truth-conditional semantics' is to give *truth-at-x* conditions for every $x \in \mathcal{S}$, for every type $\mathcal{S}$. In 'normal-worlds semantics', such 'truth conditions' do not vary across different types; all types, at least with respect to the usual connectives, are treated the same. But this is just the usual run of things. There's nothing prohibiting the discovery of a conditional that has *different* truth-in-x conditions for different types $\mathcal{S}$. In *abnormal*-worlds semantics (or, more generally, 'multiple-world-type semantics'), this is exactly what happens. The point, though, is that, contrary to the objection, there's no reason to think that we are talking about different connectives. We've got one connective; it's just that, to give its *full* truth conditions, one needs to give different 'partial conditions' at various (different) types of points.

Objection: conditional and the hook. Field's conditional is intimately related to the hook. Yours isn't. For example, as in Chapter 4, Field's conditional gives us

1. $\alpha, \neg\beta \vdash \neg(\alpha \to \beta)$
2. $\alpha \supset \beta \vdash \alpha \to \beta$
3. $\alpha \lor \neg\alpha, \beta \lor \neg\beta \vdash (\alpha \supset \beta) \leftrightarrow (\alpha \to \beta)$

but none of these hold in your BX theory. Such a disconnect with the hook makes your conditional suspect.

Reply. It's true that none of these holds in my theory, but this is to be *expected*, and perhaps even *desired*. After all, the hook itself does not detach, given the glutty spandrels of *ttruth*. Since, unlike Field, I recognize the essentially exhaustive nature of negation, we should neither expect nor want something like (3), at least given the inevitable gluts. So, the force of this objection is not strong.

Perhaps it is worth noting that, while (2) and (3) are not achieved, (1) is achieved over a restricted fragment. Given the base-language restrictions in play (see Chapter 1), we do have (1); if one restricts models to those for which the base language is classical, then (1) holds over the given classical fragment.

Objection: restricted generalizations in BXTT. One of the chief motivations for your truth theory BXTT is that our truth predicate is nothing more than a see-through device introduced for practical, expressive purposes. Common— indeed, paradigm—examples of *ttruth* doing its job are restricted generalizations such as *everything Max said is ttrue*. Such common examples involve restricted-quantification claims like *All As are Bs*, where this appears to involve a conditional $\mapsto$ as in $\forall x(A(x) \mapsto B(x))$. The trouble is that the 'suitable conditional' in BXTT (viz., the BX conditional) is not suited to serve as the target 're-stricted conditional' $\mapsto$ (i.e., the conditional involved in restricted-quantification claims). In short, the BX conditional $\to$ is simply too strong for typical re-stricted generalizations. The BX conditional requires an all-worlds connection between antecedent and consequent: $\alpha \to \beta$ is true at a (normal) world just if there's no world at which α but not β is true. This sort of all-worlds connection is too strong for a restricted conditional; all As might be Bs at the actual world without *all worlds* having this connection.

Another way of seeing the problem with the BX conditional is to notice that a critical rule involved in common restricted generalizations is *Conditional Weakening*. Where $\mapsto$ is our target restricted conditional, Conditional Weakening (henceforth, CW) has the following form.

$$\text{CW.} \quad \beta \vdash \alpha \mapsto \beta$$

This rule is common when restricted generalizations are in play. For example, from *everything is B* it is common to infer that *all As are Bs*. This is invalid if $\mapsto$ is taken to be $\to$, our 'suitable conditional' in BXTT.

One might, of course, point to the hook $\alpha \supset \beta$, defined as $\neg\alpha \vee \beta$, as a candidate for $\mapsto$ (our required restricted conditional). This will give us CW, since we have the following in BXTT.

$$\beta \vdash \alpha \supset \beta$$

The trouble is that the hook fails to detach; it fails to satisfy MPP. (See Chapter 1.) And if we cannot detach from our restricted generalizations, it is difficult to see how they're useful. And if they're not generally useful, then it's far from clear why we should introduce *ttruth*—and, hence, its spandrels—for purposes of restricted generalizations!

The current objection, in short, is that BXTT's driving philosophical motivation stands in stark tension with its resources.[8] The philosophical motivation adverts to common generalizations involving *ttruth*. Such common generalizations involve restricted quantification, where this involves a 'restricted conditional' (as above). The BX conditional is too strong; it fails to deliver rules such as CW. The hook is sufficiently weaker, but it fails to detach in BXTT.

Reply. I agree that, given its philosophical motivation, BXTT requires an adequate restricted conditional.[9] In what follows, I offer three avenues of reply. Before doing so, it is worth setting some bare desiderata for the target restricted conditional. What we need, at a minimum, is a 'restricted conditional' that can be *non-trivially* added to BXTT. At the very least, we want the following, bare-minimum desiderata met.

d1. Modus Ponens (MPP). $\alpha, \alpha \mapsto \beta \vdash \beta$

d2. Conditional Weakening (CW). $\beta \vdash \alpha \mapsto \beta$

d3. No Contraposition. $\alpha \mapsto \beta \nvdash \neg\beta \mapsto \neg\alpha$.

d4. Non-triviality. We want a non-triviality proof for the resulting theory— namely, BXTT plus the restricted conditional, whatever it is.

One might want more than d1–d4, but I think that they serve as bare-minimum desiderata for any candidate restricted conditional, and so shall focus on these. With respect to d3, I should note that Contraposition, combined with MPP and CW and a glutty β, yields triviality. By CW and Contraposition we get

$$\beta \vdash \neg\beta \mapsto \neg\alpha$$

---

[8] I am grateful to Vann McGee, who, in correspondence, pressed a version of this objection.

[9] One might suggest, as Sam Butchart (2008) has done, that common restricted quantification involves a different sort of quantifier (viz., so-called binary quantifiers) instead of a 'restricted conditional' (as I'm calling it). If this is right, then it would provide an adequate reply to the current objection. But it must be done right, including avoiding Curry-like problems. (It is not known whether Butchart's own proposal avoids Curry-related problems, at least in the cited draft.) For now, I assume the fairly standard idea—at least in philosophical logic (though perhaps not linguistics)—that restricted generalizations involve a conditional (what I'll call a *restricted conditional*).

If, as we want, $\mapsto$ detaches, then a glutty β yields triviality: $\neg\alpha$ for all α. (If $\neg\alpha$ is ttrue for all α, then Double Negation Elimination, which we enjoy, gives the ttruth of *all* α.) So, our restricted conditional cannot contrapose. (Our BX suitable conditional contraposes and satisfies MPP, but it fails to satisfy d2, which 'failure' saves us from the given sort of triviality just mentioned but which 'failure' also drives the current search for a restricted conditional.)

With our bare desiderata d1–d4 in hand, I turn to three candidate restricted conditionals.

« *Parenthetical remark.* An option that I do not discuss here might be to add a version of the 'Melbourne conditional' discussed in Beall, Brady, Hazen, Priest and Restall 2006. (The conditional is so called due to its being the result of a Melbourne-based collaborative project.) This conditional gives us d1–d3 (and much else), but d4 remains open (as of the time of writing). As such, I set this option aside, leaving details to the cited paper. *End parenthetical.* »

» *Ackermann constant.* One option invokes the so-called Ackermann constant t (Anderson and Belnap, 1975). The idea, for present purposes, is to add t as a logical constant axiomatized via the two-way rule TR, namely,

TR. $\alpha \dashv\vdash t \to \alpha$

If we add TR to the logic, we get $\vdash t$ and, most importantly,

$$\beta \vdash t \wedge \alpha \to \beta$$

Hence, we can define our restricted conditional in terms of t as follows.

$$\alpha \mapsto \beta := \alpha \wedge t \to \beta$$

This is the approach that Graham Priest (2006*b*) endorses for his own (non-transparent) truth theory. Each of the desiderata d1–d3 is achieved, though I skip the proofs here.

What of desideratum d4, the non-triviality of the resulting theory? Let BXTT$^+$ be the theory that results from adding TR to BXTT. The question is whether BXTT$^+$ is non-trivial. That BXTT$^+$ is non-trivial may be established by showing that it is covered by a slight modification of the Chapter 2 (appendix) construction. I show as much below. *Note well: in what follows, talk of 'the construction' refers to the construction in the appendix to Chapter 2. Readers who skipped the Chapter 2 appendix should skip the following proof!*

» *The proof (sketch).* The strategy is to add a semantic-value constant b to the language, where b gets its face-value value (viz., $\frac{1}{2}$) everywhere, and then interpret our (Ackermann) constant t via b. (The constant, then, preserves the requisite monotonicity of the construction, viz., M below.)

In what follows, ν_i^* is a (Kripke) fixed point of base model ν_i. I reserve ν_κ for the least fixed point of the construction, and so $\nu_\kappa^* = \nu_\kappa = \nu_{\kappa+1}$ for the given (transparent) model. Recall from Chapters 1–2 (appendices) that the proof that ν_κ^* exists relies on the following monotonicity.

$$\text{M.} \quad i \le j \text{ implies } \nu_i^* \preceq \nu_j^*$$

The proof of M, as noted in Chapter 2 (appendix), relies on a particular ground model ν_0. (More generally: the proof relies on the right sort of ground model, but I simply assume the ground model ν_0.) The ground model ν_0 is the standard model for the arithmetic fragment;[10] ν_0 assigns $\frac{1}{2}$ to all conditionals and sentences of the form $Tr(n)$ where n is the code of a sentence, and assigns $Tr(n)$ to 0 where n is not the code of a sentence.

In what follows, $\Rightarrow$ is the RM_3 conditional (see Chapter 2 appendix). Recall that the *reset rule for conditionals*, for ordinals $j > 0$, is as follows.

$$\nu_j(\alpha \to \beta) = \begin{cases} 1 & \text{if } \forall i < j\,[\nu_i^*(\alpha) \Rightarrow \nu_i^*(\beta)] = 1 \\ 0 & \text{if } \exists i < j\,[\nu_i^*(\alpha) \Rightarrow \nu_i^*(\beta)] = 0 \\ \frac{1}{2} & \text{otherwise.} \end{cases}$$

The following two facts are useful.

F1. The value of $b \Rightarrow v$ is v for all $v \in \{1, \frac{1}{2}, 0\}$, where $\Rightarrow$ is RM_3.

F2. $\nu_i^*(b) = \frac{1}{2}$ for all i.

Applying F1 and F2 to the *reset rule for conditionals* (see above) implies what we may call the *b-relative reset rule*, namely, where $j > 0$

$$\nu_j(b \to \beta) = \begin{cases} 1 & \text{if } \forall i < j\,[\nu_i^*(\beta) = 1] \\ 0 & \text{if } \exists i < j\,[\nu_i^*(\beta) = 0] \\ \frac{1}{2} & \text{otherwise.} \end{cases}$$

This reset rule is really the only one that matters for the following proof that BXTT$^+$ is non-trivial. The proof is as follows.

1. Let t be b in the construction (i.e., interpret constant t as our constant b).

2. Prove: TR holds in ν_κ^*, i.e. $\nu_\kappa^*(\alpha) \in \{1, \frac{1}{2}\}$ iff $\nu_\kappa^*(\text{t} \to \alpha) \in \{1, \frac{1}{2}\}$.

   (a) LRD. We prove the contrapositive. By the *b*-relative reset rule, if $\nu_\kappa(b \to \alpha) = 0$ then $\nu_i^*(\alpha) = 0$ for some $i < \kappa$. Principle M tells us that if $i < \kappa$ then $\nu_i^* \preceq \nu_\kappa^*$, and so $\nu_\kappa^*(\alpha) = 0$. Hence, the LRD of TR holds in fixed point ν_κ.[11]

---

[10] Recall that, to make things easier, I am using the language of arithmetic rather than set theory, and assuming a truth predicate $Tr(x)$ rather than $\in$.

[11] Reed Solomon notes that one cannot strengthen TR to $\nu_\kappa(\alpha) = \nu_\kappa(b \to \alpha)$. To see this, let $\nu_0^*(\alpha) = \frac{1}{2}$ and $\nu_\kappa(\alpha) = 1$. One can then show that $\nu_\kappa(b \to \alpha) = \frac{1}{2}$, in which case $\nu_\kappa(\alpha) \ne \nu_\kappa(b \to \alpha)$. This also bears against strengthening TR to conditional form—e.g., replacing the turnstile with the arrow.

(b) RLD. We invoke the fact that κ is a fixed point of the construction, that is, that $\nu_\kappa^* = \nu_\kappa = \nu_{\kappa+1}$. Assume, towards proving the contrapositive, that $\nu_\kappa^*(\alpha) = 0$. By the b-relative reset rule, $\nu_{\kappa+1}(b \to \alpha) = 0$. But, then, since κ is a fixed point of the construction, $\nu_\kappa(b \to \alpha) = 0$, and hence $\nu_\kappa^*(b \to \alpha) = 0$.[12]

So, we have non-triviality for BXTT$^+$, and hence have not only our desiderata d1–d3 but also desideratum d4. This seems to provide at least one viable option for accommodating restricted generalizations in the overall transparent truth theory. What is worth noting, however, is that there is also another option—a hook-like descendant—that is already available in BXTT.

» *Hook-like descendant.* Consider the hook, namely, $\alpha \supset \beta$ defined as $\neg\alpha \vee \beta$. This would be nice for restricted quantification if it only detached, but it doesn't detach in the logic of BXTT. (See Chapter 2.) Still, it is worth considering a hook-like option. The hook itself is true (at a point) just if one of the following disjuncts is true (at the point).

» $\alpha \wedge \beta$
» $\neg\alpha \wedge \beta$
» $\neg\alpha \wedge \neg\beta$

The hook fails to detach due to the third case, which is satisfied even when α is glutty but β 'just false'. (In the formal picture: we can have $@ \models \neg\alpha \wedge \neg\beta$ and $@ \models \alpha$ but $@ \not\models \beta$.)

What is surprising is that a fairly simple tweak gives us a detachable, hook-like conditional. In what follows, I discuss the hook-like descendant in BXTT.

Let $\bot$ be any unsatisfiable sentence, say '1 = 0', so that $@ \not\models \bot$ for all relevant models. (Recall that, as developed in Chapters 1–2, the theory has such sentences; the restricted account in §1.5.4 'kicks out' any would-be BX models that have the semantic-free fragment of the language glutty at $@$.) Now, define our restricted conditional $\alpha \mapsto \beta$ along hook lines but with a tweak in the third case.

$$\alpha \mapsto \beta := (\alpha \wedge \beta) \vee (\neg\alpha \wedge \beta) \vee (\neg\alpha \wedge \neg\beta \wedge (\alpha \wedge \neg\alpha \to \bot))$$

Our restricted conditional, then, is true at a point just if at least one of r1–r3 is true at the point.

r1. $\alpha \wedge \beta$
r2. $\neg\alpha \wedge \beta$
r3. $\neg\alpha \wedge \neg\beta \wedge (\alpha \wedge \neg\alpha \to \bot)$

The only difference with the hook comes at r3. This might look a bit kludgey, but it delivers d1–d4 as follows. (Recall that, in the formal picture, validity is defined only over all base or 'actual' worlds of all models.)

---

[12] A simpler proof of the RLD of TR arises from the facts that $\nu_\kappa^*(b) = \frac{1}{2}$ and that 'detachment' of $\to$ holds in ν_κ^*, that is, that if $\nu_\kappa^*(\alpha)$ and $\nu_\kappa^*(\alpha \to \beta)$ are designated, so is $\nu_\kappa^*(\beta)$.

d1. MPP: suppose $@ \models \alpha$ and $@ \models \alpha \mapsto \beta$. Suppose, for reductio, that $@ \not\models \beta$, in which case we're dealing with r3. Since r3 requires $@ \models \neg\alpha$, we have $@ \models \alpha \wedge \neg\alpha$. But, then, we have a point (viz., $@$) at which $\alpha \wedge \neg\alpha$ is true but $\perp$ not. (Recall that $\perp$ is unsatisfiable.) Hence, $@ \not\models \alpha \wedge \neg\alpha \rightarrow \perp$. But this is impossible.

d2. CW: suppose $@ \models \beta$. Since $@ \models \alpha$ or $@ \models \neg\alpha$, we get either r1 or r2. Either way, we get CW.

d3. Contraposition fails in cases you expect, namely, when you've got a glut in the works. Consider the following.

» $@ \models \alpha$ and $@^{\star} \models \alpha$
» $@ \models \beta$ and $@^{\star} \not\models \beta$ (so β is glutty at $@$)
» Hence, $@ \models \alpha \wedge \beta$ and, so, $@ \models \alpha \mapsto \beta$.
» But since $@ \not\models \neg\alpha$, we have $@ \models \neg\beta \mapsto \neg\alpha$ only if we also have $@ \models \neg\neg\beta \wedge \neg\neg\alpha \wedge (\neg\beta \wedge \neg\neg\beta \rightarrow \perp)$, which we don't have.

d4. We have non-triviality for the resulting theory, since the resulting theory is simply BXTT (for which, as in Chapter 2, we have non-triviality).

So, the hook-like connective gives us our bare desiderata d1–d4.

A notable—and prima facie awkward—feature of the conditional is failure of (Conditional) Identity.

$$\not\vdash \alpha \mapsto \alpha$$

Identity fails due to spandrels of *ttruth* that are actually not true but are glutty at certain abnormal (though non-trivial) points. (Consider, e.g., a sentence γ that says $\neg\gamma \wedge (\gamma \wedge \neg\gamma \rightarrow \perp)$.) With the loss of Identity, we similarly lose (Conditional) Simplification.

$$\not\vdash \alpha \wedge \beta \mapsto \beta$$

Accordingly, it fails to be a matter of logic alone that, for example, *all cats are cats* or *all black cats are cats*, at least if such claims employ the given hook-like descendant.

While the noted 'failures' are prima facie problematic for the given hook-like conditional qua candidate for restricted conditional, I think that the problem is not serious. We *can* truly say things like *all cats are cats* and so on; it's just that, as above, such claims are not true as a matter of logic alone. But it seems to me that we wanted a conditional that doesn't require a logical or, more simply, all-worlds connection between antecedent and consequent; we wanted something much closer to the hook—something we have with the hook-like descendant. Moreover, if we want to assert *logically true* claims like *all cats are cats* or *all black cats are cats*, we can use our 'suitable conditional' (the BX conditional) for which both $\forall x(Cx \rightarrow Cx)$ and $\forall x(Bx \wedge Cx \rightarrow Cx)$ are valid. In the end, then, the noted 'failures' may be addressed by recognizing another hook-like conditional already in BXTT. In particular, where $\mapsto$ is our r1–r3 conditional above and $\rightarrow$ our 'suitable' BX conditional, we define $\hookrightarrow$ as follows.

$$\alpha \hookrightarrow \beta := (\alpha \mapsto \beta) \vee (\alpha \rightarrow \beta)$$

Not only does this satisfy d1–d4, but—in virtue of the right disjunct—it also satisfies Identity and Simplification.

» *Simple Addition* There is one more option that not only yields all of the desiderata, but is also both more general and simpler than the options discussed above.[13] As with the hook-like descendent (above), we define our restricted conditional $\mapsto$ out of resources already available in BXTT. The notable difference is that we needn't invoke anything beyond disjunction and our BX conditional $\rightarrow$. In particular, we define $\mapsto$ without invoking $\perp$ (or the need to add t or etc.); we define it via simple addition.

$$\alpha \mapsto \beta := (\alpha \rightarrow \beta) \vee \beta$$

Immediately, the desiderata are satisfied. (Recall that, in the formal picture, validity is defined only over all base or 'actual' worlds of all models.)

d1. MPP: suppose $@ \models \alpha$ and $@ \models \alpha \mapsto \beta$, in which case either $@ \models \alpha \rightarrow \beta$ or $@ \models \beta$. In the former case, we detach to get what we want, viz., $@ \models \beta$, which is what we already have in the latter case.

d2. CW: suppose $@ \models \beta$. Addition (and commutation of disjunction) gives $@ \models (\alpha \rightarrow \beta) \vee \beta$.

d3. Contraposition fails. The Chapter 2 non-triviality proof for BXTT establishes as much, given that $\mapsto$ satisfies MPP and CW; however, a simple countermodel is the following.

» $@ \models \alpha$ and $@^\star \models \alpha$
» $@ \models \beta$ and $@^\star \not\models \beta$ (so β is glutty at $@$)
» Hence, $@ \not\models \alpha \rightarrow \beta$ since $@^\star \models \alpha$ but $@^\star \not\models \beta$, and so Contraposition for $\rightarrow$ (or just that $@ \models \neg\beta$ but $@ \not\models \neg\alpha$) gives that $@ \not\models \neg\beta \rightarrow \neg\alpha$.
» This is a model in which $(\alpha \rightarrow \beta) \vee \beta$ is true but $(\neg\beta \rightarrow \neg\alpha) \vee \neg\alpha$ not true, and hence in which $\alpha \mapsto \beta$ is true but $\neg\beta \mapsto \neg\alpha$ untrue.

d4. We have non-triviality for the resulting theory, since the resulting theory is simply BXTT (for which, as in Chapter 2, we have non-triviality).

Also notable, in contrast with the hook-like descendent, is that this approach enjoys features of Simplification and, in turn, Identity: $\vdash \alpha \wedge \beta \mapsto \beta$ and $\vdash \alpha \mapsto \alpha$. (Proofs go via the given features of the BX conditional, and in turn Addition, i.e., $\alpha \vdash \alpha \vee \beta$, after which the current proposal is named.)

---

[13] I am particularly grateful to Greg Restall for discussion that led to this simplification, and also to Graham Priest and Ross Brady, and to participants at the 2008 World Congress of Paraconsistency IV in Melbourne.

Hence, the simple-addition conditional, which is simpler and more general than the other discussed options, is another prima facie adequate candidate for our restricted conditional. (On generality, note that the proposal should also work in Field's non-paraconsistent, paracomplete theory. See Chapter 4.)

Summing up: the current objection is met if either we can non-trivially extend BXTT to a theory that enjoys a 'restricted conditional' or, perhaps contrary to initial appearances, we already have a restricted conditional in BXTT. The foregoing reply shows that both options are viable: we already have a restricted conditional in BXTT (in fact, at least two), but we can also non-trivially extend BXTT to BXTT$^+$.

5.4   Base-language gluts?

This section takes up a few objections to the 'modest' or conservative aspect of my position according to which our base language (free of 'ttrue' and related notions like 'true of', 'denotes', etc.) is classical.

Objection: legal gluts.   Priest (2006*b*) has argued that there are gluts in our base language that arise not from spandrels of *ttruth* (or related notions) but, rather, from the way legislatures actually work. In a recent synopsis, Priest puts the matter as follows.

> Consider, for example, the argument based on legal contradictions. A duly constituted legislature passes a law to the effect that anyone in category A has the right to vote, but nobody in category B has the right to vote. Maybe there was no reasonable expectation at the time that someone in both categories was possible. But suppose that such a person does then turn up. Until the law is changed, that person both does and does not have the right to vote. The issues here are simpler and much less technical than those involved in the paradoxes of self reference. For that reason, I think, it is much harder to object to the argument. Moreover, the basis of the contradiction—fiat—is transparent. There are no deep metaphysical complications. (Priest, 2007)

Pending a response to this sort of all-too-common situation, it looks as if you are stuck with gluts in the base language—gluts that have nothing to do with the spandrels of *ttruth* or related notions.

Reply.   I admit that this is a common phenomenon, but I think that, contrary to Priest, the phenomenon is not one that requires countenancing base-language gluts. What we have, in such cases, is exactly what Priest says: *according to legislative body* X, those in category A have the right to vote but those in B do not have the right to vote. But this, I suggest, is not a contradiction. The 'according to X' is essential to laws, and—importantly—the 'according to X' does not enjoy appropriate Release features. In particular, letting $\mathbb{A}_X$ be our 'according to X' operator, we do *not* have

$$\text{Release for } \mathbb{A}_X\colon \quad \mathbb{A}_X(\alpha) \text{ implies } \alpha$$

If $\mathbb{A}_X$ did enjoy Release, then Priest's example wouldn't require an agent unexpectedly sitting in $A \cap B$. Just witness Australia and the USA. According to

Australian law, it's illegal to drive on the right. According to USA law, it's legal to drive on the right. We don't infer a glut—namely, that it's legal and not legal to drive on the right—because we do not take the legal 'according to' operators to Release. Argument that such operators do Release is required.

Priest might reply that if, instead of having two different legislative bodies (e.g., Oz and US), we have only one such body, then Release is more plausible; but I do not see any reason to think it more plausible. Indeed, it is precisely in *fiat*-determined matters that Release is in question. Fiction is fiat-determined, much as laws. The latter have more practical weight, but the fiat-drivenness is much the same in both cases. And in both cases, Release is generally dubious (at best).

Pending good reason to think that Release is in force in such legal (or similar) cases, I maintain that the argument for 'legal gluts' fails to generate base-language gluts.

« *Parenthetical remark.* I admit that if God made the relevant laws, the situation might be different. The 'according to God', in such a case, might well Release. But I think that serious argument is required to run this line towards legal, base-language gluts. (I'm confident that Priest himself would not run this theological line.)

Secretaries Liberation. I should also note that I give the same response with respect to Chihara's 'Secretary Liberation Club' (1979). For any such club, the rules are embedded in an 'according to' operator that fails to Release. (According to this Club, x is a member of the club just if x is a secretary who is not allowed to join clubs of which x is a member.) An alternative response, for those who think (for what reason?) that the relevant operator Releases in this particular case, is to accept that the club cannot have a secretary. This reply would probably bar a 'functionalist' approach to *secretaries* (wherein 'secretary' is defined by functional role), but I leave the matter there. *End parenthetical.* »

Objection: motion and change. Priest has argued that physical motion, which is plainly not in the 'merely semantic' realm, is inconsistent. (For his latest discussion of this, see Priest 2006*b*.) Priest advocates something along a Hegelian account of motion, where, in Hegel's words—as Priest (2006*b*, p. 175) quotes—the basic idea is that

> motion itself is contradiction's immediate existence. Something moves not because at one moment of time it is here and at another there, but because at one and the same moment it is here and not here ...

Priest argues that something (exact details aside) along the Hegelian, inconsistent account of motion should be endorsed over the more standard, Russellian account, where, in Russell's words—as Priest (2006*b*, p. 173) quotes—the basic account is that

> [m]otion consists in the fact that, by the occupation of a place at a time, a correlation is established between places and times; when different times, throughout any period, however short, are correlated with different places, there is motion;

when different times throughout some period, however short, are all correlated with the same place, there is rest.

While Priest acknowledges that the received, Russellian account is in line with the current scientific account, he nonetheless argues that the account faces a serious problem brought out by Zeno's paradox of the arrow. (This is directly related to the other objection that Priest mentions concerning 'an intrinsic state of motion'. For the sake of brevity, I focus only on the arrow objection, which is easier to specify concisely, and is also what Priest takes to be the stronger objection.)

Zeno's arrow paradox, in short, involves (say) the point of an arrow in uniform motion—a journey—from one point to another point. At each instant of the arrow's motion, the arrow makes no progress towards its destination point, since progress requires more than an instant of time. But the temporal period of the journey is made up of such progress-less instants. Hence, the arrow never makes progress on its journey to the (say) target. Absurd.

The standard, Russellian reply involves rejecting the final step from *that at each instant the arrow fails to make progress* to *that the arrow makes no progress*. The (alleged) problem is that rejecting the given step is too implausible. Priest puts the chief objection in a rhetorical question:

> How can going somewhere be composed of an aggregate of going nowheres? (Priest, 2006b, p. 175)

The trouble, according to Priest, is not in the standard mathematics behind the Russellian account (involving standard measure functions for length of sets of points); it is the (allegedly) loud clash with fundamental philosophical 'intuitions' about motion (and change, more generally). As Priest puts it,

> That one can prove a small mathematical theorem or two is one thing; but it does not ease the discomfort that one finds (or at least, that I find) when one tries to understand what is going on physically, when one tries to understand how the arrow actually achieves its motion. At any point in its motion it advances not at all. Yet, in some apparently magical way, in a collection of these [individual points of advancing not at all] it advances. Now a sum of nothings, even infinitely many nothings, is nothing. So how does it do it? (Priest, 2006b, p. 175)

If Priest is right, then your 'merely semantic inconsistency' is far too narrow since there will be base-language gluts (concerning motion).

Reply.   My reply is fairly straightforward. To begin, I am inclined to leave motion—like much (though not all) else—to science. The Russellian account (or something in the vicinity) sits naturally with current science of motion. Of course, some scientific theories are unintuitive, but 'intuition', especially about the physical world, sometimes needs to be re-schooled. Motion and change may well be cases in which re-schooling is required. With Russell, I do not share the basic 'intuition' to which Priest's objection appeals—namely, that motion requires an aggregate of going somewheres (as it were)—but, if I did, I would think re-schooling along Russellian lines advisable.[14] Indeed, I think that the guiding 'intuition' has problems on its own.

The principal intuition behind Priest's objection(s) is that, as he puts it, 'a sum of nothings ... is nothing' (2006*b*, p. 175). On the surface, this is plainly wrong if 'sum' is used along the lines of 'collection' (as it seems to be in the context). After all, a collection of nothing is nonetheless a collection, which is something. Of course, 'a sum of nothings ... is nothing' is (probably) just a catchier way of putting the target intuition cited above: namely, that going somewhere must be composed of 'going somewheres' (or, perhaps, of somethings other than 'going nowheres'). However the intuition be put, it seems to be one that ought be put away—re-schooled. Consider, for example, the all-too-common 'intuition' that intelligence cannot be the 'sum' of unintelligence. 'How can intelligence be composed of an aggregate of unintelligence?', one might (rhetorically) ask. More directly: a sum of dim bulbs is at most dim.

The analogy, of course, is slightly exaggerated, but I think that it is on target. It is difficult to see what is special about the motion case that is lacking in cases like (e.g.) evolution or the mind in particular. More generally, we have learned that many 'intuitions' about composition-like—or aggregation-like—principles are simply unfounded in reality in general. I think that the composition-like intuition to which Priest points is similarly unfounded. At the very least, I think it a prima facie likely candidate for re-schooling.

Objection: unified approach. Field's paracomplete framework provides a unified response to both vagueness (and soritical paradox) and the *ttruth*-theoretic paradoxes. Unless you're willing to sanction base-language gluts, your theory simply forbids such a unified approach. This would seem to be a defect of your approach.

Reply. While some philosophers (Colyvan, 2009; Hyde, 1997; Priest, 2008; Routley, 1992) have advocated a dialetheic approach to vagueness, I don't. Moreover, I do not see the prima facie attraction—let alone desideratum—of a unified approach to both soritical and *ttruth*-theoretic paradoxes. The latter arise from spandrels of our logical devices (or 'semantic' notions); the former arise, as I've suggested (see §5.2), from conflating negation with something else. Even if I'm wrong about the prospects of a (non-epistemic) classical response to the sorites, the connection between the sorites and *ttruth*-theoretic paradoxes is very far from clear. Admittedly, if, unlike me, one rejects the essential exhaustiveness of negation, then it might be prima facie attractive to approach both vagueness and *ttruth*-theoretic paradox as phenomena that arise out of negation's less than

---

[14]Notably, as Priest (2006*b*, p. 173) points out, Russell himself is happy enough in rejecting an 'intrinsic state of motion', and indeed suggests that thinking—or perhaps 'intuiting'—otherwise is responsible for quagmires in the philosophy of change. While, with Russell, I lack the driving intuition behind Priest's charge, I am largely neutral on whether it is the causal source of philosophical quagmire.

exhaustive behavior. But if, like me, one accepts the exhaustiveness of negation, there seems to be no obvious reason to treat vagueness and *ttruth*-theoretic paradox the same way—at least as far as I can see.

5.5   Orthodoxy: Priestly dialetheism

For those unfamiliar with Graham Priest's work, beyond the mere slogan 'true contradictions', it is worthwhile briefly highlighting the chief differences between Priest's dialetheic theory and my own. Some of the differences and some of the similarities have been indicated throughout this chapter and the book at large, but I hope it useful to put together a few salient differences in one spot. Instead of doing 'objections and replies' here, let me simply close by highlighting points of difference. My hope is that, in some ways, this closing section will serve to summarize highlights of my own position, and not only contrast them with the 'orthodox', Priestly dialetheism with much of which I agree, and to all of which I owe a great deal.

My aim is not to go through all of the detailed differences, but rather only point to a few salient ones. I should warn that Priest might reject my characterization of our differences—and, indeed, might point to more than I'm highlighting. In the end, the best way to compare the positions is to turn to Priest's work (2006*b*). That said, the following gives a snapshot of *some* of the differences as I see them.

5.5.1   *Philosophical, in general*

Perhaps one of the 'big' differences is largely philosophical. Priest's dialetheism, as I see it, stems from a recognition of 'possible gluts' in general. Indeed, Priest has long recognized even the 'possibility' of trivialism, a 'world', however impossible, in which everything is true. If one recognizes the possibility of gluts, in general, then the thought that some sentences are actually glutty is a natural course to follow. And Priest has followed the course, not only with respect to truth theory (on which more below), but on other matters—indeed, as indicated above, even in the base language (free of 'true' and the like).

I am not sure how to argue against such a liberal (or, from Priest's perspective, liberated) position; I simply do not share it. I do not accept gluts out of a prior acknowledgement of their possibility. Instead, I see them as arising, for the most part, out of our own doing. As in Chapter 1, we could have done without *ttruth* but it would have been a practical burden. Once we brought in the device, spandrels—in concert with the 'prior' logic (and notably exhaustive negation)—dragged in gluts. They were forced on us by the see-through device that we enjoy.

Once we have our gluts, we acknowledge the possibility of gluts. Need we now recognize the possibility of *base-language gluts*—let alone trivialism? On this point, I stand with most theorists and give a negative answer. Priest's arguments for base-language gluts are to be taken seriously, but I do not take them to establish their goal.

There is more to say, but it might be better to turn to slightly more concrete matters. Let me turn to a few truth-related points.

5.5.2   *Truth: philosophical*

Priest endorses a 'teleological' conception of truth, according to which truth is the aim of assertion. This needn't be a 'substantive' account of truth (whatever, in the end, that might mean), but it is certainly a conception that goes beyond the 'transparent conception' that, in the spirit of methodological disquotationalism, I've advocated. For example, on my conception, *ttruth* is simply a constructed, logical device introduced for practical convenience—expressive convenience, but practical convenience nonetheless. There's no property in the world that 'ttrue' was introduced to name. On Priest's conception, 'true' was introduced to name an important property, namely, *telos of assertion*. This might seem like a minor difference, but, as developed by Priest, it generates a very different dialetheic theory from the 'transparent' one advocated here. At the very least, there is a logical difference that emerges.

5.5.3   *Truth: logical*

The difference in philosophical conception brings about a difference in logic of truth. For me, negation and 'ttrue' essentially commute, since the predicate is simply see-through. For Priest, this isn't so. In particular, where $T(x)$ is his truth predicate, Priest rejects that

$$T(\ulcorner \neg \alpha \urcorner) \rightarrow \neg T(\ulcorner \alpha \urcorner)$$

holds for all α. Since Priest's theory, like mine (and Field's), enjoys the T-schema, Priest's suitable conditional, which differs from BX, fails to contrapose.

Contraposition is contestable, and I shall not dwell on that issue. The current issue concerns the behavior of Priest's truth predicate and its interaction with negation. Since, on my theory, truth is transparent, we certainly get the equivalence of $Tr(\ulcorner \neg \alpha \urcorner)$ and $\neg Tr(\ulcorner \alpha \urcorner)$. As above, Priest rejects this. Why? This brings out a methodological difference that, in the end, goes back to the different conception(s) of truth.

5.5.4   *Truth: methodological*

According to Priest, we should not multiply contradictions beyond necessity (Priest, 2006*b*). I agree with the principle in general, but disagree with Priest's application. According to Priest, if $T(\ulcorner \neg \alpha \urcorner)$ implied $\neg T(\ulcorner \alpha \urcorner)$, then we would have gluts galore: every glut $T(\ulcorner \alpha \urcorner) \wedge T(\ulcorner \neg \alpha \urcorner)$ would yield another glut, namely, $T(\ulcorner \alpha \urcorner) \wedge \neg T(\ulcorner \alpha \urcorner)$. This is correct, but the application makes sense only if one takes truth to be more than our see-through device *ttruth*. If, as on my position, truth is transparent (viz., our see-through device *ttruth*), then $Tr(\ulcorner \neg \alpha \urcorner)$ and $\neg Tr(\ulcorner \alpha \urcorner)$ are logically the same with respect to consequences. One ought not, as far as I can see, try to rid the virtues of *ttruth* in the name of Ockham-like concerns.

5.5.5 *Dialetheism: rationally mandated*

There are other, detailed points of both logical and philosophical difference; however, I shall close with one conspicuous philosophical difference between Priest's
(philosophical) position and my own. The point concerns truth, once again.

As I understand him, Priest (2006*b*) thinks that dialetheism is rationally
forced upon us. Some of the arguments come from non-truth-related topics, but
the strongest argument (at least in my opinion) concerns truth. With respect
to truth, Priest thinks that dialetheism is rationally mandated. On this, I am
not so sure. Priest is right in one sense: inasmuch as there are gluts (hence,
true gluts), and rationality mandates acceptance of truth, then dialetheism is
rationally forced upon us. With that, I agree. On the other hand, I think that
the matter is much less clear than Priest seems to think. In particular, I think
that dialetheism is rationally mandated only given our practical decision to enjoy
ttruth. Again, as in Chapter 1 (and above), we could have lived without the
device; it just would have been rather inconvenient. Given that we have it, we
have gluts. But this is different from the way that Priest sees the matter.

For Priest—at least on my understanding—one's conception of truth, so long
as it's arguably a conception of *truth*, is really neither here nor there. (I ignore
conceptions that impose ad hoc restrictions against gluts. This isn't at issue.)
Priest—perhaps with many philosophers—thinks that, whatever it may be, truth
plays Capture and Release, at least in rule form (i.e., RC and RR). This, as mentioned in §5.3, is highly questionable. Granted, traditional truth theorists have
typically said that the given property—correspondence, coherence, whatnot—
yields CC and CR (i.e., *T*-biconditionals) or, at the very least, RC and RR. But if
the given property is some natural property in the world, it's not obvious that one
can easily generalize from a few (normal) cases to all cases; it may well be that
the property of correspondence (whatever it is!) fails to yield RC and RR across
the board, especially for certain oddities like the paradoxical sentences. Indeed,
traditional truth theorists, as Priest himself will acknowledge, have rarely offered
a plausible story on the paradoxes. Perhaps the right story, for such properties,
is that RC and RR are not ultimately valid; they hold only over some restricted
front.

Against this, one might say that any such rejection of RC and CC, especially
if done in the face of paradoxes, is simply an ad hoc rejection of gluts. This
might be the story, but it might not be. My point is that, when it comes to
properties in the world, generalization from normal cases might well go wrong.
Despite the long tradition of simply assuming RC and RR for various (alleged)
properties of truth, it seems to me to be a genuinely open matter as to whether
such properties (whatever they are) really do yield RC and RR.

If this is right (and I think that it is, though I am not sure), then the rational
mandate of dialetheism is questionable—at least as far as the truth-theoretic
issues are concerned.

The situation is very different with *ttruth*. Here, there's no question about
RC and RR, at least if we have $\alpha \vdash \alpha$. (Similarly, there's no question about CC

and CR if we have $\vdash \alpha \rightarrow \alpha$.) After all, at least on my conception, *ttruth* was *constructed to be see-through*; it was brought in to satisfy TP over the whole (resulting) language. That's the job of the device; that's what it does. Inasmuch as we have it in a language with the basic logical features that we enjoy, we have gluts. Is dialetheism thereby *rationally mandated* for truth-theoretic reasons? Well, as above, the answer is 'yes and no'. Yes: given that we have the device (in a language such as we have), we have gluts, and rationality mandates that we embrace the ttruth. No: if we got rid of the device, it is not clear that any remaining *truth*-theoretic reasons would yield gluts.

APPENDIX A

OVERLAP WITHOUT INCONSISTENCY?

This is an alternative approach that I considered but eventually rejected on the grounds that it wasn't as natural as the modest dialetheic route proposed in this book. This appendix, which offers an improvement on Beall 2006*a* (from which some of this appendix is directly drawn), simply lays out the idea without further discussion. The improvement is in §A.2, but the background from Beall 2006*a* sets the stage. I should note that the approach sketched (and merely sketched) here deviates from the account that I've endorsed in this book. I include it here only as an option that others might explore.

The background aim of the following approach(es) is to have a paracomplete, *non-paraconsistent* theory in which we have 'exhaustive characterization' (see Chapter 4), but we reject that the characterization is to be done in terms of ttruth. Indeed, we reject that the sentences (mainly, paradoxical spandrels) 'beyond ttruth and tfalsity' are to be characterized in any significant way at all. The idea is overlap without inconsistency.

« *Parenthetical remark.* One related project is to take Field's framework and impose a 'coverall' *determinately* operator 'on top', one that implies all others, and satisfies Excluded Middle. This will require overlap of the sort discussed here, but it may well be able to avoid inconsistency. Details of this project are yet to be worked out. *End parenthetical.* »

A.1 Philosophical picture: paranormal

What the Liar (and its ilk) teaches us is that besides the ttrue sentences and tfalse sentences, there are paranormal sentences. One might now wonder: what is it to be a 'paranormal' sentence?

The suggestion is that we set the question aside. For present purposes, it suffices merely to 'tag' the target sentences (e.g., Liars) as such, namely, as *paranormal*. Ultimately, there may well be no interesting property of *being paranormal*, and accordingly no hope of informative 'analysis' or explication of 'paranormal'. But the term may nonetheless serve to give us the sort of 'exhaustive characterization' desired, just by giving us a 'logical device' of sorts with which to 'classify' the target sentences. My suggestion is that we resist questions concerning 'the nature' of paranormals, seeing it merely as a tag (a logical category) introduced for the target sentences.

Notice that even at this stage—without giving much more than a 'classifying role' for the device—Liar phenomena already arise.

√ The ticked sentence in §A.1 is either not ttrue or paranormal.

And such a sentence itself is surely among the very sort for which we introduced the tag 'paranormal', and indeed the usual Liar reasoning will suggest as much given the relevant version of EC (see §4.1): namely, that every sentence (hence, the ticked one) is ttrue, tfalse (true negation), or paranormal.

The upshot is that *paranormality and ttruth apparently overlap*. And my suggestion is that we simply accept as much. After all, we want a simple, exhaustive characterization, one that is consistent. And we can enjoy as much by acknowledging that some paranormal sentences—just in virtue of the role of 'paranormal' and the basic expressive job of 'ttrue'—turn out to be ttrue.

Likewise, of course, various paranormal sentences will inevitably be tfalse, for example,

⋆ The starred sentence in §A.1 is not paranormal.

If we have it—via the relevant version of EC—that the starred sentence is ttrue, tfalse, or paranormal, then it's ttrue iff not paranormal (and, so, not ttrue and paranormal). So, the sentence (just reasoning intuitively, at the moment) is paranormal, and so. . . a tfalse paranormal.

One might press for analysis or explication: what is it to *be* paranormal?! The suggestion is that we resist the question. Truth itself (at least on a suitably deflationary conception) affords little by way of informative analysis. On the usual picture, we began with our Tr-free fragment and had no problems except expressive ones due to our finite limitations. We could neither implicitly nor explicitly assert everything that we wanted to assert. Towards that end, our 'ttruth'-device was introduced. But once 'ttrue' was introduced (into the grammatical environment of English), various unintended sentences emerged—typical Liars and so on. Towards 'classifying' *those* sentences, 'paranormal' is introduced. But given the job of 'paranormal', there's little reason to expect—let alone demand—an informative analysis. Indeed, as is evident, there is even less to say about 'paranormal' than 'ttrue'.[1]

Notice that by allowing 'overlap' between the paranormal and the ttruths, we thereby avoid the need to invoke infinitely many (non-unifiable) 'stronger truth' predicates. Once 'paranormal' is introduced, unintended by-products of it emerge—*this sentence is paranormal*, etc. The suggestion is that we simply let such sentences be among the paranormal, even though—given the role and rules of 'ttrue'—they may likewise be ttrue. (Similarly for 'tfalse'.) If our chief concern is to 'exhaustively characterize' or 'classify' in a *consistent* and *simple* way, then such overlap is harmless, provided that 'ttrue' and 'tfalse' avoid overlap.

There are undoubtedly philosophical issues to be sorted out, but they must wait for another time. For now, I briefly turn to a simple, formal sketch of the idea.

---

[1]But see §A.1.2 for an alternative picture.

A.1.1 *A formal picture*

The picture is along familiar many-valued lines. Our 'semantic values' (in the *formal story*) are elements of $\mathcal{V} = \{1, \frac{3}{4}, \frac{1}{2}, \frac{1}{4}, 0\}$, with designated elements in $\{1, \frac{3}{4}\}$. Logical consequence—semantic validity—is defined as usual in terms of designated values. I skip the definition here.

Our atomics are interpreted via a function ν in the usual way, extended to compounds along familiar lines: $\nu(\alpha \wedge \beta)$ is the minimum of $\nu(\alpha)$ and $\nu(\beta)$, and $\nu(\alpha \vee \beta)$ the maximum. (Quantifiers can be treated similarly, as generalized conjunction and disjunction.) Negation is likewise familiar: $\nu(\neg\alpha) = 1 - \nu(\alpha)$. Hence, negation is fixed at $\frac{1}{2}$ but otherwise toggles designated and undesignated values; it is thus 'normal' in the usual (formal) sense.

We assume a special predicate $Tr(x)$ to be interpreted as a ttruth predicate: $\nu(Tr(\ulcorner\alpha\urcorner)) = \nu(\alpha)$ for any 'admissible' ν. Falsity, in turn, is derivative: $\nu(F(\ulcorner\alpha\urcorner)) = \nu(Tr(\ulcorner\neg\alpha\urcorner))$.

Finally, we add a unary connective π (our 'paranormal' device), which is interpreted as follows. (Note that I use 'π' for both the connective and the operator, trusting context to do its clarifying job.)

$$\nu(\pi\alpha) = \begin{cases} 0 \text{ if } \nu(\alpha) \in \{1, 0\} \\ \frac{3}{4} \text{ otherwise.} \end{cases}$$

Note that—letting 'P' be our 'paranormal' predicate—the extension of P, namely,

$$\mathcal{P}^+ = \left\{ \alpha : \frac{1}{4} \leq \nu(\alpha) \leq \frac{3}{4} \right\}$$

may well be negation-inconsistent; it may well contain both α and $\neg\alpha$ for some α. (Indeed, for typical π-free Liars, that will be the case.) In this respect, *being paranormal* differs from *ttruth* (similarly, *tfalsity*), as the extension of the latter, namely,

$$\mathcal{T}^+ = \left\{ \alpha : \frac{3}{4} \leq \nu(\alpha) \right\}$$

is always negation-consistent.

« *Parenthetical remark.* A consistency proof cannot be done in the usual fashion, given that π is non-monotonic, but such a proof is available. (Thanks to Tim Bays and Greg Restall for their interest in the idea; each of them independently suggested different proof sketches.) *End parenthetical.* »

A.1.2 *Comments*

What the 'paranormal' approach yields is a simple, consistent way towards achieving exhaustive characterization in the target sense, one that employs a unified 'paranormal' predicate. Liars, one and all, may safely be classified as paranormal, even though some paranormals may also be ttrue or tfalse. And, in general, we achieve 'unified exhaustive characterization', in that every sentence will fall under one of our three semantically significant predicates: either ttrue, tfalse, or paranormal. What we don't have, obviously, is any significant 'inferential' constraints on *being paranormal*. The next section presents a way of getting slightly more constraints—though the basic idea remains the same.

A.2   An alternative picture: merely instrumental gluts

One common way of characterizing the difference between paracomplete and (dialetheic, strong) paraconsistent accounts of paradox is that, as a familiar caricature goes, the former see 'gaps' where the latter see 'gluts'. In standard cases, such terminology (especially 'gaps') is entirely misleading, but the caricature is right in spirit. The paracomplete theorist rejects certain—say, *paranormal*, or *defective*, or whathaveyou—sentences *and* their negations (e.g., Liars and the like), while the (strong) paraconsistent theorist accepts such sentences *and* their negations. In effect, the appropriate pair of paracomplete and paraconsistent theorists agree on what's true (only), false (only), and on what goes into the 'paranormal' category. The disagreement emerges on what to say about the paranormal sentences.

A familiar problem facing paracomplete theorists concerns characterization. Assuming a normal Boolean framework (e.g., Strong Kleene),[2] the paracomplete theorist has a problem classifying or characterizing the 'paranormal' sentences (e.g., Liars). Saying that such sentences are neither true nor false is non-sensical, at least given transparent (intersubstitutable) truth—which, for present purposes, is what is assumed throughout. So, what to say?

Various things might be said, but I'll focus on a simple suggestion: paracomplete theorists should just invoke the suitable paraconsistent counterpart. In short: the paranormal sentences are the ones that are provably glutty 'in the corresponding story'. The basic idea is as follows.

A.2.1   *Three steps*

The three steps are as follows.

1. LOCATE A DUAL STORY. When we're dealing with K_3, the natural dual is LP. To simplify (here), we consider an LP-based story according to which the Tr-free fragment is classical and, note well, anything 'ungrounded' is a glut.[3]

---

[2]Here, 'Boolean' is used as per Ch. 1, picking out only the basic Boolean connectives.

[3]This means that, e.g., truth-tellers are gluts, as are sentences that say of themselves only that they're true and false, and so on. One can add all of this as extra axioms to the relevant 'LP story' (theory). (At the Boolean level, one can make this precise by first looking at, e.g., Kripke's least-fixed-point-empty-ground model, getting the resulting 'ungrounded' sentences, and then constructing a distinct LP model in which all of *those* sentences are in the extension and anti-extension of 'ttrue' at the ground level. Adding a suitable conditional changes things. (See A.2.4.))

2. CONSTRUCT A TRANSLATION SCHEME. Here, we want some 'translation' function that takes us from our sentences to their relevant LP-story counterparts (or, more accurately, a function from our sentences to what serve as the LP counterparts). Where α is a sentence of our (paracomplete) language, we let $[\alpha]^\dagger$ be the LP counterpart of α.

3. INVOKE THE LP STORY. Finally, we use the LP story to give a 'characterization' of our paranormal sentences. Let Π be our paranormal operator (or, given ttruth, what comes to the same, our paranormal predicate). We say

$$\Pi(\alpha) \text{ iff } \vdash_{LP} [\alpha]^\dagger \wedge \neg[\alpha]^\dagger$$

where '$\vdash_{LP} \alpha$' means that α is provable in the LP story.

« *Parenthetical remark.* With respect to the second step—constructing a translation scheme—what is written above may be slightly misleading. There are really two ways of thinking about what's going on: one invokes a distinct language (or theory), and the other is entirely within our own language, but we invoke a distinct proof theory—namely, that of our 'dual' theory. The latter is the approach here, although the alternative is also viable. Still, as will be evident in §A.2.4, it is important to focus on the 'right' (in particular, Boolean!) sentences—hence, the 'translation' and 'story' talk.

A similar qualification is in order regarding the third step—invoking the LP story. What's given isn't quite broad enough. To get the full story—in particular, 'contingent' cases—we will need to have provability in LP *together with all empirical and mathematical truths.* (Thanks to Hartry Field for discussion on this point.) *End parenthetical.* »

A.2.2   *How is Π to be 'translated'?*

The account above is clear enough until we consider 'Π'-ful sentences. How, in the end, is Π to be 'translated' into the LP 'story'? The natural answer, I think, is that

$$[\Pi(\alpha)]^\dagger := \alpha \wedge \neg\alpha$$

After all, the LP story goes the traditional route of explicating the 'paranormal' relative to truth. In short, the LP theorist equates the paranormal sentences with *gluts.* Accordingly, just as $\alpha \supset \beta$ *abbreviates* $\neg\alpha \vee \beta$ in the LP (and, similarly, Strong Kleene) language, so too $\Pi(\alpha)$ *abbreviates* $\alpha \wedge \neg\alpha$ in the LP story (but, obviously, not in Kleene).

Anticipating objections (but not really answering them here), I should say that it's not surprising that 'paranormal' will get a different treatment in the two stories. After all, it's precisely the paranormal sentences over which disagreement emerges between the paracomplete and paraconsistent camps.

A.2.3 *Overlap without inconsistency*

One immediate upshot is that some truths are paranormal, as are some false-hoods. Consider, for example, a sentence β that says $\neg\beta \vee \Pi(\beta)$. By the going account, we have

$$\Pi(\alpha) \text{ iff } \vdash_{LP} [\alpha]^\dagger \wedge \neg[\alpha]^\dagger$$

As in §A.2.2, $[\Pi(\beta)]^\dagger := \beta \wedge \neg\beta$, and so, for our given β,

$$[\neg\beta \vee \Pi(\beta)]^\dagger := \neg\beta \vee (\beta \wedge \neg\beta)$$

Accordingly, we have

$$\Pi(\beta) \text{ iff } \vdash_{LP} (\neg\beta \vee (\beta \wedge \neg\beta)) \wedge \neg(\neg\beta \vee (\beta \wedge \neg\beta))$$

It is not hard to see that, by its construction (and empirical-cum-mathematical facts), β is provably glutty in the *LP* story. Hence, we conclude that β is para-normal, in which case, by construction, β has a true disjunct, and so β is true. There are true paranormals. And similar examples reveal false paranormals.

While our chief semantic classes overlap, there is no inconsistency (i.e., no true and false sentences). Paracomplete theorists have no reason to object.

A.2.4 *What about a serious conditional?*

I have so far ignored the critical issue of a suitable conditional, where a suitable conditional $\rightarrow$ is a conditional that satisfies at least the following desiderata (and probably more). (See Chapter 2.)

» $\vdash \alpha \rightarrow \alpha$ for all α
» $\alpha \wedge (\alpha \rightarrow \beta) \vdash \beta$
» Curry is not a problem (and, hence, $\nvdash \alpha \wedge (\alpha \rightarrow \beta) \rightarrow \beta$, etc.)!

For present purposes, I assume something along the lines of Chapter 2, though a range of alternatives would do.

In effect, the proposal of §A.2.1 is really so far restricted to the Boolean level. Let $\rightarrow$ be our suitable conditional. Then, in effect, the proposal so far is really rather

$$\Pi(\alpha) \text{ iff } \vdash_{LP} [\alpha]^\dagger \wedge \neg[\alpha]^\dagger \text{ for all `}\rightarrow\text{'-free } \alpha$$

Such a restriction raises an obvious issue. The issue concerns how to square the above account (in §A.2.1) with the existence of a suitable conditional. After all, the 'duality' at issue is mathematically plain only at the *Boolean* level; however, a suitable conditional will go well beyond the Boolean level.

Another way of looking at the issue is to consider Curry. (See Chapter 2.) Curry paradox isn't a genuine threat at the Boolean level. Curry is a threat once a 'serious' conditional is added. We're now assuming that we've got a serious conditional (vs merely Boolean). Now, paracomplete theorists will want to treat (real) Curry sentences and their negations as paranormal. On the proposed ac-count of 'paranormal' (in §A.2.1), a Curry sentence γ is paranormal if and only if

$\vdash_{LP} [\gamma]^{\dagger} \wedge \neg[\gamma]^{\dagger}$. In other words, the going account would require the LP theory to treat Curry sentences as gluts. But that, on pain of the LP story being trivial, won't be the case if $[\gamma]^{\dagger}$ involves a suitable conditional.

The question, then, is how to square the 'according to LP' account of the paranormal with the existence of genuine Curry sentences—ones that use a suitable conditional. The question, in other words, is how to extend the account to cover—to characterize—the paranormal '$\rightarrow$'-ful sentences.

The natural idea, I think, is to just concentrate on LP's Boolean conditional, namely, the hook (defined via negation and disjunction). After all, what the paracomplete theorist wants to say about 'real Curry' is that they and their negations are paranormal; and that is exactly what the LP theorist says about Boolean Curry (i.e., disjunctive Liars). The suggestion, then, is to keep the going account of §A.2.1, but 'translate' our suitable conditional as a hook 'inside' the LP story. In short, I propose

$$[\alpha \rightarrow \beta]^{\dagger} := [\alpha]^{\dagger} \supset [\beta]^{\dagger}$$

In turn, we carry the same account as previously discussed, namely,

$$\Pi(\alpha \rightarrow \beta) \text{ iff } \vdash_{LP} ([\alpha]^{\dagger} \supset [\beta]^{\dagger}) \wedge \neg([\alpha]^{\dagger} \supset [\beta]^{\dagger})$$

Accordingly, a Curry sentence is paranormal just if the corresponding 'Curry hook' is provably inconsistent in the LP story. Example: let 'c' denote the sentence '$Tr(c) \rightarrow \bot$', where $\bot$ is explosive.[4]

$$[Tr(c) \rightarrow \bot]^{\dagger} := (Tr(c) \supset \bot) :=: (\neg Tr(c) \vee \bot)$$

As before, we have

$$\Pi(Tr(c) \rightarrow \bot) \text{ iff } \vdash_{LP} (Tr(c) \supset \bot) \wedge \neg(Tr(c) \supset \bot)$$

Quick reflection shows that $\vdash_{LP} (Tr(c) \supset \bot) \wedge \neg(Tr(c) \supset \bot)$. Hence, $Tr(c) \rightarrow \bot$ is paranormal, and similarly c's negation is paranormal.

A.2.5 *The proposal, in general*

In general, then, assuming $[\varphi(\alpha)]^{\dagger} :=: \varphi(\alpha)$ for all connectives φ except Π and $\rightarrow$, we have the following account.

$$\Pi(\alpha) \text{ iff } \vdash_{LP} [\alpha]^{\dagger} \wedge \neg[\alpha]^{\dagger}$$

The proposal offers neither a substantive account of the *paranormal* sentences nor an account of the paranormals in terms of ttruth. On the other hand, the proposal does give the paracomplete theorist something by way of classifying the

---

[4]The 'translation scheme' is extended to singular terms in the natural way. In this case, where c, in our language, is '$Tr(c) \rightarrow \bot$', 'c' denotes the *translation* of '$Tr(c) \rightarrow \bot$' in the LP story.

target sentences, of having a 'unified' predicate that affords 'exhaustive characterization'.

« *Parenthetical remark.* I should note that Carrie Jenkins (2007) argues that this approach fails to give the target 'exhaustive characterization', since it cannot consistently express, for example, *has a designated value.* I will not discuss the matter here, but, were I to defend this sort of approach (versus the dialetheic approach endorsed in this book), I would say that Jenkins is conflating model-dependent notions with the 'absolute' notions that our 'formal modeling' purports to serve. (See Chapter 3.) I largely agree with the reply to Jenkins in Caret and Cotnoir (2008). *End parenthetical.* »

APPENDIX B

LIST OF COMMON ABBREVIATIONS

BIV. $\vdash Tr(\ulcorner\alpha\urcorner) \vee Tr(\ulcorner\neg\alpha\urcorner)$.

CC. $\vdash \alpha \rightarrow Tr(\ulcorner\alpha\urcorner)$

CR. $\vdash Tr(\ulcorner\alpha\urcorner) \rightarrow \alpha$

DS. $\alpha \vee \beta, \neg\alpha \nvdash \beta$.

EC. Every sentence (in the language) is either ttrue, tfalse, or *Other*.

EFQ. $\alpha, \neg\alpha \vdash \beta$.

LEM. $\vdash \alpha \vee \neg\alpha$.

MMP. $\alpha, \alpha \supset \beta \nvdash \beta$.

MPP. $\alpha, \alpha \Rightarrow \beta \vdash \beta$

PMP. $\alpha \wedge (\alpha \rightarrow \beta) \rightarrow \beta$

RC. $\alpha \vdash Tr(\ulcorner\alpha\urcorner)$

RR. $Tr(\ulcorner\alpha\urcorner) \vdash \alpha$

SP. For any object o and predicate $\varphi(x)$, there is a semantical property $\mathcal{Y}$ such that o exemplifies $\mathcal{Y}$ iff $\varphi(x)$ is ttrue of o.

TP. Let β be any sentence in which sentence α occurs. Then the result of substituting $Tr(\ulcorner\alpha\urcorner)$ for any occurrence of α in β has the same semantic value or same semantic status as β.

WT. $w \models Tr(\ulcorner\alpha\urcorner)$ iff $w \models \alpha$ for all α and $w \in \mathcal{W}$.

REFERENCES

Anderson, Alan Ross and Belnap, Nuel D. (1975). *Entailment: The Logic of Relevance and Necessity*, Volume 1. Princeton University Press, Princeton.

Anderson, Alan Ross, Belnap, Nuel D., and Dunn, J. Michael (1992). *Entailment: The Logic of Relevance and Necessity*, Volume 2. Princeton University Press, Princeton.

Asenjo, F. G. (1966). A calculus of antinomies. *Notre Dame Journal of Formal Logic*, **16**, 103–105.

Barwise, Jon (1989). Situations, facts, and true propositions. In *The Situation in Logic*, Number 17 in CSLI Lecture Notes, pp. 221–254. CSLI Publications, Stanford, CA.

Barwise, Jon and Perry, John (1983). *Situations and Attitudes*. MIT Press, Bradford Books, Cambridge, MA.

Beall, Jc (2004). True and false—as if. In *The Law of Non-Contradiction* (ed. G. Priest, J. Beall, and B. Armour-Garb), pp. 197–216. Oxford University Press, Oxford.

——— (2005*a*). Negation's holiday: double-aspect dialetheism. In *A Logical Approach to Philosophy* (ed. D. DeVidi and T. Kenyon). Kluwer Academic Publishers, Dordrecht.

——— (2005*b*). Transparent disquotationalism. In *Deflationism and Paradox* (ed. J. Beall and B. Armour-Garb), pp. 7–22. Oxford University Press, Oxford.

——— (2006*a*). True, false, and paranormal. *Analysis*, **66**(290), 102–114.

——— (2006*b*). Truth and paradox: a philosophical sketch. In *Philosophy of Logic* (ed. D. Jacquette), Volume X of *Handbook of the Philosophy of Science*, pp. 187–272. Elsevier, Dordrecht.

——— (2007*a*). Prolegomenon to future revenge. In *Revenge of the Liar: New Essays on the Paradox* (ed. J. Beall), pp. 1–30. Oxford University Press, Oxford.

Beall, Jc (ed.) (2007*b*). *Revenge of the Liar*. Oxford University Press, Oxford.

Beall, Jc (2008). Curry's paradox. In *The Stanford Encyclopedia of Philosophy* (ed. E. N. Zalta).

——— (2009). 'Unsettledness' in a bivalent language: a modest, non-epistemic approach. In *From Truth to Reality* (ed. H. Dyke), pp. 17–28. Routledge, Oxford.

Beall, Jc and Armour-Garb, B. (2003). Should deflationists be dialetheists? *Noûs*, **37**(2), 303–324.

Beall, Jc, Brady, Ross, Hazen, Alan, Priest, Graham, and Restall, Greg (2006). Relevant restricted quantification. *Journal of Philosophical Logic*, **35**(6), 587–598.

Beall, Jc and Restall, Greg (2005). *Logical Pluralism.* Oxford University Press, Oxford.

Beebee, Helen and Dodd, Julian (ed.) (2005). *Truthmakes: the Contemporary Debate.* Oxford University Press, Oxford.

Białynicki-Birula, A. and Rasiowa, H. (1957). On the representation of quasi-boolean algebras. *Bulletin de l'Académie Polonaise des Sciences,* **5**, 259–261.

Brady, Ross T. (1989). The non-triviality of dialectical set theory. In *Paraconsistent Logic: Essays on the Inconsistent* (ed. G. Priest, R. Routley, and J. Norman), pp. 437–470. Philosophia Verlag.

Butchart, Sam (2008). Binary quantifiers for relevant paraconsistent logic. To appear. Presented at the Australasian Association for Philosophy conference in Melbourne, 2008.

Caret, Colin and Cotnoir, Aaron (2008). True, false, designated? *Analysis,* **68**, 238–244.

Chellas, Brian F. (1980). *Modal Logic: An Introduction.* Cambridge University Press, Cambridge.

Chihara, Charles (1979). The semantic paradoxes: A diagnostic investigation. *The Philosophical Review,* **88**(4), 590–618.

Colyvan, Mark (2009). Vagueness and truth. In *From Truth to Reality* (ed. H. Dyke), pp. 29–40. Routledge, Oxford.

Curry, Haskell B. (1942). The inconsistency of certain formal logics. *Journal of Symbolic Logic,* **7**, 115–117.

da Costa, N. C. A. and Alves, E. H. (1977). A semantical analysis of the calculi C_n. *Notre Dame Journal of Formal Logic,* **18**, 621–630.

Dowden, Bradley (1984). Accepting inconsistencies from the paradoxes. *Journal of Philosophical Logic,* **13**, 125–130.

Dummett, Michael (1978). Truth. In *Truth and Other Enigmas* (ed. M. Dummett). Duckworth, London.

Dunn, J. Michael (1969). Natural language versus formal language. Presented at the joint APA–ASL symposium, New York, December 27, 1969.

—— (1999). A comparative study of various model-theoretic treatments of negation: A history of formal negation. In *What is Negation?*, pp. 23–51. Kluwer Academic Publishers, Dordrect.

—— (2000). Partiality and its dual. *Studia Logica,* **65**, 5–40.

Dunn, J. Michael and Restall, Greg (2002). Relevance logic. In *Handbook of Philosophical Logic (2nd Edition)* (ed. D. M. Gabbay and F. Günthner), Volume 6. D. Reidel, Dordrecht.

Feferman, Solomon (1984). Toward useful type-free theories, I. *Journal of Symbolic Logic,* **49**, 75–111. Reprinted in Martin 1984.

Field, Hartry (1994). Deflationist views of meaning and content. *Mind,* **103**, 249–285. Reprinted in Field 2001.

—— (2001). *Truth and the Absence of Fact.* Oxford University Press, Oxford.

—— (2003). The semantic paradoxes and the paradoxes of vagueness. In *Liars and Heaps: New Essays on Paradox* (ed. J. Beall), pp. 262–311. Oxford University Press, Oxford.

—— (2004). The consistency of the naïve (?) theory of properties. *The Philosophical Quarterly*, 78–104.

—— (2005*a*). Is the liar both true and false? In *Deflationism and Paradox* (ed. J. Beall and B. Armour-Garb), pp. 23–40. Oxford University Press, Oxford.

—— (2005*b*). Reply to McGee. *Philosophical Studies*, **124**, 105–128. This is part of a book symposium on Field 2001.

—— (2005*c*). Variations on a theme by Yablo. In *Deflationism and Paradox* (ed. J. Beall and B. Armour-Garb), pp. 53–74. Oxford University Press, Oxford.

—— (2006). Truth and the unprovability of consistency. *Mind*, 567–605.

—— (2008). *Saving Truth from Paradox*. Oxford University Press, Oxford.

Fine, Kit (1974). Models for entailment. *Journal of Philosophical Logic*, **3**, 347–372. Substantially reprinted in Anderson, Belnap and Dunn 1992.

—— (1975). Vagueness, truth and logic. *Synthese*, **30**, 265–300.

Fitting, Melvin (1986). Notes on the mathematical aspects of Kripke's theory of truth. *Notre Dame Journal of Formal Logic*, **27**, 75–88.

Glanzberg, Michael (2001). The liar in context. *Philosophical Studies*, **103**, 217–251.

—— (2003). Against truth-value gaps. In *Liars and Heaps*, pp. 151–194. Oxford University Press, Oxford.

—— (2004). Truth, reflection, and hierarchies. *Synthese*, **142**, 289–315.

Gould, Stephen Jay and Lewontin, Richard C. (1978). The spandrels of San Marco and the Panglossian paradigm: a critique of the adaptationist programme. *Proceedings of the Royal Society of London*, **205**, 581–598.

Grim, Patrick (1991). *The Incomplete Universe*. MIT Press, Cambridge, MA.

Gupta, Anil and Belnap, Nuel (1993). *The Revision Theory of Truth*. MIT Press, Cambridge, MA.

Hájek, Petr, Paris, Jeff, and Shepherdson, John (2000). The liar paradox and fuzzy logic. *Journal of Symbolic Logic*, **65**, 339–346.

Halbach, Volker and Horsten, Leon (2006). Axiomatizing Kripke's theory of truth. *Journal of Symbolic Logic*, **71**, 677–712.

Halldén, Sören (1949). *The Logic of Nonsense*. Uppsala Universitets Arsskrift, Uppsala.

Hartry Field (2003). A revenge-immune solution to the semantic paradoxes. *Journal of Philosophical Logic*, **32**, 139–177.

Herzberger, Hans (1982). Notes on naive semantics. *Journal of Philosophical Logic*, **11**, 61–102. Reprinted in Martin 1984.

Hilbert, David and Bernays, Paul (1939). *Grundlagen der Mathematik*. Springer Verlag, Berlin.

Hyde, Dominic (1997). From heaps and gaps to heaps of gluts. *Mind*, **106**, 641–660.

Jenkins, C. S. (2007). True, false, paranormal and designated: a reply to Beall. *Analysis*, **67**, 80–84.

Kleene, S. C. (1952). *Introduction to Metamathematics*. North-Holland.

Kremer, Michael (1988). Kripke and the logic of truth. *Journal of Philosophical Logic*, **17**, 225–278.

Kremer, Philip (2000). 'Semantics' for languages with their own truth predicates. In *Circularity, Definition and Truth* (ed. A. Chapuis and A. Gupta), pp. 217–246. Indian Council of Philosophical Research, New Delhi.

Kripke, Saul (1965). Semantical analysis of modal logic II: Non-normal modal propositional calculi. In *The Theory of Models* (ed. J. W. Addison, L. Henkin, and A. Tarski), pp. 206–220. North-Holland Publishing Co, Amsterdam.

———— (1975). Outline of a theory of truth. *Journal of Philosophy*, **72**, 690–716. Reprinted in Martin 1984.

Kroon, Fred (2004). Realism and dialetheism. In *The Law of Non-Contradiction* (ed. G. Priest, J. Beall, and B. Armour-Garb), pp. 245–263. Oxford University Press, Oxford.

Lynch, Michael P. (ed.) (2001). *The Nature of Truth*. MIT Press, Cambridge, MA.

Mares, Edwin (1996). Relevant logic and the theory of information. *Synthese*, **109**, 345–360.

———— (2004a). *Relevant Logic: A Philosophical Interpretation*. Cambridge University Press, Cambridge.

———— (2004b). Semantic dialetheism. In *The Law of Non-Contradiction* (ed. G. Priest, J. Beall, and B. Armour-Garb), pp. 264–275. Oxford University Press, Oxford.

Martin, Robert L. (ed.) (1984). *Recent Essays on Truth and the Liar Paradox*. Oxford University Press, New York.

Martin, Robert L. and Woodruff, Peter W. (1975). On representing 'true-in-L' in L. *Philosophia*, **5**, 217–221. Reprinted in Martin 1984.

Maudlin, Tim (2004). *Truth and Paradox: Solving the Riddles*. Oxford University Press, New York.

McGee, Vann (1989). Applying Kripke's theory of truth. *Journal of Philosophy*, **86**, 530–539.

———— (1991). *Truth, Vagueness, and Paradox*. Hackett, Indianapolis.

———— (1992). Maximal consistent sets of instances of Tarski's schema (T). *Journal of Philosophical Logic*, **21**, 235–241.

———— (2005). Two conceptions of truth? *Philosophical Studies*, **124**, 71–104.

Meyer, Robert K., Routley, Richard, and Dunn, J. Michael (1979). Curry's paradox. *Analysis*, **39**, 124–128.

Mortensen, Chris (1995). *Inconsistent Mathematics*. Kluwer Academic Publishers.

Myhill, J. (1975). Levels of implication. In *The Logical Enterprise* (ed. A. R. Anderson, R. C. Barcan-Marcus, and R. M. Martin), pp. 179–185. Yale University Press, New Haven.

―――― (1984). Paradoxes. *Synthese*, **60**, 129–143.

Preyer, G. and Peters, G. (ed.) (2002). *Logical Form and Language*. Oxford University Press, Oxford.

Priest, Graham (1979). The logic of paradox. *Journal of Philosophical Logic*, **8**, 219–241.

―――― (1980). Sense, entailment and modus ponens. *Journal of Philosophical Logic*, **9**, 415–435.

―――― (1984). Logic of paradox revisited. *Journal of Philosophical Logic*, **13**, 153–179.

―――― (1987). *In Contradiction: A Study of the Transconsistent*. Martinus Nijhoff, The Hague.

―――― (1991). Intensional paradoxes. *Notre Dame Journal of Formal Logic*, **32**, 193–211.

―――― (1992). What is a non-normal world? *Logique et Analyse*, **35**, 291–302.

―――― (1997). On a paradox of Hilbert and Bernays. *Journal of Philosophical Logic*, **26**, 45–56.

―――― (1998). What is so bad about contradictions? *Journal of Philosophy*, **XCV**(8), 410–426. Reprinted in Priest, Beall and Armour-Garb 2004.

―――― (1999). Semantic closure, descriptions and triviality. *Journal of Philosophical Logic*, **28**, 549–558.

―――― (2000*a*). Could everything be true? *Australasian Journal of Philosophy*, **78**, 189–195.

―――― (2000*b*). Truth and contradiction. *The Philosophical Quarterly*, **50**(200), 305–319.

―――― (2002). Paraconsistent logic. In *Handbook of Philosophical Logic (2nd Edition)* (ed. D. M. Gabbay and F. Günthner), Volume 6, pp. 287–393. Kluwer Academic Publishers, Dordrecht.

―――― (2005). *Towards Non-Being*. Oxford University Press, Oxford.

―――― (2006*a*). *Doubt Truth To Be A Liar*. Oxford University Press, Oxford.

―――― (2006*b*). *In Contradiction* (Second edn). Oxford University Press, Oxford.

―――― (2006*c*). The paradoxes of denotation. In *Self-Reference* (ed. T. Bolander, V. F. Hendricks, and S. Andur Pedersen), pp. 137–150. CSLI, Stanford, CA.

―――― (2007). Replies to Beall, Bueno, and Field. To appear. Paper presented at the book symposium on Priest 2006*b* and Priest 2006*a*, Pacific APA, San Francisco USA.

———— (2008). Inclosures, vagueness, and self-reference. To appear. Paper presented at the Fourth World Congress of Paraconsistency, Melbourne, Australia.

Priest, Graham, Beall, Jc, and Armour-Garb, B. (ed.) (2004). *The Law of Non-Contradiction.* Oxford University Press, Oxford.

Priest, Graham and Routley, Richard (1989). Systems of paraconsistent logic. In *Paraconsistent Logic: Essays on the Inconsistent* (ed. G. Priest, R. Routley, and J. Norman), pp. 151–186. Philosophia Verlag.

Priest, Graham, Routley, Richard, and Norman, Jean (ed.) (1989). *Paraconsistent Logic: Essays on the Inconsistent.* Philosophia Verlag.

Priest, Graham and Sylvan, Richard (1992). Simplified semantics for basic relevant logics. *Journal of Philosophical Logic*, **21**, 217–232.

Read, Stephen (2008*a*). Further thoughts on Tarski's T-scheme and the Liar. In *The Modern Relevance of Medieval Solutions to the Liar Paradox* (ed. S. Rahman, T. Tulenheimo, and E. Genot), pp. 205–225. Springer Verlag.

———— (2008*b*). The truth schema and the Liar. In *The Modern Relevance of Medieval Solutions to the Liar Paradox* (ed. S. Rahman, T. Tulenheimo, and E. Genot), pp. 3–17. Springer Verlag.

Reinhardt, William N. (1986). Some remarks on extending and interpreting theories with a partial predicate for truth. *Journal of Philosophical Logic*, **15**, 219–251.

Restall, Greg (1992). Arithmetic and truth in Łukasiewicz's infinitely valued logic. *Logique et Analyse*, **139–140**, 303–312.

———— (1993*a*). How to be *Really* contraction-free. *Studia Logica*, **52**, 381–391.

———— (1993*b*). Simplified semantics for relevant logics (and some of their rivals). *Journal of Philosophical Logic*, **22**, 481–511.

———— (1994, January). *On Logics Without Contraction.* Ph.D. thesis, The University of Queensland.

———— (1995). Information flow and relevant logics. In *Logic, Language and Computation: The 1994 Moraga Proceedings* (ed. J. Seligman and D. Westerståhl), pp. 463–477. CSLI Publications.

———— (1999). Negation in Relevant Logics: How I Stopped Worrying and Learned to Love the Routley Star. In *What is Negation?* (ed. D. Gabbay and H. Wansing), Volume 13 of *Applied Logic Series*, pp. 53–76. Kluwer Academic Publishers.

———— (2000). *An Introduction to Substructural Logics.* New York: Routledge.

Routley, Richard (1980). Problems and solutions in the semantics of quantified relevant logics — I. In *Proceedings of the Fourth Latin American Symposium on Mathematical Logic* (ed. A. I. Arrduda, R. Chuaqui, and N. C. A. da Costa), pp. 305–340. North Holland.

———— (1992). Ubiquitous vagueness without embarrassment. typescript.

Routley, Richard and Loparić, A. (1978). Semantic analyses of Arrudada Costa P-systems and adjacent non-replacement systems. *Studia Logica*, **37**, 301–320.

Routley, Richard and Meyer, Robert K. (1973). Semantics of entailment. In *Truth, Syntax, and Modality* (ed. H. Leblanc), pp. 194–243. North Holland. Proceedings of the Temple University Conference on Alternative Semantics.

Routley, Richard and Routley, Valerie (1972). Semantics of first-degree entailment. *Noûs*, **3**, 335–359.

Shapiro, Stewart (2005). Proof and truth: Through thick and thin. *Journal of Philosophy*, 493–521.

Simmons, Keith (1993). *Universality and The Liar*. Cambridge University Press.

——— (2003). Reference and paradox. In *Liars and Heaps: New Essays on Paradox* (ed. J. Beall). Oxford University Press, Oxford.

Skyrms, Brian (1970). Return of the liar: Three-valued logic and the concept of truth. *American Philosophical Quarterly*, **7**, 153–161.

——— (1984). Intensional aspects of semantical self-reference. In *Recent Essays on Truth and the Liar* (ed. R. M. Martin), pp. 119–131. Oxford University Press, Oxford.

Smullyan, Raymond M. (1992). *Gödel's Incompleteness Theorems*, Volume 19 of *Oxford Logic Guides*. Oxford University Press, New York.

——— (1993). *Recursion Theory for Metamathematics*, Volume 20 of *Oxford Logic Guides*. Oxford University Press, New York.

Soames, Scott (1999). *Understanding Truth*. Oxford University Press, New York.

Sorensen, Roy (2001). *Vagueness and Contradiction*. Clarendon, Oxford.

Urquhart, Alasdair (1972). Semantics for relevant logics. *Journal of Symbolic Logic*, **37**, 159–169.

van Fraassen, Bas C. (1966). Singular terms, truth-value gaps, and free logic. *Journal of Philosophy*, **63**, 481–495.

——— (1969). Facts and tautological entailments. *Journal of Philosophy*, **66**, 477–487. Reprinted in Anderson and Belnap 1975.

Varzi, Achille (1999). *An Essay in Universal Semantics*, Volume 1 of *Topoi Library*. Kluwer Academic Publishers, Boston.

Visser, Albert (1984). Four valued semantics and the liar. *Journal of Philosophical Logic*, **13**, 181–212.

——— (2004). Semantics and the liar paradox. In *Handbook of Philosophical Logic* (Second edn) (ed. D. M. Gabbay and F. Günthner), pp. 149–240. Kluwer Academic Publishers, Dordrecht.

Weir, Alan (2005). Naive truth and sophisticated logic. In *Deflationism and Paradox* (ed. J. Beall and B. Armour-Garb), pp. 218–249. Oxford University Press, Oxford.

White, R. B. (1979). The consistency of the axiom of comprehension in the infinite-valued predicate logic of Łukasiewicz. *Journal of Philosophical Logic*, **8**, 509–534.

Williamson, Timothy (1994). *Vagueness*. Routledge, Oxford.

Woodruff, P. (1984). Paradox, truth, and logic. *Journal of Philosophical Logic*, **13**, 213–252.

Yablo, Stephen (2003). New grounds for naïve truth theory. In *Liars and Heaps: New Essays on Paradox* (ed. J. Beall), pp. 313–330. Oxford University Press, Oxford.

INDEX

a priori, 107, 113
AAL, xi
abnormal worlds, 8–10, 28, 29, 31, 34, 79
Ackermann constant, 121
admissible models, 12
Agnes, 2
Aiehtela, 2
Aiehtelanu, 2
all-points detachment, 30
Anderson, Alan R., 10, 103
Armour-Garb, B., xi
asymmetry, 15

Barwise, Jon, 99, 117
base language, 3, 14–17, 24, 32, 41, 47
    restrictions, 119
base-language facts, 15
base-points detachment, 30
Batens, D., 61
Bays, Tim, 136
Belnap, Nuel, ix, 10, 20, 74, 83, 103
Berry's paradox, 114
Białynicki-Birula, A., 7
Bivalence, 3, 9, 66, 142
Boolean connectives, 6, 7, 9, 25
Brady, Ross, xi, 20, 32, 42, 43, 57, 121,
    125
Bricker, Phillip, xi
Bueno, Otávio, xi
Butchart, Sam, 120
BX, 31
    axioms, 31
BXTT, 32
    hook-like conditional, 123
    non-triviality proof, 42, 47
BXTT$^+$, 121
    non-triviality proof, 121

Capture, 5, 14, 25, 49, 56, 62
    Conditional, 14, 142
    Rule, 14, 142
Caret, Colin, xi, 141
CC, see Capture (Conditional)
Chellas, B., 86
Cheyne, Colin, xi
Chihara, C., 127
classical constraint, 8–10, 12

classical star model, 8
Colyvan, Mark, xi, 4
conceptual truth, 16
contraction, 27, 28, 31
Cotnoir, Aaron, xi, 141
$CPL^\star$ validity, 8
CR, see Capture (Rule)
Curry paradox, 27, 35, 78, 79, 83, 89, 113
    and Liars, 33
    semantical properties, 113
    sets, 113
Curry sentences, 27, 33

da Costa, N., 60, 108
definability, 115
detachment
    all-points, 30
    base-points, 30
dialetheic, 5, 6, 17, 51, 52, 130
dialetheism, 1, 5, 98, 111, 115
    deflated, 17
    merely semantic, 6, 16
Disjunction Principle, 49
Disjunctive Syllogism, 10, 16, 142
disquotationalism, 2
Dowden, B., 7, 20
DP, see Disjunction Principle
DS, see Disjunctive Syllogism
Dunn, J. Michael, xi, 10, 103, 117

ECP, see Exhaustive Characterization
    Project
Elder, Crawford, xi
equivalents replacement, 28, 29, 31
Ex Falso Quodlibet, see Explosion
Excluded Middle, 3, 10, 78, 79, 81–83, 89,
    91, 100–104, 107, 134, 142
exhaustion, 9
exhaustive characterization, 142
Exhaustive Characterization Project, 66,
    74, 76, 77, 79, 80
Explosion, 10, 16, 99, 142
extensional connectives, see Boolean
    connectives

falsity, 3
FDE, 10

many-valued, 103
Feferman, S., 75, 77, 78
Field, Hartry, viii, ix, xi, xii, 2–4, 39, 43,
　　57, 79, 80, 82–90, 92, 101, 103,
　　112, 116, 118, 126
Fine, Kit, 5, 31, 67
Fitting, M., 20
free logic
　negative, 115

Gödel quotes, ix
Gödel's 2nd incompleteness theorem, 115
Gödel, Kurt, 112
gappy, 10
gappy worlds, 10, 105
gaps, 98, 104, 105
　abnormal gaps, 8, 10
Garfield, Jay, xi
Glanzberg, Michael, ix, xi, 16, 103
glut, 6, 10, 15
gluts, 5, 6, 8, 10, 13, 15, 17, 34, 51, 115
　base-language, 98, 126–128
　merely semantic, 14, 16
glutty, 10, 24, 47, 105
God, 1
Greenough, Patrick, xi
Grelling's paradox, 115
Grim, Patrick, xi, 66
Gupta, Anil, xi, 20, 74, 83

Hájek, P., 27
Halbach, Volker, 75, 77
Halldén, S., 18
Hardegree, Gary, xi
Hazen, A., 121
Herzberger, H., 83
Higgins, Katrina M., xii
holiday, 10
hook, 25, 119
　Hook Capture, 26
　Hook Release, 26
Horsten, Leon, 75
Hyde, Dominic, xi, 4, 67

idealization, 53
Identity (Conditional), 27
incoherent operators, 48, 50, 62

Jenkins, Carrie, xi, 16, 141
just true, 48, 52, 62
　as ttruth, 51, 52, 57

König's paradox, 114
Kremer, Michael, 74
Kremer, Philip, 75

Kripke, Saul, 6, 20, 30, 44, 74–80, 83, 85,
　　87, 89, 91
Kroon, Fred, xi

LEM, *see* Excluded Middle
Lewis, C. I., 30
Lewis, David, xi
LLL, xi
logical pluralism, 37
Loparić, A., 28
LP, 10, 11, 13
　many-valued, 20
LP⋆, 9, 10, 12
　admissible interpretations, 16
　models, 12
　quantification, 11
LPTT, 13, 20
　non-triviality proof, 18, 21
Łukasiewicz, Jan, 27
Lycan, William, xi
Lynch, Michael, xi

Mares, Edwin D., xi, 6, 16, 30, 117, 118
Martin, R. L., 74
material conditional, *see* hook
Material Modus Ponens, 10, 142
Maudlin, T., 75, 77
Max, 1, 2, 52
Maximum Leader, xi
McGee, Vann, ix, xi, 3, 67, 75, 77, 80, 120
McKinnon, Ross, xi
Melbourne Logic Group, xi
metaphysics, 98
methodological deflationism, 118
methodological disquotationalism, 2, 3,
　　118
Meyer, Robert K., xi, 30
MMP, *see* Material Modus Ponens
model language, 53–56
model-dependent notion, 55
Modus Ponens, 26, 30, 142
Mortensen, Chris, xi, 112
MPP, *see* Modus Ponens
Myhill, John, 37, 112

natural, 32
natural models, 13
negation, 3–5, 7, 9–11, 16, 17, 98–104,
　　108, 109, 111, 119, 129–131
Nolan, Daniel, xi, 16
non-extensional negation, *see* negation
non-paraconsistent, 134
non-triviality, 13, 24, 26, 32, 66
Non-Triviality Project, 66, 74, 77, 79, 80,
　　87
normal exhaustion, 8, 10

normal worlds, 9
NTP, *see* Non-Triviality Project

Ockham, 2
oddities, 17
overactivity, 10, 17
Owings, Doug, xi
Oz, xi

paracomplete, 67, 76–80, 82, 83, 87, 89,
        91, 134
paraconsistent, 66, 67
paranormal, 134–137
Paris, J., 27
Plumwood, Val, xi
PMP, *see* pseudo modus ponens
Priest, Graham, vii, ix, xi, xii, 4, 5, 10,
        15, 20, 29–31, 33, 42, 48, 52,
        98, 101, 103, 114, 115, 121,
        125, 127
probability, non-classical, 100, 101
pseudo modus ponens, 28, 142

Quine quotes, ix

Rasiowa, H., 7
rationality, 99–101, 105, 132, 133
Rayo, Augustín, xi
RC, *see* Release (Conditional)
Read, Stephen, ix, xi
Reasoning by Cases, 5, 49
Reinhardt, W. N., 67, 75
Release, 5, 14, 25, 48, 49, 56, 62, 127
    Conditional, 14, 142
    Rule, 14, 142
Restall, Greg, ix, xi, xii, 27, 31, 37, 79,
        117, 121, 125, 136
restricted generalizations, 119
revenge, 52, 54, 56
Richard's paradox, 114
Ripley, David, xi, 117
RM_3, 43
Rossberg, Marcus, xi
Routley, Richard, 4–7, 28, 30
Routley, Valerie, 6, 7
RR, *see* Release (Rule)
Russell's paradox, 112, 113
    semantic properties, 112, 113
    sets, 112
Russell, Gillian, xi

Schechter, Josh, xi
Secretary's Club, 127
see-through device, 3, 14, 17
see-through truth, 1, 2
see-through-ness, 12

Seligman, Jerry, xi
semantic terms, 6
semantical properties
    schema, 113
semantical property schema, 142
Shapiro, Lionel, xi, 111
Shapiro, Stewart, xi, 3
Shepherdson, J., 27
Simmons, Keith, ix, 114
Smullyan, R., 48
Soames, Scott, 67
Solomon, Reed, xi, xii
Sorensen, Roy, 107
spandrels, 5, 6, 9–11, 13–15, 17, 36, 47,
        99–101, 105, 111, 114, 115,
        119, 120
star, 7, 8, 105
star mate, 9, 105, 106
star worlds, 8, 116
star-many-valued translation, 20
Strong Kleene, 6, 75, 77–79, 83, 84, 86
subsitutivity of equivalents, *see*
        equivalents replacement
suitable conditional, 27
    abnormal condition, 29, 30
    normal condition, 27, 29, 30
    restricted conditional, 120
supervene, 15
supervenience, 15, 16, 75
Sylvan, Richard, xi, 31, 101
symmetry, 15, 34

T-biconditionals, 26, 27, 31
T-schema, 26
Tanaka, Koji, xi
Tarski's Theorem, 48
Tarski, A., 69, 77
ternary relation, 29, 117
tfalsity, 3
TP, *see* Transparency Principle
Transparency Principle, 12, 14, 32, 121,
        142
transparent device, *see* ttruth
transparent truth, vii, 1, 3, 4, 9
trivial world, 34
trivialism, 48
trivialist, *see* trivialism
triviality, 35
    Curry-generated, 27
trivialize, 50
true falsehoods, 17
true of
    ttrue of, 115
truth, 76
    determinate, 83, 89–92
    strong (-er), 81–83, 85, 89–91, 135

truth preservation, *see* validity and truth
    preservation
truth-tellers, 15
ttruth, 1, 3, 5, 7, 9, 10, 12, 14–17, 48, 57,
    74, 77–80, 82–84, 87, 89,
    134–136
ttruth-ineliminable sentences, 14, 15, 24,
    34, 47

UConn Logic Group, xi
uniformity, 15
Urquhart, Alasdair, xi, 6, 7, 117

vagueness, 4, 107
validity, 37
    2-step definition, 39
    partial, 40
    primitive, 38
validity and truth preservation, 34, 35

    and the hook, 35
validity and truth-preservation, 116
valuation scheme, 68
van Fraassen, Bas, xi, 74, 99
Varzi, Achillé, xi, 67
Visser, A., 7

Weak Kleene, 74
weak transparency, 12, 142
Wheeler, Sam, xi
Williams, J. Robert G., xi
Williams, Robbie, xi
Williamson, Timothy, xi, 107
Woodruff, P., 7, 20, 74
worlds, 6, 7, 27, 68, 85, 86
Wright, Crispin, xi
WT, *see* weak transparency

Yablo, Steve, xi, 48, 88

Lightning Source UK Ltd.
Milton Keynes UK
UKHW021600120521
383160UK00012B/310